MAN AND HIS ENVIRONMENT
GENERAL SCIENCE BOOK II

SECONDARY SCIENCE SERIES

The books in this series adopt the latest approach to science teaching for secondary schools and the new middle schools. The students are encouraged to discover as much as possible for themselves rather than simply to verify what they are told to be true. Scientific knowledge is acquired through a largely experimental approach, related always to everyday life and experience.

Most of the experiments are simple and require the minimum of equipment. To help readers who do not have access to full laboratory facilities, the conclusions to be drawn from investigations are incorporated later in the text. At the end of most chapters there is a *Test Your Understanding* section to reinforce knowledge and understanding of important points.

SI units have been used throughout the series.

These volumes, **Matter and Energy**, General Science Book I, and **Man and His Environment**, General Science Book II, are designed to follow on from the first volume, **Foundation Science** (formerly **Common Core Science**), which provides a two-year course in basic science. They are intended to take pupils up to the standard required by the CSE General Science examination. The majority of topics required by the various GCE boards, particularly with regard to the newer syllabuses, has also been covered.

The parallel volumes are:

Science: the Basic Skills;
Chemistry (revised edition);
Biology Book I: **General Plant and Animal Biology**;
Biology Book II: **Human Biology and Hygiene**;
Physics Book I: **Force and Energy**;
Physics Book II: **Atoms and Waves**.

These volumes are already available.

SECONDARY SCIENCE SERIES

MAN AND HIS ENVIRONMENT

General Science Book II

N. E. Savage and R. S. Wood

Illustrated by David and Maureen Embry

London, Boston and Henley
Routledge & Kegan Paul

First published 1972
Reprinted 1974
Reprinted with corrections 1976
This revised edition published in 1979
by Routledge & Kegan Paul Ltd
39 Store Street, London WC1E 7DD,
Broadway House, Newtown Road,
Henley-on-Thames, Oxon. RG9 1EN and
9 Park Street, Boston, Mass. 02108, U.S.A.
Printed in Great Britain by
Butler & Tanner Ltd, Frome and London

ISBN 0 7100 0067 7

SECONDARY SCIENCE SERIES

SERIES EDITORS

L. J. Campbell, B.Sc., A.M.B.I.M.
R. J. Carlton, B.Sc.

CONTRIBUTORS TO THE SERIES

L. J. Campbell, B.Sc., A.M.B.I.M.
Assistant Education Officer, Isle of Wight.
Formerly Head of Science Department, Hinchley Wood C.S. School.
Formerly Chairman, Science Panel, South East Regional Examination Board for the C.S.E.

R. J. Carlton, B.Sc.
Senior Assistant Master and Head of Science Department, Ashford North Boys' School.
Correspondent, Science Panel and Physics sub-Panel, South East Regional Examinations Board for the C.S.E. 1962 to 1966.
Chief Moderator in Physics, South East Regional Examinations Board for the C.S.E. 1967 to 1973.
Sometime member of Kent Teachers Panel for Metrication.

E. J. Ewington, B.Sc.
Headmaster, Howard of Effingham School.
Formerly Senior Master, Hinchley Wood C.S. School.

R. H. Stone, M.Sc., C.Chem., M.R.I.C.
Senior Chemistry Master, The Judd School, Tonbridge.

D. W. H. Tripp, B.Sc., A.R.C.S., Teacher's Diploma (Lond.)
Senior Science Master, Brighton, Hove and Sussex Sixth Form College.
Sometime member of the Radiochemistry Committee, Association for Science Education.

R. S. Wood
Science Master, Faversham C.S. School.
Formerly Chairman of the Science Panel, South East Regional Examinations Board for the C.S.E.
Chairman of the Physics and Engineering Science Panel, South East Regional Examinations Board for the C.S.E.

FORMER CONTRIBUTORS TO THE SERIES

The late D. F. Moore, B.Sc., M.I.Biol.
Late Senior Lecturer, Hockerill College of Education.
Formerly member of Biology sub-Panel, South East Regional Examinations Board for the C.S.E.

The late N. E. Savage
Late Senior Physics Master, Technical High School for Girls, Canterbury.
Formerly member, Science Panel and Physics and Integrated Science sub-Panels, South East Regional Examinations Board for the C.S.E.

Contents

Introduction

The authors believe that a sound training in basic science is essential for any educated person living in the modern world. This course has been written for pupils preparing for examinations in General Science or Integrated Science at CSE level and, for this reason, the authors have borne in mind the requirements of the various Examination Boards. The text will also prove to be of considerable value to pupils preparing for the General Certificate of Education at Ordinary level in these subjects.

This course in science is man based in concept. It will give to the school leaver an appreciation and understanding of the rapid developments in science and technology and of their consequences. With this in mind, the course is intended to develop the critical faculty of the pupil, so that he can use his own judgment to enable him to evaluate a given set of circumstances. It is for this reason that an investigational approach has been used wherever it has been considered of educational advantage to do so.

All scientific experiments must be carried out with care. In order to help teachers and students, hazard signs and warnings have been used in the margin in many cases. These signs and warnings give guidance to some possible dangers but safe working in a laboratory must, of necessity, rest with the teacher in charge. It is emphasized that the use of these signs and warnings in no way relieves teachers (and students) from their responsibilities in this respect. The fact that no sign or warning is given in a particular case does not imply the absence of risk.

It is assumed that safety glasses will be used at all times and no symbol for their use has been incorporated.

Teachers are advised always to try out an experiment before the class is allowed to undertake it.

Information about hazardous chemicals may be obtained from various reference books. *Hazards in the Chemical Laboratory*, published by the Chemical Society, is one of the most complete.

The authors hope that their approach to the subject will encourage many pupils to continue their scientific studies after they have worked through the complete course that is contained in Books I and II of General Science: *Matter and Energy* and *Man and His Environment.*

The books are intended to be used by the pupils and are couched in language which they will easily understand. The SI system of units has been used throughout and a brief summary of the principal units is given in Appendix 1. Appendices 2, 3 and 4 give tables of the elements, of solutions, and of common chemical substances, respectively. In Book II there is, additionally, a fifth Appendix listing some famous scientists.

We wish to acknowledge the work done by our fellow authors in this series, who have found the time to read and criticize the original manuscript; and to the artists, for their willing co-operation in producing excellent drawings from our rough sketches.

N. E. S.
R. S. W.

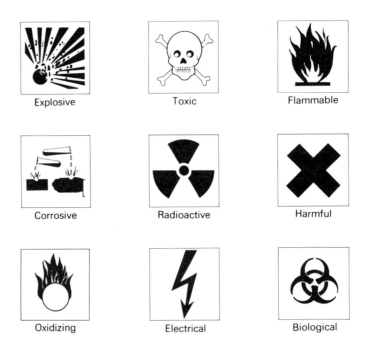

Explosive	Toxic	Flammable
Corrosive	Radioactive	Harmful
Oxidizing	Electrical	Biological

Chapter 1

Classification

Man is constantly striving to create order out of chaos. If we look at the immense variety of things around us, we notice that certain things have features in common with each other. It is these similarities that enable us to put things into logical groups. When we group things together, we start with the most obvious similarities and then separate these large groups into smaller groups according to less obvious similarities.

In a lending library, books are arranged in two main groups: fiction and non-fiction. The fiction books are arranged in alphabetical order, according to the surnames of the authors, while the non-fiction books are arranged according to subject. Table 1.1 shows a skeleton classification chart of the books in a library.

TABLE 1.1. LIBRARY CLASSIFICATION

How could you find a particular book in a library if the books were put back in the shelves in the order in which other borrowers returned them? If you want to find a particular piece of information in a reference book, such as an encyclopaedia, what a difficult task it would be if the items were not in any logical order.

If you are a philatelist (stamp collector), you will know that the object of the hobby is not just to collect as many stamps as possible. A philatelist sorts his stamps into groups. In the first sorting he arranges them in countries, then into sets of the same issue and, finally, he arranges each issue into an order according to the face value of the stamps. Table 1.2 shows a skeleton classification chart of a stamp collection.

TABLE 1.2. STAMP CLASSIFICATION

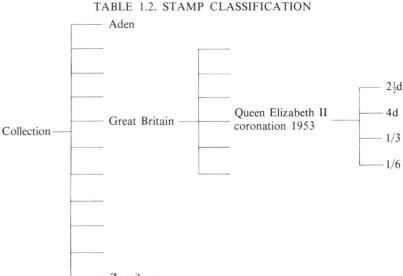

You will notice that, in both of these examples, groups which are bracketed together all have something in common which links them with the group heading on the left of the bracket, although each group has subdivisions. As you follow one of these charts from left to right, the variations between one group and another become more detailed and more clearly defined. To find an individual item involves a process of elimination. For example, if you were looking for a book about the development of films, you would look on the non-fiction shelves in a library. This makes your search simpler because you have no need to look on the fiction shelves. Then you find the fine arts section and, within this section, the books dealing with photography. Having proceeded so far, it is a simple matter to find the particular book that you are looking for.

Although these two examples of classification charts have been

2

simplified, and the groups have not been completed, they will serve to explain the principles of classification. If either of these charts was completed down to the very smallest items on the right-hand side, a very large sheet of paper would be needed.

Matter can be classified in a similar manner. Although there are

TABLE 1.3. CLASSIFICATION

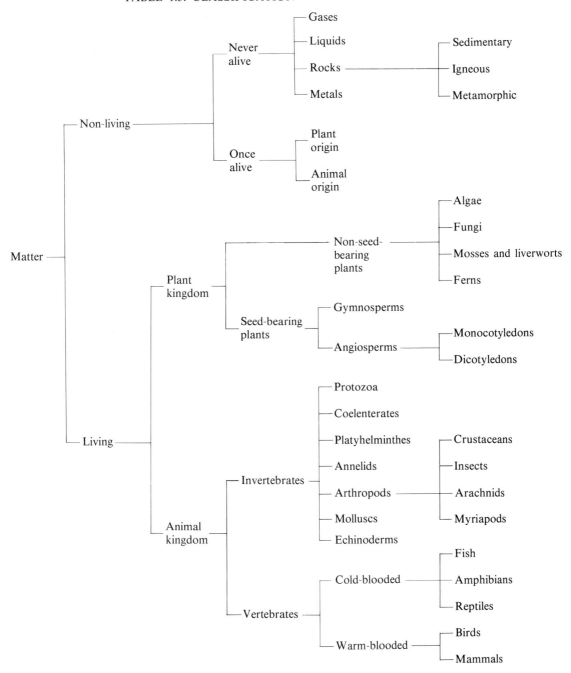

many methods of making the first large division (e.g. the division into solids, liquids and gases), for the purpose of this chapter we have decided to make the first division between living and non-living things. Table 1.3 shows a classification chart based on this major division.

1.1. Living and non-living things

At first sight, it appears very easy to tell the difference between something that is living and something that is non-living. With many things, the difference is obvious: trees, grass, daisies, buttercups, ants, worms, mice, canaries, dogs and goldfish are living; tables, chairs, bricks, books, carpets, concrete, bread, coal and cars are non-living. Is there anything that the living things have in common with each other that does not apply to the non-living things? If so, we can use the common factor to separate the living from the non-living. Let us now consider the functions performed by all living things and compare these to what happens with non-living things:

a. **Feeding** means the taking in of some sort of raw materials. In the case of many plants, these raw materials take the form of water and carbon dioxide. However, a car needs petrol to make it work, but a car is not alive; so feeding is not, by itself, a deciding factor.

b. **Respiration** is a process of oxidation which enables a living organism to obtain energy from its food by combining it with oxygen. A car engine oxidizes petrol vapour in the cylinders. The way in which air is taken into a car engine is often called, by motor mechanics, the 'breathing' of the engine.

c. **Excretion** means getting rid of the waste products of oxidation. Plants and animals excrete, but so does a car engine, which gets rid of carbon monoxide, carbon dioxide and water (all of which are waste products) through the exhaust pipe.

d. **Growth** means developing from a simple structure to a more complicated structure and increasing in size. In plants and animals, this is achieved by the constant subdivision of cells. In the non-living group, most substances expand when they are heated, although they do not increase in mass; stalactites and stalagmites 'grow'; crystals will 'grow' in a saturated solution (see Investigation 1a) and crystals will appear to 'grow' in a chemical 'garden'.

e. **Movement** is more obvious in animals than in plants. Most animals are able to move from place to place; this movement is under their own control. Of course, many non-living things move: cars, buses, trains, ships and aeroplanes all move, but they are certainly not living things.

f. **Response** involves reacting to a stimulus. Plant stems grow away from the force of gravity and towards light; plant roots grow towards the force of gravity and towards water. Animals respond to many stimuli: watch the reaction of a dog or a cat when a sudden noise is made behind it. A car responds to pressure on the accelerator or brake pedal, but it is not alive.

g. **Reproduction** is the ability of living organisms to produce off-spring very similar to themselves. This cannot be done by non-living things: books do not produce leaflets, carpets do not produce rugs and loaves of bread do not produce rolls.

Some of these functions are performed by non-living things but never all of them. You will notice that of all these functions, the only one that is completely satisfactory as a deciding factor is reproduction. If objects can reproduce themselves, they are living; if they cannot, they are non-living.

Investigation 1a. 'Growing' crystals

Put about 250 cm³ of distilled water into a 400 cm³ beaker. Dissolve as much aluminium potassium sulphate(VI) (potash alum) as possible in the water and then heat the solution to about 50 °C. Add more aluminium potassium sulphate(VI) and stir until no more will dissolve—the excess settles on the bottom of the beaker. Place the beaker where it can remain undisturbed, cover it with a piece of paper to protect it from dust and leave it to cool to room temperature.

Tie a small metal nut to the end of a piece of thin string and suspend it in the saturated solution as shown in Figure 1.1(a). Leave the weighted piece of string in the solution with a cover over the beaker overnight. When you remove the weighted piece of string, you should find that it is covered with small crystals. These crystals are called seed crystals. Select the largest of the seed crystals and tie it to a piece of cotton. Re-saturate the solution by heating it, adding more aluminium potassium sulphate(VI) until the excess settles on the bottom of the beaker, and allow it to cool. Now suspend your seed crystal in the solution, cover it with a piece of paper, as shown in

Figure 1.1 'Growing' crystals

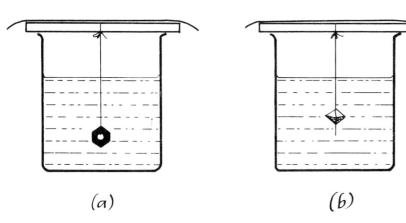

(a)　　　　　　　　*(b)*

5

Figure 1.1(b), and place the beaker where it can be left undisturbed at a steady temperature. Look at your crystal daily and note any change in size. If there is very little increase in size, remove the crystal, re-saturate the solution, allow it to cool and replace the crystal.

Harmful

You will notice that the crystal 'grows' by adding layers to the outside—very different from the way in which living things grow. Try growing crystals of copper(II) sulphate(VI) or sodium carbonate (washing soda), using the same method.

1.2. Plant and animal life

What is the difference between a dog and a tree? What is the difference between an elephant and a mushroom? What is the difference between an earthworm and the green slime on the surface of stagnant water?

In each of these pairs of living things, one is a member of the animal kingdom and the other is a member of the plant kingdom. How do we tell which is which? Is the deciding factor size, colour, shape, type of movement or method of reproduction, or is it a mixture of these and other factors? Table 1.4 shows the main characteristics of plants and animals by which they can be identified. In some cases, particularly the microscopic organisms, these differences are so small that it is difficult to distinguish with complete certainty between plants and animals.

TABLE 1.4. PLANT AND ANIMAL CHARACTERISTICS

	Plant	Animal
Body	Spreading, with a large surface area compared with volume.	Compact, with a small surface area compared with volume.
Movement	Restricted to growth and small slow changes of position of parts.	Normally able to move from place to place.
Feeding	Intake of simple substances to form more complicated substances. Most plants contain chlorophyll and are food-producers.	Intake of complicated substances which are broken down into simpler substances. No animals are food-producers; they contain no chlorophyll.
Cells	Plant cells have cell walls which are thick and are mainly cellulose.	Animal cells do not have a cell wall, only a cell membrane.
Response to Stimuli	Slow and, even then, only when the stimulus is applied over a period of time.	Fast response to a short application of the stimulus.

PLANT LIFE

1.3. Plants without seeds

If a plant does not produce seeds, it must be able to reproduce by some other means. Single-celled plants reproduce by division. If we assume that the cell is the shape of a cube and regular growth occurs, the volume increases faster than the surface area, as shown in Table 1.5.

TABLE 1.5. VARIATION OF SURFACE AREA AND VOLUME

Length of Cube Side	Surface Area	Volume	Ratio of Surface Area to Volume
1 mm	6 mm^2	1 mm^3	6 : 1
2 mm	24 mm^2	8 mm^3	3 : 1
3 mm	54 mm^2	27 mm^3	2 : 1
4 mm	96 mm^2	64 mm^3	3 : 2
5 mm	150 mm^2	125 mm^3	6 : 5
6 mm	216 mm^2	216 mm^3	1 : 1

The maximum size of a cell is limited by the ratio between the surface area and the cell volume, since all food and oxygen needed to maintain the cell must be taken in through the surface of the cell. At some stage in the growth of a cell, the surface area will become too small to maintain the rapidly increasing volume and, at this stage, the cell will reproduce by dividing into two completely independent daughter cells.

Other plants without seeds reproduce by means of spores. If you examine the underside of the leaf of a fern such as bracken, you will notice some brown markings. These are made up of thousands of spores, each of which is capable of growing into a plant, provided that it lands on a suitable surface under the correct conditions of temperature and humidity.

Plants without seeds include:

a. **Algae** are minute single-celled plants which include those that form the green slime in stagnant water. Because they contain chlorophyll, they are able to produce food by photosynthesis. They reproduce by simple division. Seaweeds are multi-celled algae with holdfasts which serve only to anchor them to the sea-bed.

b. **Fungi** are plants which do not contain chlorophyll, so they cannot produce food by photosynthesis. Because of this, they are either **parasites** (living on, and obtaining their food from, living animals or plants) or **saprophytes** (living on, and obtaining their food from, dead animals or plants). Fungi generally grow from spores, which germinate to produce thin thread-like structures called **hyphae**. The hyphae penetrate the material on which the spores fall and extract food from it in the form of a liquid. As the hyphae grow and intermingle, they form a mesh called the **mycelium**. In the case of **moulds**, a type of fungus which grows on rotting food, rotten wood and manure, slightly thicker hyphae with bulbous ends grow upwards from the mycelium. These bulbous ends contain spores which are released when the spore-case bursts. In the case of mushrooms, two or more hyphae join together to form a vertical growth which is bulbous at the top (we call this a 'button' mushroom), but as it develops, the lower part of the bulb breaks away from the stem (columella) to reveal a large number of delicate pink gills. These gills gradually darken in colour to a rich brown; spores are then released from between the gills. (See Figure 1.2.)

Figure 1.2 Moulds and mushrooms

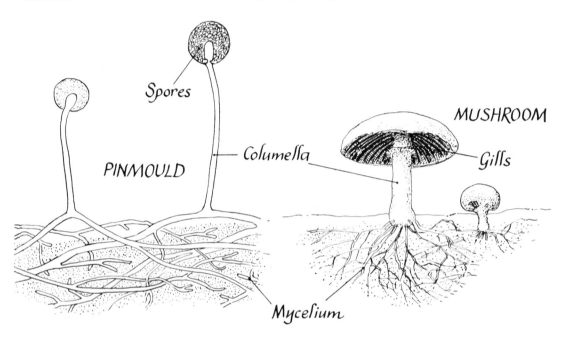

c. **Bacteria** are minute plants (for want of a better word) which contain no chlorophyll. Some bacteria perform useful functions while others cause disease. Among the useful bacteria are those which convert nitrogen into soluble nitrates for plant food and others which feed on dead plant and animal remains.

Certain types of bacteria serve a useful purpose within the bodies of animals. For example, in the caecum of a rabbit, bacteria break down the cellulose in the cell walls of the plants which the rabbit eats; bacteria perform the same function in the **rumen** (one of the compartments of the stomach of a ruminant, such as the cow, sheep, goat, deer, etc.). In this way, bacteria and the animal host assist each other; the bacteria break down the cellulose in return for a steady supply of food and ideal surroundings.

Among the harmful bacteria are those which produce toxins (poisons) when they enter the bloodstream. Other bacteria cause

8

many common diseases, such as chicken pox, pneumonia, diphtheria and tuberculosis.

Although there are many varieties of bacteria, there are three main types (see Figure 1.3) which can be identified by their general shape: **cocci** (pronounced 'cock eye'), **bacilli** (pronounced 'bass ill eye') and **spirilla.**

Figure 1.3 The main types of bacteria

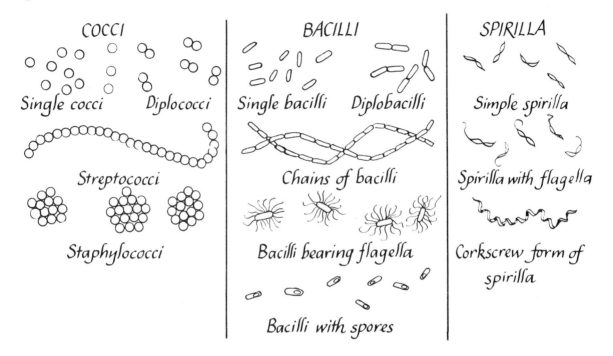

d. **Mosses and liverworts** are grouped together because they both contain chlorophyll, have no true roots and reproduce in two stages. These stages are:

1. The **gamete plant** of moss is the green, feathery-leaved plant which has male and female sex organs. It is called the gamete plant because the sex cells of any living organism which reproduces sexually are called **gametes.** For fertilization of the ova (female gametes) to take place, the male gametes must have a thin layer of water through which they can swim to reach the ova. This is why moss grows in damp places.

2. The **spore plant** grows from the gamete plant as a result of fertilization, and is a stalk with a spore capsule at the end. When the spores are ripe, they disperse and give rise to new gamete plants.

Liverworts require more moisture for fertilization than mosses and are frequently found growing in or near streams and waterfalls.

e. **Ferns** have true roots and, like the mosses and liverworts, reproduce in two stages. Fern spores grow into a gamete plant called

9

the **prothallus**, which is small and compact in comparison with the spore plant. The ova are fertilized in the same way as in the mosses. The spore plants, which are the well-known green fronds with the spore cases on the underside of the leaves, grow from the fertilized ova and the prothallus dies.

1.4. Plants with seeds

Gymnosperms are plants which produce their seeds in cones. Pine, fir, spruce, cedar and larch are all examples of gymnosperms and are all evergreen except the larch, which is **deciduous** (sheds its leaves in winter).

All other seed-bearing plants are **angiosperms**. There are two main groups: **monocotyledons** and **dicotyledons** (often called monocots and dicots). A cotyledon is a fleshy, seed leaf. In the seed of a monocot there is one cotyledon while in the seed of a dicot there are two cotyledons. Other differences between monocots and dicots are shown in Table 1.6.

TABLE 1.6. CHARACTERISTICS OF MONOCOTS AND DICOTS

	MONOCOTYLEDONS	DICOTYLEDONS
SEED	One cotyledon	Two cotyledons
STEM	Very little tapering from ground level to the top	Thicker at ground level than at the top
ROOT	Fibrous 'tufty' roots	Tap-rooted with lateral roots
LEAVES	Long narrow leaves with parallel veins, generally starting at ground level	Broad leaves with mid-rib (main vein) and lateral veins
FLOWER	Flower parts usually occur in threes	Flower parts usually occur in fours or fives

10

Investigation 1b. Examination of a dicot seed

Soak a broad bean or runner bean seed in water for several days. Remove the seed from the water and examine it. Can you see the place where it was attached to the pod? Are there any small holes in the outer coat? Gently squeeze the seed and note what happens. Carefully remove the outer coat and separate the cotyledons. Examine the cotyledons, particularly at the point where they are 'hinged'. Compare what you have seen with Figure 1.4.

Figure 1.4 External and internal features of a broad bean seed

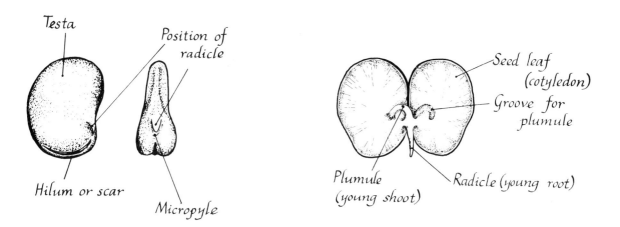

The **testa** protects the seed before and during germination. The **hilum** is the part of the seed that was attached to the pod of the parent plant. The **micropyle** is the small hole through which water is absorbed during germination. As the seed germinates, the cotyledons (which are 'hinged' at a point near the micropyle) absorb water and swell. This swelling splits the testa and the **radicle** then grows downwards while the **plumule** grows upwards. The young seedling uses the food stored in the cotyledons until the root is sufficiently developed to absorb water and mineral salts and the first leaves are able to photosynthesize. In some plants the cotyledons wither away at this stage while in others they form the first leaves.

ANIMAL LIFE

1.5. Invertebrates

Invertebrates are animals without a spinal column (backbone). There are over a million different species of invertebrates, the main groups including the following:

a. **Protozoa** are minute single-celled animals, such as the amoeba, which live in water and reproduce by division. Their size is

11

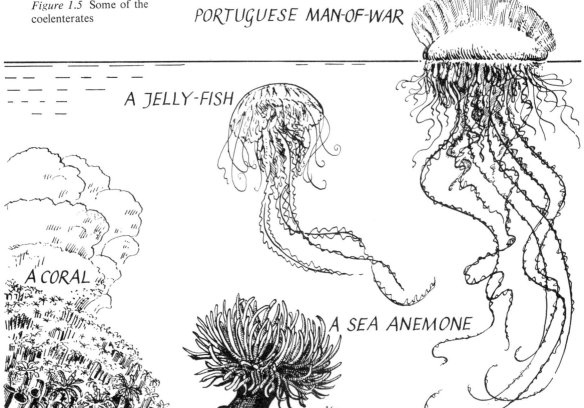

Figure 1.5 Some of the coelenterates

PORTUGUESE MAN-OF-WAR

A JELLY-FISH

A CORAL

A SEA ANEMONE

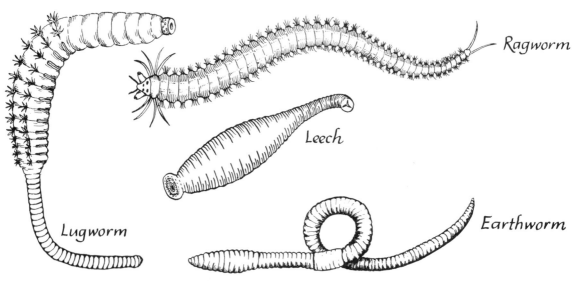

Figure 1.6 Some of the annelids

Ragworm

Leech

Lugworm

Earthworm

limited by the same factors that limit the size of single-celled plants (see Section 1.3).

b. **Coelenterates** are water animals which have only two cell layers, an outside layer and an inside layer. The coelenterates include hydra, jellyfish, sea anemone, etc. (see Figure 1.5).

c. **Platyhelminthes** are flat worms, often parasitic, such as the tapeworm and the liver fluke.

d. **Annelids** are round worms with segmented bodies, such as the earthworm (see Figure 1.6). Many annelids are **hermaphrodite** (bi-sexual—each animal having both male and female sex organs) and reproduce by laying eggs.

e. **Arthropods** have segmented bodies with jointed legs and a hard outer covering called an exoskeleton. There are four main groups of arthropod:

(i) **Crustaceans**, such as shrimps, prawns, crabs, lobsters and crayfish, which all breathe by means of gills and live mainly in water. They reproduce by laying eggs. There are about 35 000 species of crustaceans (see Figure 1.7).

Figure 1.7 Some of the crustaceans

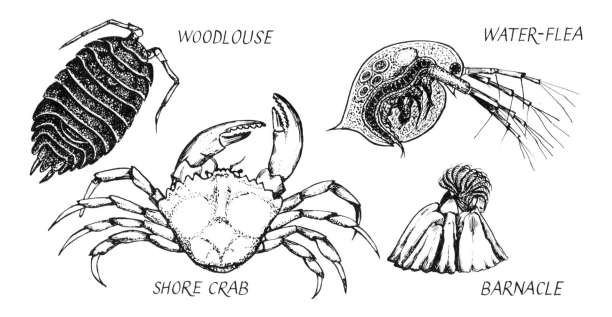

WOODLOUSE

WATER-FLEA

SHORE CRAB

BARNACLE

(ii) **Insects** are by far the largest group of arthropods, having about 850 000 species. Insects include flies, ants, beetles, moths and butterflies, a few of which are shown in Figure 1.8.

The body of an insect can be identified by having three distinct parts: the head, thorax and abdomen. The head has simple eyes and compounds eyes, a mouth and antennae (feelers). The thorax has three pairs of legs and, in many species, two pairs of wings. In some species, one pair of wings has become

13

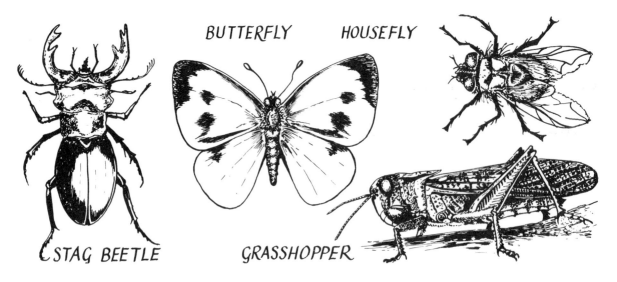

STAG BEETLE   BUTTERFLY   HOUSEFLY   GRASSHOPPER

Figure 1.8 Some of the insects

Figure 1.9 The external features of an insect

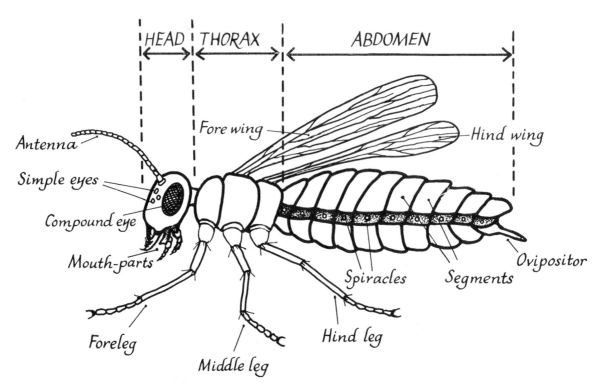

HEAD | THORAX | ABDOMEN

Antenna

Simple eyes

Compound eye

Mouth-parts

Fore wing

Hind wing

Spiracles

Segments

Ovipositor

Foreleg

Middle leg

Hind leg

14

modified to form wing cases. The abdomen has spiracles (pores) between the segments, through which the insect breathes, and, in the female insect, an ovipositor (an egg-laying tube). The main features of an insect are shown in Figure 1.9.

Reproduction usually occurs in a four-stage cycle (see Figure 1.10), although some species reproduce in a three-stage or even a two-stage cycle. The four-stage cycle starts with the egg. The egg hatches into a **larva** (grub, maggot or caterpillar) which spends most of its time eating and growing, shedding its skin several times to allow for its growth. Before the last shedding, the larva moves to a sheltered place and spins a cocoon round itself to form a **pupa** or chrysalis. During this stage, there is very little movement, but many changes take place within the pupa. Eventually the **imago** (mature adult) emerges from the pupal case.

The length of time an insect spends in each of the stages of development varies considerably. For example, the speckled wood butterfly lays its eggs at any time from early May until late July. If the eggs are laid in early May, from egg to larva takes about two weeks, from larva to pupa takes about three weeks and from pupa to imago takes between three and four weeks. If the eggs are laid in late July, from egg to larva takes about four weeks, from larva to pupa takes about eight weeks and from pupa to imago takes about six weeks. Can you

Figure 1.10 Life cycle of the cabbage-white butterfly

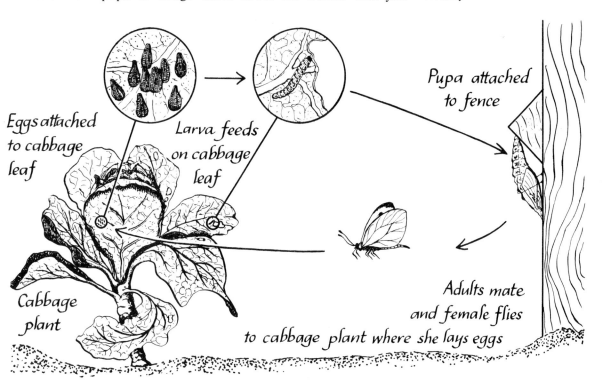

Eggs attached to cabbage leaf

Larva feeds on cabbage leaf

Pupa attached to fence

Cabbage plant

Adults mate and female flies to cabbage plant where she lays eggs

suggest what conditions may be responsible for these variations in time?

Different varieties spend the winter months in different stages. For example, the brown fritillary butterfly winters as an egg, the clouded yellow butterfly winters as a larva and the swallow-tail butterfly winters as a pupa.

(iii) **Arachnids**, which include spiders, have two parts to the body, the front part being the head and thorax combined and the rear part being the abdomen. The front part has simple eyes only and four pairs of legs. At the rear end of the abdomen of a spider are **spinnarets**, which produce a liquid that solidifies on contact with air to form a web. Spiders reproduce by laying eggs which hatch out into minute spiders. The arachnids also include mites, ticks and scorpions (see Figure 1.11).

Figure 1.11 Some of the arachnids

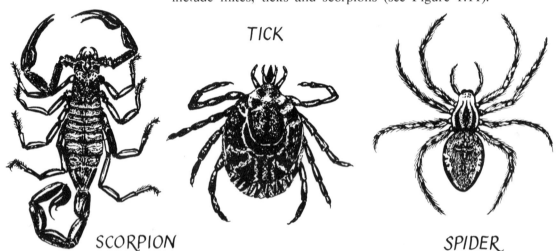

TICK

SCORPION

SPIDER

(iv) **Myriapods** are many-legged animals, including about 1 000 species of centipedes (one pair of legs per segment) and about 1 000 species of millipedes (two pairs of legs per segment).

f. **Molluscs** have soft unsegmented bodies, often with a protective shell. The shell can be either single, as in the case of snails, winkles, etc., or double (hinged), as in the case of oysters, clams, cockles, mussels, etc. Some types, such as slugs, cuttlefish, octopuses and squids have no protective shell (see Figure 1.12).

g. **Echinoderms** have a circular body with a mouth in the centre and five or more extensions radiating from it. Typical examples are the starfish, brittle star and sea urchin (see Figure 1.13).

1.6. Vertebrates

A vertebrate is an animal with a spinal column. Some vertebrates are cold-blooded (poikilothermic). A cold-blooded vertebrate's

16

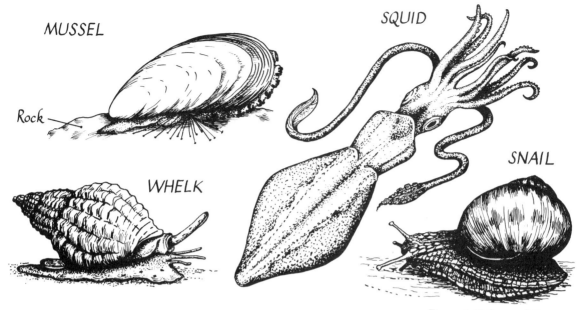

Figure 1.12 Some of the molluscs

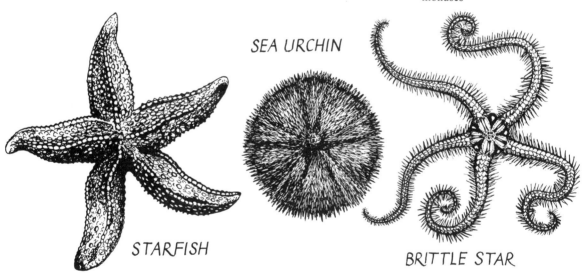

Figure 1.13 Some of the echinoderms

blood temperature varies with the temperature of its surroundings, usually being one or two degrees higher. For example, the blood temperature of a fish swimming in water at 20 °C will be about 22 °C. There are three main groups of cold-blooded vertebrate:

a. **Fish** have a covering of overlapping scales, and fins for propulsion and manoeuvring. Along each side is a lateral line, which enables the fish to detect changes in pressure. Some fish, such as the shark and the skate, are cartilaginous (have a skeleton of cartilage or gristle), while others, such as the herring, have a bony skeleton. The main features of a fish are shown in Figure 1.14.

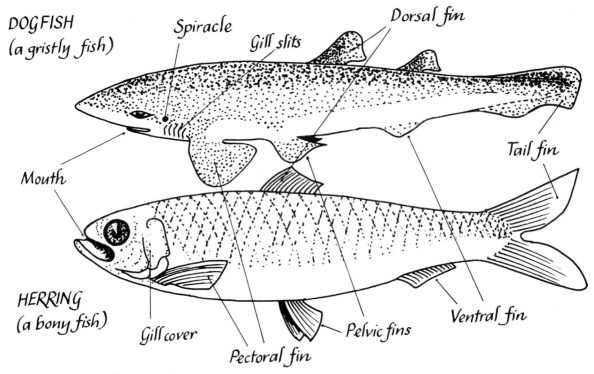

DOGFISH
(a gristly fish)

Spiracle

Gill slits

Dorsal fin

Mouth

Tail fin

HERRING
(a bony fish)

Gill cover

Pectoral fin

Pelvic fins

Ventral fin

Figure 1.14 The external features of a fish

Figure 1.15 Sculling a boat

18

Fish breathe by taking in water through the mouth and passing it out through the gills. Water contains dissolved oxygen, and the function of the gills is to extract this oxygen from the water. In running water, a fish usually faces upstream so that there is a flow of water from head to tail. This is the direction in which the scales overlap and the flow extracts water from the gills after the dissolved oxygen has been removed. In still water, the pectoral fins quiver to keep water flowing in this direction past the gill covers.

A fish swims by moving its tail fin from side to side in the same way as a boat can be moved forward by sculling (moving an oar from side to side at the stern of the boat), as shown in Figure 1.15.

Most fish reproduce by laying eggs, which are fertilized in the water by the sperms in the milt, which the male fish ejects into the water. A few species of fish are viviparous (reproduce by live birth).

b. **Amphibians** are animals which, in their early stages, live entirely in water and breathe by means of gills. Later, they develop legs and lungs and are able to live on land, although they frequently return to water, particularly for breeding. Details of the life cycle of the frog, a typical amphibian, will be found in Chapter 12. Other amphibians include toads and newts (see Figure 1.16).

Figure 1.16 Some of the amphibians

Spotted salamander

Tree frog

Crested newt

19

LIZARD

CHAMELEON

TURTLE

SNAKE

Figure 1.17 Some of the reptiles

c. **Reptiles** are animals which have hard, scaly skins and breathe with lungs. Some examples of reptiles are shown in Figure 1.17.

Some reptiles do not have legs (snakes) and move with a crawling action. Reptiles with legs move diagonally opposite legs together— left front leg with right rear leg and right front leg with left rear leg. This action causes the body to twist as the reptile moves, as shown in Figure 1.18.

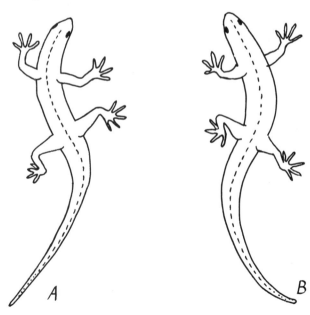

A

B

Figure 1.18 How a reptile moves

Most reptiles live on land (lizards, slow-worms, snakes, etc.) but a few (crocodiles, turtles, etc.) live in water. Most reptiles reproduce by laying soft-shelled eggs on land, which are then left under suitable conditions to hatch. A few bear forth their young alive.

The remaining two groups of vertebrates are warm-blooded (homothermic). The blood temperature of a warm-blooded animal remains constant, to within a degree or so, no matter what the temperature of its surroundings is. The blood temperature of man is about 37 °C, whether he is in the tropics with the air temperature at 45 °C or in the Arctic with the air temperature at -15 °C. In order to achieve this stability of blood temperature, warm-blooded animals have become adapted to control heat loss from the body.

a. **Birds** are animals which are covered with feathers, have wings, lay hard-shelled eggs and breathe with lungs. The bones of a bird's skeleton are less dense than the bones of most other animals because of the large air spaces within the bones. Most birds can fly, but there are some species which use their wings for other purposes: penguins have modified wings which are used for swimming; ostriches, emus, kiwis, domestic fowl, etc., use their wings to enable them to run faster on land. Some examples of birds are shown in Figure 1.19.

Figure 1.19 Some of the birds

HERON

SWALLOW

KESTREL

PENGUIN

Birds control heat loss from the body in two ways:
1. In spring, most birds moult; this reduces the thickness of the insulating layer of feathers.
2. The angle between the shafts of the feathers and the skin can be varied. In cold weather, the angle is increased, thus increasing the thickness of the insulating layer; in warm weather, the feathers lie flatter against the skin (see Figure 1.20). Common garden birds, such as sparrows, thrushes and blackbirds, all appear to be fatter in winter than in summer. This is because their feathers are 'fluffed out' to reduce heat loss.

WINTER

Figure 1.20 Feather angle in warm and cold weather

SUMMER

The feathers of swimming birds are coated with a water-repelling grease. This enables them to float on the layer of air which is trapped between the skin and the outer surface of the feathers. The grease is produced by a gland on the back, just in front of the bird's tail. You may have seen a duck scratching its back and then its underside with its beak. This is how the grease is applied to the feathers.

You will have noticed that the beaks of birds vary a great deal. This variation depends largely on the bird's diet and, to a lesser extent, on the way it moves when it is not flying. Compare the way in which canaries and budgerigars move about in their cages. They can both fly but a budgerigar also uses its beak. Some of the ways in which birds' beaks have become adapted are shown in Figure 1.21.

b. **Mammals** are the most advanced and the most complicated of all the groups of animals. Mammals have a covering of hair or fur, the thickness of which is controlled in the same way as the feathers of a bird. All mammals are lung breathers and live bearers. The ovum is fertilized and the embryo develops inside the mother's body. After birth the young is suckled (fed with milk from the mother's breast). The milk is produced by mammary glands in the breast,

EAGLE - *flesh eater*

FLAMINGO - *water strainer*

PELICAN - *fish eater*

HUMMING BIRD - *nectar eater*

GOLDFINCH - *seed and insect eater*

MACAW - *seed eater*

Figure 1.21 Some beak adaptations

hence the term 'mammal'. (The duck-billed platypus is classified as a mammal because its young are suckled in spite of the fact that it lays eggs.)

There are many types of mammal (see Figure 1.22); their size, shape and features are adapted to their particular way of life (what they eat, how they obtain their food and how they avoid their natural enemies). The main types of mammal are:

1. **Swimming mammals**, such as whales and porpoises.
2. **Flying mammals**, such as bats.
3. **Marsupials (pouched mammals)**, such as kangaroos and wallabies, where after birth the young are transferred to the pouch and are suckled there.
4. **Insectivorous mammals**, such as anteaters, hedgehogs and moles which live on a diet of insects.
5. **Rodents (gnawing mammals)**, such as rats, mice, beavers and squirrels.
6. **Carnivorous (flesh-eating) mammals** which include all members of the cat and dog families, such as tigers, leopards, wolves and foxes. You will notice that all carnivorous mammals have long, sharp fangs for tearing flesh.
7. **Hoofed mammals** which are all herbivorous (plant-eating). Some have a single hoof, such as horses, while others have a double or cloven hoof, such as cattle, sheep, pigs, deer and antelope. Most

23

BAT

KANGAROO

DUCK-BILLED
PLATYPUS

GIRAFFE

SHREW

CHIMPANZEE

Figure 1.22 Some of the mammals

of the cloven-hoofed mammals chew the cud and are able to digest cellulose. These mammals are called **ruminants**.

8. **Primates** are man-like mammals with a well-developed brain. They have pentadactyl (five-fingered or five-toed) limbs in which the thumb and big toe can move in opposition to the rest of the fingers and toes. This ability is an important evolutionary development (see Chapter 14). All primates have eyes which look forward and most have the ability to stand erect. Primates include lemurs, monkeys, chimpanzees, gorillas, baboons and man.

1.7. Webs of dependence

All animals eat plants. Is this statement true or false? If we consider herbivorous animals, it is obviously true. What about carnivorous animals? Foxes eat ducks, ducks eat worms and worms eat dead leaves, which were once part of a plant. This is known as a food chain, and no matter which animal you start with, the final food will be some kind of plant life. All carnivorous animals prey on other (usually smaller) animals and all animals have natural enemies. The defensive methods used by animals against their natural enemies are many and varied. Camouflage and immobility (stillness), speed, the ability to burrow, fly, climb, swim or look very ferocious, physical strength and size are all defensive methods used by animals in their struggle for existence.

Animal life also depends on plant life for its constant supply of oxygen, because it is produced when green plants photosynthesize. Plant life depends on animal life for its constant supply of carbon dioxide and, to a lesser degree, nitrogen compounds.

In order to exist, green plants need sunlight, water, carbon dioxide and certain mineral salts, all of which are non-living. Carbon dioxide is constantly produced by the process of respiration in animals and plants, and water and mineral salts are a part of the soil in which the plants grow.

NON-LIVING THINGS

1.8. The soil

One of the surest ways of annoying a gardener or a farmer is to call soil 'dirt'. Soil is a complicated mixture of substances in varying proportions.

Investigation 1c. The solids in soil

Remove the large stones from a sample of soil and put the sample in a gas jar to a depth of about 3 cm. Pour water into the gas jar until it is about half full and shake the soil and water thoroughly. Put the gas jar on a level surface and leave for some time to allow the soil to settle. Now, compare the appearance of your gas jar with Figure 1.23. You will notice that the first particles to settle were the

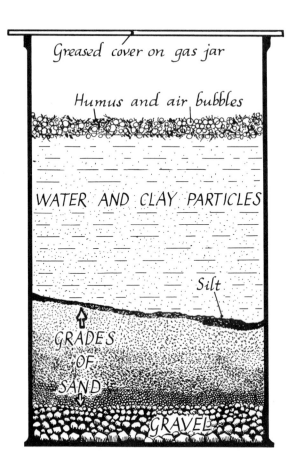

Figure 1.23 Separation of the solids in soil

larger ones and the last to settle were the fine particles. The larger particles are sand while the smaller particles are clay. The humus, which consists of decayed and decaying plant and animal remains, floats on top of the water but later may become waterlogged and sink to the bottom.

From this investigation you will see that the main constituents of soil are clay, sand and humus.

Investigation 1d. To separate sand from clay

Put a sample of soil in a beaker, and half fill the beaker with water. Stir the soil, allow it to settle and remove the floating humus from the surface. An alternative method of removing the humus is to put the

26

sample in a metal container, such as a tin lid, heat it strongly with a bunsen burner and allow it to cool. If you use this method, note the smell of the burning humus.

When the humus is removed, stir the soil with some water in a beaker and decant (carefully pour off) the muddy water into a large container, such as a bucket. Add more water to the soil remaining in the beaker, stir and decant. Repeat this process until the water clears almost immediately when you stop stirring. The material left at the bottom of the beaker is sand and the material which settles to the bottom of the bucket is clay. These materials can be dried by decanting the water and spreading the damp sand and clay on sheets of newspaper in a warm place. What are the proportions of sand and clay in your sample of soil? If a microscope is available, examine some dry sand and some dry clay. Which contains the larger particles?

In addition to sand, clay and humus, many soils contain chalk.

Investigation 1e. Chalk in soil

Cover the bottom of a beaker with soil to a depth of about 5 mm. Now, cover the soil with dilute hydrochloric acid and note any effervescence. Be careful not to confuse air bubbles rising to the surface with carbon dioxide produced by the reaction between the acid and the chalk. If chalk is present in the soil, you will be able to hear the effervescence and the bottom of the beaker will become slightly warm.

Harmful

Soil which has a large proportion of clay is called a **heavy clay soil**. Soil which has a large proportion of sand is called a **light sandy soil**. Soil which has about equal amounts of sand and clay is called a **loam**. Soil which contains a large proportion of humus is called a **peaty soil**. Soil containing a large amount of chalk is called a **marl**.

Investigation 1f. Air in soil

Pour some air-dried soil into a 200 cm³ measuring cylinder until it reaches the 100 cm³ mark. From another measuring cylinder, pour 100 cm³ of water into the cylinder containing the soil. Now, carefully shake the cylinder to allow the water to saturate the soil and displace the air from it. Note the level of the water in the measuring cylinder. The difference between this level and the 200 cm³ mark is the volume of air displaced from your 100 cm³ sample of soil (i.e. the percentage). Repeat this investigation, using samples of dry sand and dry clay. Which has the greater percentage of air-space? Is there any connection between the percentage of air-space and particle size?

27

Can you explain why a clay soil is described as 'heavy' and a sandy soil is described as 'light'?

Investigation 1g. Soil retention and drainage

Place a small wad of cotton wool in the neck of each of two equal-sized filter funnels. Fill the funnels to within 1 cm of the top, one with dry clay and the other with dry sand. Rest the funnels in 100 cm³ measuring cylinders, as shown in Figure 1.24, and pour 100 cm³ of

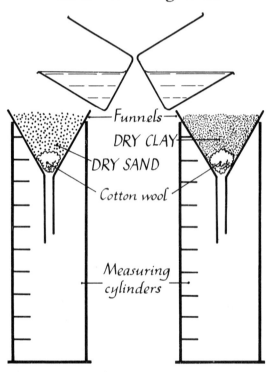

Figure 1.24 Soil retention and drainage

water slowly into each funnel, being careful not to allow the water to overflow. Note the speed at which the water drains through and also the total volume that collects in each of the measuring cylinders. Which type of material retains the greater volume of water? Which type drains better? Is there any connection between the results of Investigations 1f and 1g?

Investigation 1h. Capillarity in soil

The ability of a substance to soak up water (or any other liquid) against the force of gravity is called **capillarity**.

Take two pieces of glass tubing, about 30 cm long and at least 2 cm in diameter. Plug one end of each tube with a wad of cotton

28

wool and tie pieces of muslin over the ends to secure the cotton wool. Fill one tube with dry clay and the other with dry sand. Place both tubes simultaneously (at the same time) in a container of water, as shown in Figure 1.25. Watch the water rising in each of the tubes.

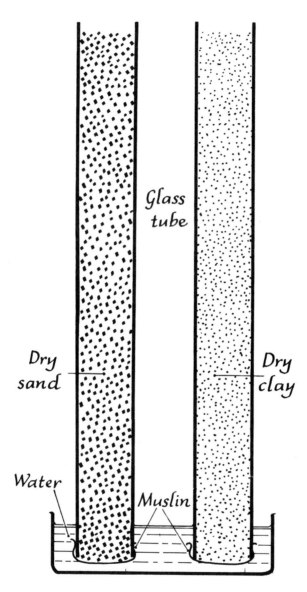

Figure 1.25 Capillarity in soil

In which does the water rise faster? In which tube does the water rise higher? Which type of soil is less likely to dry out during a drought?

Living organisms in soil are many and varied. By far the most numerous organisms in soil are bacteria, which maintain the

29

fertility of the soil by decomposing animal and plant remains, producing humus and soluble salts for plant nutrition.

1.9. Soil formation

Soil is formed by erosion (breaking down) of rocks. Erosion occurs in a number of ways:

a. **Temperature variation**. When the surface of rock is exposed to the radiant heat of the sun, the temperature of its surface layer rises. This layer expands. The lower layers heat up more slowly, do not reach such a high temperature and expand less than the surface layer. This difference in expansion produces stresses between the layers, causing thin flakes of rock to become detached. At night, the surface cools faster than the lower layers and contracts. This contraction causes the surface to crack.

b. **Frost**. When water freezes to form ice, it expands. When water seeps into cracks in the rocks and then freezes, the force of expansion is sufficient to crack the rock still further, thus making a wider and deeper crack. This process continues until eventually the rock splits.

c. **Rain**. When drops of rain fall through the air, they absorb a small amount of carbon dioxide. A solution of carbon dioxide in water is a weak acid called carbonic acid, which is capable of dissolving certain mineral salts in rocks. Even without the action of carbonic acid, rain constantly beating against rock over a long period of time will erode it.

d. **Rivers and streams.** Constantly moving water will erode rocks: very slowly in the case of the harder rocks and faster in the case of the softer rocks. Once small particles of rock have been dislodged, they are carried downstream and cause further erosion by impact. As the rivers reach lower and more level ground, the speed of the water decreases and the particles of rock drop to the bottom to form a silt or sediment. The larger particles drop first and, as the speed of the water decreases still further, the smaller particles fall to the bottom to form a fine mud. Soil deposited in this way is called **alluvial soil**.

e. **Moving ice**. During the ice age, the slow-moving glaciers and sheet ice broke away the rock surface. This material was carried by the moving ice and deposited as the ice melted.

f. **Wind**. In predominantly dry areas, a strong wind can carry small particles for considerable distances. When this occurs, it is called a duststorm or a sandstorm. When fast-moving air containing these particles hits solid rock, the particles wear away the rock by a scouring action.

1.10. Types of rock

Although rocks vary in their chemical composition, they can be classified into three main groups according to how they were formed. The three groups are **igneous**, **sedimentary** and **metamorphic**.

a. **Igneous rocks** are those which were formed when the surface of the earth solidified. 'Igneous' means 'formed by fire'. Most igneous rocks are crystalline in structure, the size of the crystals depending on the rate of cooling. Granite is an example of an igneous rock which has a coarse crystalline structure, because it cooled and solidified slowly, deep within the earth's crust. Basalt has a finer crystalline structure, because it cooled and solidified more rapidly on the surface of the earth's crust. Lava, which issues as a liquid from an erupting volcano and then solidifies, is an igneous rock with a fine crystalline structure. It is interesting to note that the word 'volcano' is derived from Vulcan who was the Roman god of fire. Because igneous rocks were formed long before any form of life existed on the earth, fossils are never found in igneous rocks.

b. **Sedimentary rocks** were formed later, from materials carried by water. These materials included:
 (i) Particles produced as a result of the weathering and erosion of existing rocks.
 (ii) Salts dissolved out of existing rocks and later precipitated after the solution became saturated.
(iii) Calcium carbonate from living organisms.
Typical sedimentary rocks are sandstone, rock salt, chalk, limestone and shale.

c. **Metamorphic rocks** were formed by the action of heat and pressure on existing rocks or by the action of one of these factors alone. If limestone were subjected to heat alone, it would become marble. If shale were strongly compressed, it would become slate. Typical rocks formed by the action of both heat and pressure are gneiss and schist.

Test your understanding

1. What are the main differences between living and non-living things?
2. What characteristics would you look for in a living thing to enable you to determine whether it was a plant or an animal?
3. By what methods can seedless plants reproduce?
4. What characteristics indicate that grass is a monocotyledon and an oak tree is a dicotyledon?
5. What is the function of the micropyle in a seed?
6. What are the essential differences between a butterfly and a spider?
7. Explain the meanings of 'cold-blooded' and 'warm-blooded'.

8. If you were given two bones of about the same size and shape and were told that one was the bone of a bird and the other was the bone of a mammal, how would you decide which was which?

9. How do birds keep warm in cold weather?

10. Explain how animals depend on plants and how plants depend on animals.

11. If you were given two samples of soil and were told that one was a clay soil and the other was a sandy soil, what would you do to determine which one was which?

12. When the tide is out, a sandy beach is dry but the surface of the mud in a tidal estuary is wet. Explain why this is so.

13. Make a list of the things in your living-room and classify them under the following headings: 'animal origin', 'plant origin' and 'never alive'.

14. If you were presented with a fossil, said to have been discovered in a piece of granite, why would you be suspicious?

Chapter 2

Water

About 70 per cent of the earth's surface is covered by water. All living organisms contain water: plants contain about 90 per cent water while the human body contains over 60 per cent water. The processes of life involve chemical reactions; the materials taking part in these reactions must be in solution and must be transported in order to react together. Water is the solvent in which these materials are dissolved and transported.

2.1. The impurities in water

Water is usually found to contain certain impurities. The nature of these impurities differs from one source to another.

a. **Sea water** contains insoluble particles brought down by rivers (these particles are eventually deposited on the sea-bed) and dissolved mineral salts, mainly sodium chloride.

b. **River water** contains insoluble particles of rock and dissolved mineral salts, the nature of which depends on the chemical composition of the ground through which the river and its tributaries flow. River water will also contain unnatural pollution, which includes industrial waste and treated sewage.

c. **Stream water** contributes insoluble particles of rock and dissolved mineral salts to the river into which it flows. Stream water generally has less pollution than river water.

d. **Spring water** has fewer impurities than river or stream water. Springs occur on the side of a hill in which a basin-shaped, non-porous layer (frequently clay) lies below a porous layer. Rainwater filters through the porous layer until it reaches the non-porous layer, thus saturating the porous layer. When the level of saturation reaches the rim of the basin, springs will appear along this rim. The level at which springs occur is called the spring line (see Figure 2.1).

e. **Wells** provide water which contains impurities, the amount and nature of which depends on the depth of the well and the chemical composition of the ground in which the well is sunk. If you dig down into the ground, you will eventually reach a depth at which the hole will begin to fill with water at the bottom. This is because the hole has

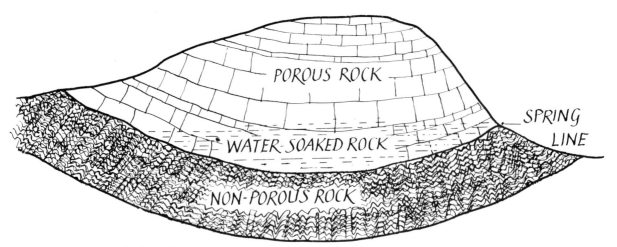

Figure 2.1 The formation of springs

reached ground which is saturated with water. The level at which water saturation occurs is called the **water table**. When a well is sunk in an area where the water table is close to the surface, the well will be a shallow one, but the water may contain pollution from the surface of the ground. Water from a deep well is less likely to contain surface pollution, because the water has filtered through a great depth in order to reach the water table.

In order to obtain water from most wells, it must be pumped to the surface. However, where a well is sunk in a basin in which the layers form a 'sandwich' of porous rock between two layers of non-porous rock, the water will gush out under pressure. Such wells are called **artesian wells** (see Figure 2.2). The first known well of this type was

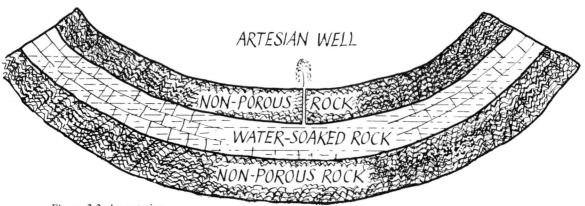

Figure 2.2 An artesian well

sunk in 1126 in the French province of Artois (formerly Artesium), hence the term, artesian well. Two examples of areas where artesian wells have been sunk are London and Paris, both of which are situated in basins. It is important to note that the water from an artesian well will only rise to the level of the water table in the porous rock.

34

f. **Rainwater** will contain dilute carbonic acid, formed when carbon dioxide dissolves in water. In industrial areas, rainwater may also contain soot particles and dilute sulphurous acid (sulphuric (IV) acid), the latter being formed when sulphur dioxide or hydrogen sulphide dissolves in water. It is the presence of these acids in rainwater which causes erosion to stone buildings.

2.2 Hardness of water

Investigation 2a. What is 'hard' water?

Wash your hands with soap in some rainwater. Does the soap produce a lather almost immediately, or does it produce a scum first? Now, wash your hands with the same type of soap in some lime-water which has turned cloudy and then clear again, after carbon dioxide has been bubbled through it. What difference do you notice?

Hard water is water in which it is difficult to produce a lather with soap. **Soft water** lathers easily with soap. Which of your samples of water was softer?

The next three investigations will compare the hardness of different types of water. To ensure that the comparisons are fair and valid, the conditions under which they are made must be the same throughout. These are the conditions:
1. All test-tubes must be of the same size (19 mm $\times$ 150 mm is suitable).
2. The same volume of water must be tested in each case (10 cm^3 is suitable).
3. All of the samples should be at the same temperature.
4. Soap must be added in standard amounts. Soap flakes may be used since, for the purpose of these investigations, they are about the same size and thickness.
5. The depth and duration of lather must be standardized (a 1-cm depth of lather lasting for fifteen seconds after the end of agitation is suitable).

Investigation 2b. Temporary hardness

Label two test-tubes 'A' and 'B'. Into tube A, put 10 cm^3 of tap water and into tube B, put 10 cm^3 of tap water which has been boiled for five minutes and allowed to cool.

Put one soap flake into tube A, close the mouth of the tube with a cork and shake the tube until the soap flake has dissolved or disintegrated. If this does not produce a standard lather, add another soap flake and shake again. Repeat this procedure until a standard lather is produced. Note the number of flakes you have added.

A convenient method of transferring a soap flake to the water in the test-tube is to pick the flake up with the moistened end of a wooden splint and then dip it into the water.

Add soap flakes, one at a time, to the water in tube B until you obtain a standard lather. Make a note of the number of flakes you have added.

You may find that tube B required fewer flakes to produce a standard lather. This indicates that boiling has removed some of the hardness from the water. The type of hardness which can be removed by boiling is called **temporary hardness**. This temporary hardness is usually caused by the presence of calcium hydrogencarbonate, which is soluble in water. When water containing calcium hydrogen-carbonate is boiled, the calcium hydrogencarbonate is decomposed into calcium carbonate, carbon dioxide and water. The calcium carbonate thus produced is insoluble and forms a deposit in the vessel in which the water is boiled.

$$Ca(HCO_3)_2 \rightarrow CaCO_3 + CO_2 + H_2O$$
(calcium hydrogen- (calcium (carbon (water)
carbonate) carbonate) dioxide)

If you found that tubes A and B required an equal number of soap flakes to produce a standard lather, the water supply in your district has no temporary hardness.

Water with artificial temporary hardness can be made by bubbling carbon dioxide through a 10 per cent solution of lime-water (one part of lime-water to nine parts of distilled or de-ionized water) until the cloudiness, which is produced at first, has disappeared. The cloudiness first produced is caused by the formation of in-soluble calcium carbonate.

$$Ca(OH)_2 + CO_2 \rightarrow CaCO_3 + H_2O$$
(lime-water) (carbon (calcium (water)
dioxide) carbonate)

By adding more carbon dioxide, the calcium carbonate is converted into calcium hydrogencarbonate.

$$CaCO_3 + CO_2 + H_2O \rightarrow Ca(HCO_3)_2$$
(calcium (carbon (water) (calcium hydrogencarbonate) dioxide) carbonate)

It is this reaction which gives water from chalky districts its temporary hardness.

Investigation 2c. Permanent hardness

Label two test-tubes 'C' and 'D'. Dissolve 5 g of magnesium sulphate(VI) in 100 cm³ of distilled or de-ionized water and put 10 cm³ of this solution into tube C. Boil the rest of the solution for five minutes, adding more distilled or de-ionized water to make up any loss by evaporation, thus maintaining the strength of the solution. Allow this solution to cool and put 10 cm³ into tube D.

Now add soap flakes, one at a time, as you did in Investigation 2b, to each of the test-tubes until you obtain a standard lather. Note the number of flakes added to each test-tube. Does boiling remove permanent hardness?

Investigation 2d. Total hardness

Label three test-tubes 'E', 'F' and 'G'. Into tube E, put 10 cm³ of distilled or de-ionized water. Into tube F, put 10 cm³ of tap water. Into tube G, put 10 cm³ of tap water which has been boiled for five minutes and allowed to cool.

Repeat the process of adding soap flakes to each tube until you obtain a standard lather in each. Note the number of flakes added to each tube.

TOTAL HARDNESS = TEMPORARY HARDNESS + PERMANENT HARDNESS

If we call the number of flakes added to each tube by its label, we can determine the proportions of temporary hardness and permanent hardness in our water supply:

$$Temporary\ hardness = G - E$$

$$Permanent\ hardness = F - G$$

$$Total\ hardness\qquad = F - E$$

2.3. Stalactites and stalagmites

In limestone caves, where water filters through the limestone and drips from the roof, **stalactites** form on the roof and **stalagmites** rise to meet them from the floor.

When rain falls, it dissolves carbon dioxide to form a weak acid called **carbonic acid.**

$$H_2O + CO_2 \rightarrow H_2CO_3$$
(water)   (carbon   (carbonic
              dioxide)   acid)

37

As this dilute carbonic acid passes through the limestone, it reacts with the limestone to form soluble calcium hydrogencarbonate.

$$CaCO_3 + H_2CO_3 \rightarrow Ca(HCO_3)_2$$

(limestone)   (carbonic   (calcium hydrogen-
acid)   carbonate)

When this solution reaches the roof of the cave, some of the water evaporates and the calcium hydrogencarbonate loses carbon dioxide. This causes it to revert to calcium carbonate, which forms the stalactites and stalagmites (see Figure 2.3).

$$Ca(HCO_3)_2 \rightarrow CaCO_3 + CO_2 + H_2O$$

(calcium hydrogen-   (limestone)   (carbon   (water)
carbonate)   dioxide)

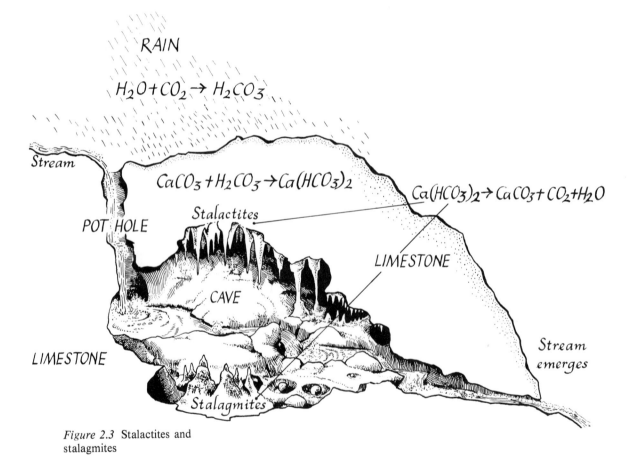

Figure 2.3 Stalactites and stalagmites

2.4. Softening water

Although mineral salts in water are desirable in our diet, their presence is a disadvantage when the water is to be used for washing.

Removing temporary hardness

a. **Boiling.** You already know (from Investigation 2b) that boiling will remove temporary hardness. Unfortunately, this precipitates calcium carbonate. When this deposit forms in a kettle, it is called **fur**. When it forms in a boiler or water pipes, it is called **scale**. The formation of these deposits reduces the capacity of kettles and boilers. When scale builds up in a pipe, the steam pressure in the boiler will increase and this could cause an explosion. Also, some of the energy normally used to heat the water is wasted in heating these deposits, thereby reducing the efficiency of the kettle or the boiler.

b. **Clark's process.** Another method of removing temporary hardness is **Clark's process**, in which a carefully calculated amount of slaked lime is added to the water. This has the effect of converting the soluble calcium hydrogencarbonate into calcium carbonate, which is precipitated.

$$Ca(HCO_3)_2 + Ca(OH)_2 \rightarrow 2CaCO_3 + 2H_2O$$

(calcium hydrogen- (slaked lime) (calcium (water)
carbonate)   carbonate)

Removing total hardness

a. **Adding soap.** When soap is added to hard water, it must first soften the water, by reacting with the soluble salts causing the hardness, and form a scum, before it can form a lather.

$$HARD\ WATER + SOAP \rightarrow SOFT\ WATER + SCUM$$

$$SOFT\ WATER + SOAP \rightarrow SOFT\ WATER + LATHER$$

Investigation 2e. Making soap

Stir 10 cm³ of olive oil with 5 cm³ of methylated spirits in a beaker and add 50 cm³ of 10 per cent sodium hydroxide (caustic soda) solution. Boil this mixture for about twenty minutes, stirring all the time and adding distilled or de-ionized water at intervals to replace water which has evaporated. Remove the heat source, add 100 cm³ of brine and stir. When the contents of the beaker have cooled, remove the solid crust from the surface and rinse it in water. This solid crust is a very crude soap. The liquid remaining in the beaker contains **glycerol (1,2,3-trihydroxypropane)**.

Toxic

Flammable

Corrosive

Soap is produced by boiling a fat or an oil with either sodium hydroxide or potassium hydroxide. The oils and fats commonly used are:
1. Olive oil (which contains glyceryl oleate).
2. Palm oil (which contains glyceryl palmitate).
3. Mutton fat (which contains glyceryl stearate).

The reactions which occur when these oils and fats are boiled with sodium hydroxide are:
1. glyceryl oleate + sodium hydroxide → sodium oleate + glycerol
2. glyceryl palmitate + sodium hydroxide → sodium palmitate + glycerol
3. glyceryl stearate + sodium hydroxide → sodium stearate + glycerol

Sodium oleate, sodium palmitate and sodium stearate are soaps. The reactions which occur when sodium oleate is added to hard water can be summarized as follows:

1. *Removing temporary hardness*

sodium oleate + calcium hydrogen-carbonate → calcium oleate + sodium hydrogen-carbonate

2. *Removing permanent hardness*

sodium oleate + calcium sulphate → calcium oleate + sodium sulphate

In each of these reactions, calcium oleate is precipitated as a scum. The sodium hydrogencarbonate and sodium sulphate(VI) do not cause hardness. Similar reactions take place when sodium palmitate and sodium stearate are used.

b. **Adding sodium carbonate.** When sodium carbonate (washing soda) is added to hard water, it reacts with the soluble salts which cause the hardness, forming insoluble calcium carbonate and soluble sodium salts, neither of which cause hardness. The reactions which occur are:

1. *Removing temporary hardness*

$$Na_2CO_3 + Ca(HCO_3)_2 \rightarrow 2NaHCO_3 + CaCO_3$$
(sodium carbonate)   (calcium hydrogen-carbonate)   (sodium hydrogen-carbonate)   (calcium carbonate)

2. *Removing permanent hardness*

$$Na_2CO_3 + CaSO_4 \rightarrow Na_2SO_4 + CaCO_3$$
(sodium carbonate)   (calcium sulphate(VI))   (sodium sulphate(VI))   (calcium carbonate)

c. **Using a water softener.** Adding soap or washing soda are efficient methods of softening water when it is to be used for washing. These methods, however, are not suitable if the water is to be boiled in order to produce steam or for cooking.

One of the commonest water softening materials is '**permutit**', which is aluminium *sodium* silicate(IV). When hard water passes through a cylinder containing 'permutit', the 'permutit' reacts with the calcium salts in the hard water, converting them into sodium salts. In time, the 'permutit' becomes converted into aluminium *calcium* silicate(IV). When this stage has been reached, no more hardness can be removed from the water until the 'permutit' has been regenerated. This is done by putting common salt into the cylinder, on top of the aluminium calcium silicate(IV), and reversing the flow of water until the water flowing out of the cylinder no longer tastes of salt. The 'permutit' process is shown in Figure 2.4.

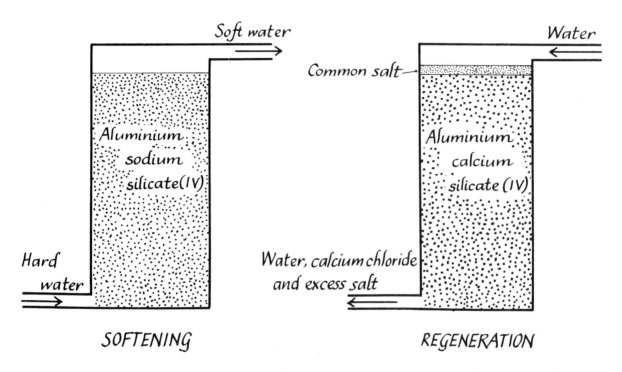

Figure 2.4 The 'permutit' process

The chemical reactions which occur in the 'permutit' process can be summarized as follows:

(1) *Softening*

$$\underbrace{\text{calcium hydrogen-carbonate} + \text{calcium sulphate(VI)}}_{\text{in water}} + \begin{array}{c}\text{aluminium}\\\text{sodium}\\\text{silicate(IV)}\end{array} \rightarrow \underbrace{\begin{array}{c}\text{sodium}\\\text{hydrogen-}\\\text{carbonate}\end{array} + \begin{array}{c}\text{sodium}\\\text{sulphate(VI)}\end{array}}_{\text{in water}} + \begin{array}{c}\text{aluminium}\\\text{calcium}\\\text{silicate(IV)}\end{array}$$

(2) *Regeneration*

$$\begin{array}{c}\text{aluminium}\\\text{calcium}\\\text{silicate(IV)}\end{array} + \underbrace{\begin{array}{c}\text{sodium}\\\text{chloride}\end{array}}_{\text{in water}} \rightarrow \begin{array}{c}\text{aluminium}\\\text{sodium}\\\text{silicate(IV)}\end{array} + \underbrace{\begin{array}{c}\text{calcium}\\\text{chloride}\end{array}}_{\text{in water and discarded}}$$

41

2.5. Surface tension

The surface of water behaves as if it has a thin transparent skin. The force which this skin exerts is called **surface tension**. By carefully adjusting a water tap, it is possible to leave a drop of water hanging from the outlet of the tap. The reason that this drop of water does not fall is that the force of surface tension is equalizing the force of gravity acting on the drop. By slowly turning the tap on, the mass of water in the drop increases, until the force of gravity acting on it is greater than the force of the surface tension supporting it. When this happens, the drop falls.

Investigation 2f. The force of surface tension

Fill a beaker with water. With a pair of tweezers, gently lower a sewing needle on to the surface of the water. (Alternatively, float the needle on a piece of blotting paper and wait for the blotting paper to sink.) Does the needle float or sink? A sewing needle is made of steel; as steel is denser than water, a steel needle should sink in water. If your needle floats, what is supporting it? If it sinks, slightly grease the needle and try again. An easy way of greasing the needle is to rub your fingers along the crease at the side of your nostrils and then run the needle between your fingers.

Investigation 2g. Does water always flow downhill?

Dip a finger in some grease and draw a ring on a sheet of glass with it. Lay the sheet of glass on a level surface and, using a pipette, pour water inside the greasy ring. Does the water immediately flow all over the glass, or does it stop at the grease and, as more water is added, build up inside the ring until, eventually, it overflows?

Many aquatic insects, such as pond-skaters and water-boatmen, rely on surface tension to support them.

2.6. Detergents

A **detergent** is a cleansing agent. Soap is a detergent, although many people tend to confuse the term 'detergent' with 'soapless detergent'. It is important to realize that detergents are used for purposes other than cleaning. One of the properties of a detergent is that it reduces surface tension.

In farming, crops are sprayed with many substances: pesticides, insecticides, fungicides, selective weed-killers, etc. Many liquid sprays are most effective when as large a surface area of the leaves as possible is covered with a thin layer of the liquid. To ensure an even coverage, a detergent is often mixed with the liquid in order to reduce the surface tension. When used in this way, the detergent is called a **spreader**. Without a spreader, the liquid would cover the leaves in small droplets and, consequently, would only be in contact with a relatively small surface area.

When developing a film, it is essential that the developer spreads evenly over the surface of the film and that there are no air bubbles trapped between the film and the developer. A detergent may be added to the developer to ensure even wetting of the surface of the film and, used in this way, it is known as a **wetting agent**. When a film has been developed, rinsed, fixed and washed, it must be allowed to dry. If the water used for the final washing has normal surface tension, the water will not run off the film when it is hung up to dry, but will remain in blobs on the film. As these blobs of water evaporate, any dissolved solids will remain on the surface of the film like tear drops. These markings will show on any prints made from the negatives. Therefore, a wetting agent may be added to the final washing water to ensure that the water runs off the film easily.

Investigation 2h. The effect of a detergent on drop size

Set a water tap dripping at a countable speed. Place a measuring cylinder so that it catches the drops and count the number of drops until there is 20 cm³ in the measuring cylinder. Now, smear the outlet of the tap with a detergent (washing-up liquid is suitable) and, after emptying the measuring cylinder, count the number of drops in 20 cm³. What difference do you notice? Does the addition of detergent increase or decrease the force of the surface tension? This effect is shown in Figure 2.5.

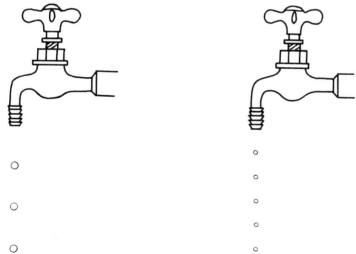

WITHOUT DETERGENT   WITH DETERGENT

Figure 2.5 The effect of a detergent on drop size

Investigation 2i. Reducing surface tension

In this investigation we shall use a detergent, because of its property of surface tension reduction.

1. Fill a sink with water. Tie the ends of a piece of waxed thread together to form a loop and float it on the water. The surface tension will pull on the thread with equal force in all directions. Now, put a drop of detergent inside the loop and note the effect. This effect is caused because the pull of surface tension round the outside of the loop is maintained while the surface tension inside the loop is reduced by the detergent, as shown in Figure 2.6.

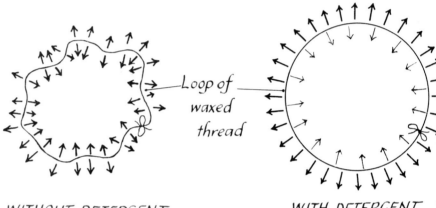

Figure 2.6 Reducing surface tension

WITHOUT DETERGENT　　　WITH DETERGENT

2. Fill a tumbler or a plastic beaker with water until it is brimming and about to overflow. Now, gently add a drop of detergent to the surface. What happens?
3. Fill a sink with water and, when the surface is still, float four wooden splints on it so that they form a square. Now, gently add a drop of detergent to the surface of the water inside the square. What happens to the splints? Explain why this happens.
4. Float a sewing needle on the surface of some water in a beaker (as you did in Investigation 2f). Add a drop of detergent to the surface and note what happens.

Investigation 2j. A detergent-powered boat

From a piece of thin card, cut out a boat shaped like the one shown in Figure 2.7. Fill a sink with water and, when the surface is still, float your boat at one end, with the bows pointing towards the other end. Now, put a drop of detergent on the surface of the water showing through the hole in the centre of the boat. Explain what happens.

Make another boat and rinse out the sink thoroughly. Repeat

the investigation, using a small piece of camphor instead of the detergent. What happens? What can you say about camphor?

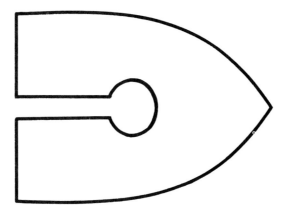

Figure 2.7 A detergent-powered boat

Investigation 2k. Water penetration and detergents

With a pipette, place a large drop of water on a piece of fabric, so that it remains on the surface and does not sink into the fabric. (You may have to try a number of different fabrics until you find one which will enable you to do this.) Look along the surface of the fabric and notice how the surface of the water holds the drop together by curling underneath it. With the point of a pencil which has been dipped in a detergent, touch the surface of the drop and note what happens.

This effect is essential when a detergent is to be used for washing fabrics, since any dirt lodged between the fibres can only be washed out if water can penetrate into the spaces between the fibres.

Unfortunately, the increased use of detergents in homes and industry has led to an increased amount of pollution by detergents in rivers and streams; the situation is aggravated as bacteria are unable to break down soapless detergents. This has had a disastrous effect on many forms of life in rivers and streams, particularly on water-fowl, such as ducks and moorhens. Ducks are able to float in water because their feathers are slightly greasy. This grease repels water, and a layer of air is trapped between the outer surface of the feathers and the skin. When the water is polluted with detergents, the surface tension is reduced and water penetrates through the feathers, displacing the layer of air and causing the duck to become water-logged.

Investigation 2l. Soaps and soapless detergents

Put 10 cm^3 of hard water into each of two test-tubes (19 mm $\times$ 150 mm). To one test-tube, add soap flakes, one flake at a

45

time, or soap solution, one drop at a time, shaking after each addition until you obtain a lather. To the other test-tube, add a soapless detergent, one drop at a time, shaking after each addition until you obtain a lather. Did the soap form a scum? Did the soap soften the water? Did the soapless detergent form a scum? Did it soften the water? Which formed a lather with the smaller amount, the soap or the soapless detergent?

Test your understanding

1. Draw a diagram to show how springs can 'dry up'.
2. What is the difference between temporary hardness and permanent hardness?
3. Why is water, obtained from chalky ground, hard?
4. Does soap remove temporary hardness, permanent hardness, or does it remove both types of hardness?
5. Why is a spreader added to crop sprays?
6. What does a wetting agent do?
7. If you repeated Investigation 2i (1) using ordinary cotton thread instead of waxed thread, what would you expect to happen? Explain your answer.
8. In Investigation 2j, why will your boat not keep going simply by adding more detergent?
9. If a fabric raincoat is washed in a detergent, why must it be re-proofed?
10. You are given two liquids and are told that one is a soap while the other is a soapless detergent. Describe an experiment you could perform to determine which is which.
11. Explain why it is possible to float a steel needle on water even though steel is denser than water.
12. You are given three test-tubes, each containing 10 cm³ of water. By adding soap flakes to the water and shaking, you obtain a standard lather in each test-tube with the following results:

Distilled water	2 flakes
Tap water	6 flakes
Boiled tap water	5 flakes

From these results, what can you deduce about the hardness of the water supply?
13. Why are stone buildings likely to last longer in a rural area than in an industrial area?

Chapter 3

Density and Water Pressure

3.1. Floating and sinking

Wood floats in water and lead sinks. Why is this so? You may be tempted to say that it is because wood is lighter than water and lead is heavier than water. Look at Figure 3.1 and you will see why this explanation is not correct.

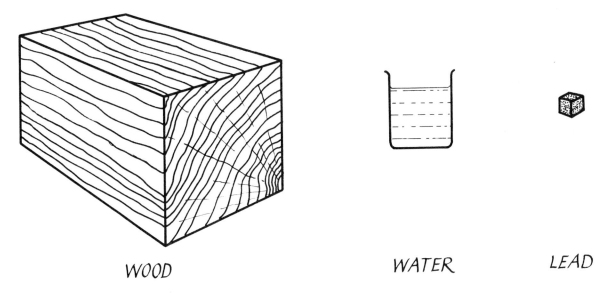

WOOD   WATER   LEAD

Figure 3.1 Which is heaviest?

Wood is lighter than water and lead is heavier than water if we consider equal volumes of each material. When we consider the mass of a known volume of a substance, we are concerned with the **density** of the substance.

The density of a substance is its mass per unit volume. Units of density are kilograms per cubic metre ($kg\ m^{-3}$) or grams per cubic centimetre ($g\ cm^{-3}$), whichever is the more convenient for the quantities involved. In the laboratory, it would be possible to find the density of a substance by finding the mass of 1 cm^3, but it is more accurate to use a larger volume and calculate the density by applying the formula:

$$\text{DENSITY} = \frac{\text{MASS}}{\text{VOLUME}}$$

You will see, therefore, that it is necessary to be able to measure (or calculate) volumes. As you know, a measuring cylinder can be used to measure the volume of a liquid. A **pipette** is an instrument which enables us to measure out a predetermined volume of liquid with a higher degree of accuracy than would be possible with a measuring cylinder. To use a pipette, the lower end is dipped into the liquid and, by removing air from the upper end, liquid enters the pipette. When the level of the liquid has risen above the scribed mark, the upper end is quickly blocked with a finger. By releasing the finger,

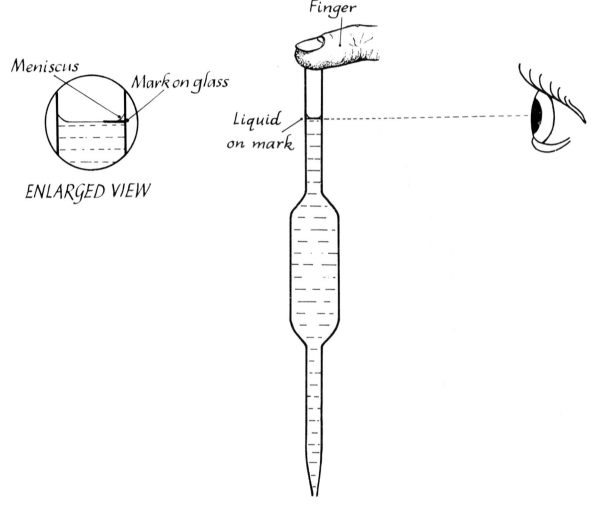

Figure 3.2 Reading a pipette

liquid is allowed to flow until the bottom of the meniscus is level with the scribed mark. The lower end should now be touched on the surface of the liquid to remove any excess. When the pipette is over the vessel into which the measured volume of liquid is to be delivered, the finger is removed and, when the liquid has stopped dripping, the lower end of the pipette is touched on the surface of the liquid in the vessel. The method of reading a pipette is shown in Figure 3.2.

The volumes of regularly shaped solids can be calculated by measuring their dimensions and applying the appropriate formula:

Volume of a prism = Area of cross-section
(including cube,   × length
rectangular block,
cylinder and
triangular prism)

Volume of a sphere $= \dfrac{4}{3}\pi r^3$

The volumes of irregularly shaped solids cannot easily be calculated from measurements, but their volumes can be found by displacement, assuming that they are not porous. If a solid is small enough to fit into a measuring cylinder, the volume of the solid can be found by pouring some water into the measuring cylinder and noting the volume of this water, and then lowering the solid into the water and noting the new reading. (The volume of the solid is the difference between the two readings.)

If the solid is too large to fit into a measuring cylinder, its displacement can be found by using a displacement can (Eureka can), as shown in Figure 3.3.

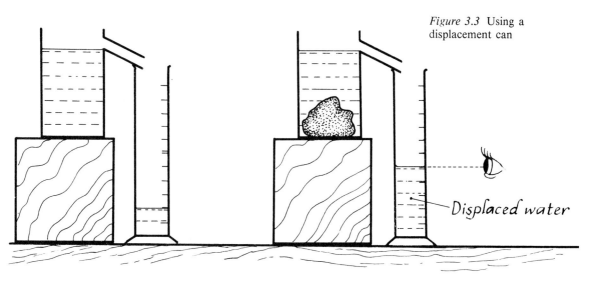

Figure 3.3 Using a displacement can

Displaced water

Investigation 3a. Finding the volume of a solid

Place a displacement can on a level surface, with the spout over a measuring cylinder. Pour water into the displacement can until it begins to overflow into the measuring cylinder. Collect the overflowing water until the dripping stops and then empty the measuring cylinder. Replace the cylinder and slowly lower the solid into the water in the displacement can. When the dripping stops, note the reading in the measuring cylinder. This is the volume of the water displaced by the solid and, consequently, the volume of the solid.

Toxic

Flammable

Investigation 3b. Finding the density of a liquid

Use the following technique to find the densities of methylated spirits, distilled water and brine (a saturated solution of sodium chloride).
1. Find the mass of an empty beaker.
2. Measure 100 cm³ of the liquid into the beaker.
3. Find the mass of the beaker with the 100 cm³ of the liquid.
4. Calculate the mass of the 100 cm³ of the liquid.
5. Calculate the density of the liquid (in g cm^{-3}) by applying the formula: $\text{Density} = \dfrac{\text{Mass}}{\text{Volume}}$.

In this investigation, 100 cm³ is suggested as a suitable volume because it simplifies the calculations, but a larger or smaller volume may be used if it is more convenient.

Investigation 3c. Finding the density of a solid

1. Find the mass of the solid.
2. Find the volume of the solid by displacement (see Investigation 3a).
3. Calculate the density by applying the formula.

How could you find the density of a solid which floats in water? (Here is a hint: before finding the volume, tie a piece of lead or other suitable sinker just below the solid.)

Investigation 3d. The upthrust of water

For this investigation you will need three spring balances (labelled 'A', 'B' and 'C' in Figure 3.4). Put a displacement can on balance B. Fill the displacement can with water, catching the overflow in a beaker until the dripping stops and then discarding this water. Note the reading on balance B. Place an empty beaker on balance C, so that it is below the spout of the displacement can. Note the reading on balance C. Now, tie a solid (choose an object which will sink in water and will fit into the displacement can) to balance A and note the reading on this balance.

While watching the balance readings, slowly lower the solid into the displacement can until it is completely immersed in water but is not touching the bottom or the sides of the displacement can. What do you notice about the reading on balance B, compared with its reading before you immersed the solid? What do you notice about the upthrust (the difference in readings of balance A before and after immersion) and the weight of the water displaced (the difference in readings of balance C before and after immersion)?

Repeat the investigation to discover if this relationship between upthrust and the weight of the displaced liquid is the same for:
1. Different-sized pieces of the same solid in water.
2. Pieces of different solids in water.
3. Solids in other liquids.

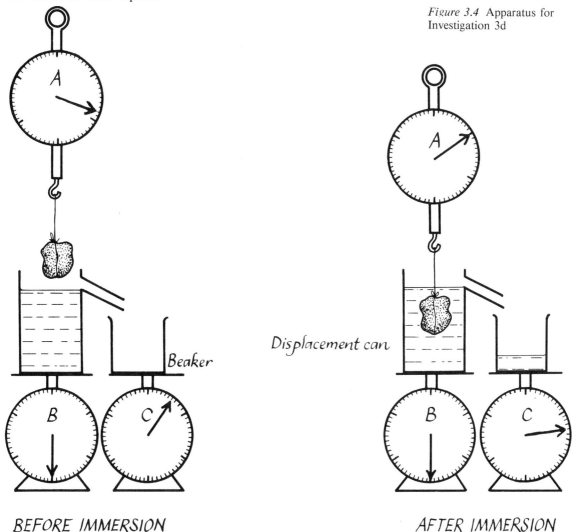

Figure 3.4 Apparatus for Investigation 3d

BEFORE IMMERSION

AFTER IMMERSION

Investigation 3e. Water displacement of a floating object

1. Find the mass of an object which will float on water and will fit into a displacement can without touching the bottom or the sides. (A piece of wood which has been painted or varnished to keep it waterproof is suitable.)
2. Put a displacement can on a level surface, fill it with water and wait until it has stopped dripping.
3. Find the mass of an empty beaker and place it under the spout of the displacement can.
4. Carefully, lower the object on to the surface of the water and then release it, so that it floats.
5. When the displacement can has stopped dripping, find the mass of the beaker with the displaced water and, by subtraction, calculate the mass of the displaced water.

Figure 3.5 Finding the mass of a ship

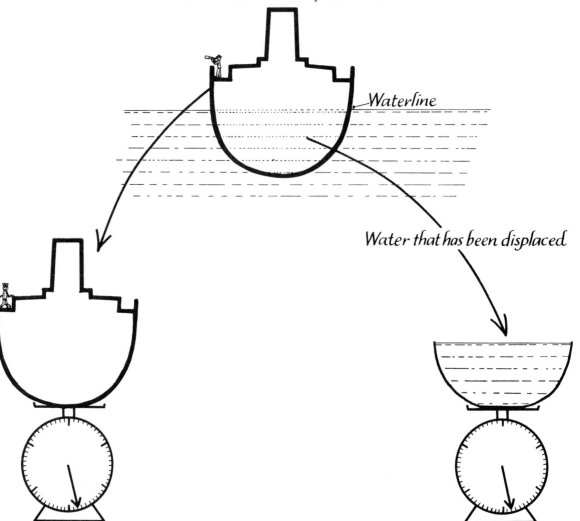

Waterline

Water that has been displaced

MASS OF SHIP = MASS OF WATER DISPLACED

What do you notice about the mass of the object and the mass of the displaced water?

Repeat the investigation, to discover if this relationship is the same for other floating objects in water and other liquids.

The relationships which you have discovered in Investigations 3d and 3e were first discovered by a famous Greek mathematician, **Archimedes** (287–212 B.C.). The facts which he (and you) discovered are known as **Archimedes' Principle**:

When a body is partly or wholly immersed in a fluid, it experiences an upthrust. The force of this upthrust is equal to the weight of the fluid displaced.

Archimedes' principle is used to find the mass of a ship. It would obviously be impossible to find the mass of a ship on a balance, so its mass is obtained by finding the volume of the ship that is below the waterline (the ship's displacement) and calculating the mass of this volume of water. This mass is called the **displacement tonnage** of the ship (see Figure 3.5).

When a ship is floating, its weight (the force of gravity on its mass) is equal to the upthrust of the water. If the ship is loaded with cargo, it will float deeper in the water and displace more water. This increased displacement will provide an increased upthrust to keep the ship afloat. Under all conditions, the upthrust is equal to the weight of the ship. Conditions in different oceans cause variations in density, so the volume of water displaced by the ship varies accordingly. To avoid overloading, all ships registered with Lloyd's have a **Plimsoll line.** This shows the level to which a ship may safely be loaded when in water of different densities. The Plimsoll line, together with a key, is shown in Figure 3.6.

Figure 3.6 The Plimsoll line

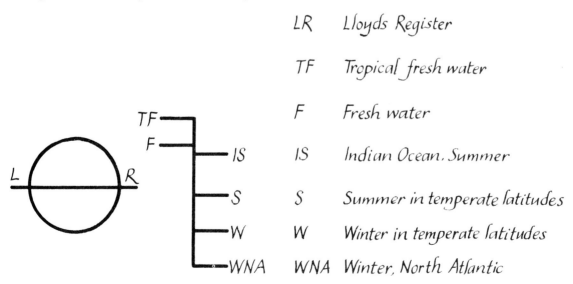

LR   Lloyds Register

TF   Tropical fresh water

F   Fresh water

IS   Indian Ocean, Summer

S   Summer in temperate latitudes

W   Winter in temperate latitudes

WNA   Winter, North Atlantic

TABLE 3.1. DENSITIES

Substance	Density/ g cm^{-3}	Substance	Density/ g cm^{-3}
Cork	0·22–0·26	Tetrachloromethane	1.6
Pine	0·5	Aluminium	2·7
Petrol	0·75	Zinc	7·1
Ethanol	0·79	Copper	8·9
Oak	0·8–0·95	Silver	10·5
Ice	0·92	Lead	11·3
Water	1·0	Mercury	13·6
Milk	1·03	Gold	19·3
Ebony	1·2	Platinum	21·45

Compare the results you obtained in Investigations 3b and 3c with the densities shown in Table 3.1. If they differ, try to discover where the inaccuracies may have occurred. How accurate was your balance? How accurate was your measuring cylinder and your reading of it? Can you be certain that the volume of the displaced water was the same as the volume of the solid? What effect does temperature have on the volume of a solid or a liquid?

Consider the following:
a. When a solid is completely immersed in water (or any other fluid), it displaces its own volume of water (or other fluid). (See Investigation 3a.)

b. The upthrust on an immersed solid is equal to the weight of an equal volume of water (or other fluid). (See Investigation 3d.)

c. The density of water is 1 g cm^{-3} (1 cm^3 of water has a mass of 1 g, 27 cm^3 of water has a mass of 27 g, etc.).

By combining these three facts, we can use a simple method to determine the density of a solid, without the need of a displacement can or a measuring cylinder, by using Archimedes' principle.

The volume of a given mass of water, expressed in cubic centimetres is *numerically equal* to its mass, in grams. Therefore, *numerically*:

$$\text{Density (in g cm}^{-3}) = \frac{\text{Mass of solid}}{\text{Mass of an equal volume of water}}$$

You will remember that mass and weight are not the same thing, but that the weight of an object is directly proportional to its mass.

Therefore:

$$\text{Density} = \frac{\text{Weight of solid}}{\text{Weight of water displaced}}$$

$$= \frac{\text{Weight of solid in air}}{\text{Apparent loss of weight in water}}$$

Investigation 3f. Finding the density by Archimedes' principle

Weigh a solid in air and then weigh it again when it is completely immersed in water. By subtraction, find the apparent loss of weight in water. Now, calculate the density of the solid by applying the formula:

$$\text{Density} = \frac{\text{Weight of solid in air}}{\text{Apparent loss of weight in water}}$$

This will give the density in g cm⁻³. This method of finding the density of a solid is shown in Figure 3.7.

Figure 3.7 Apparatus for Investigation 3f

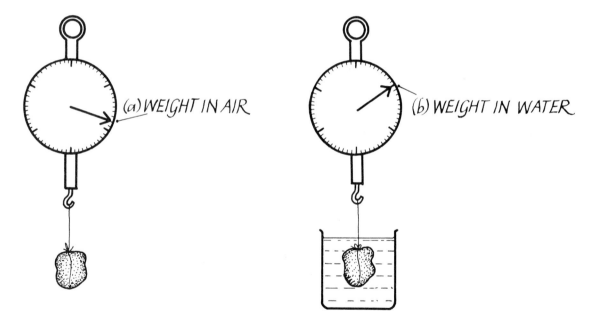

By using this method, find the densities of aluminium, zinc, copper and lead. If possible, use several pieces of each metal and then find the average of your results. Enter your results as shown in Table 3.2. (*Note.* The densities which you have obtained are expressed in g cm⁻³, but the results give the densities of the materials *relative to water*, no matter what units are used.)

TABLE 3.2. RESULTS OF INVESTIGATION 3f

Material	Weight in Air (a)	Weight in Water (b)	Apparent Loss of Weight (a−b)	Density $\left(\dfrac{a}{a-b}\right)$	Average/ g cm^{-3}
Aluminium					
Aluminium					
Aluminium					
Zinc					
Zinc					
Zinc					

3.2. Hydrometers

A **hydrometer** is an instrument for measuring the density of a liquid. If an object floats in a liquid, the volume which is below the surface depends on the density of the liquid.

Investigation 3g. Making a simple hydrometer

Toxic   Flammable

Seal one end of a drinking straw. A waxed paper straw may be sealed with 'Sellotape', while some plastic straws may be sealed by melting one end and squashing it with pliers until it is cool.

Drop some lead shot into the straw until it floats upright in methylated spirits, with about a quarter of its length showing above the surface. Mark the level of the surface of the spirits on the straw. Now, float the straw in water and mark the new level on the straw. What do these two levels tell you about the density of methylated spirits? Put a third mark on the straw when it is floating in brine. What does this third mark tell you about the density of brine?

In each liquid, the mass of the liquid displaced was equal to the mass of the hydrometer. (See Figure 3.8.)

Special-purpose hydrometers are used to determine the densities of particular liquids. A **lactometer** is a hydrometer for measuring the density of milk relative to that of water. Because milk contains fats, which have a lower density than water, the fat content of a sample of milk can be determined by measuring its density; the lower the density, the higher the fat content.

Probably the most familiar use of a hydrometer is in the measurement of the 'strength' of the acid in a car battery (see Figure 3.9).

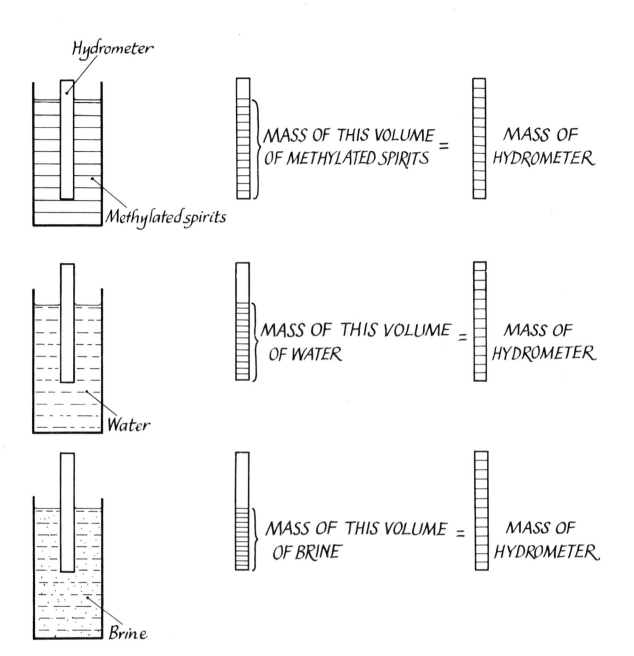

Figure 3.8 Comparing densities with a hydrometer

Charging a battery increases the 'strength' of the acid. Concentrated sulphuric(VI) acid has a density of 1·84 g cm^{-3}, so the density of the acid in a battery is an indication of the state of charge, provided that the battery is in good condition. Other tests must be used to establish this. When a battery is fully charged, the density of the acid is about 1·25 g cm^{-3}. When the battery is discharged, the density falls to about 1·15 g cm^{-3}.

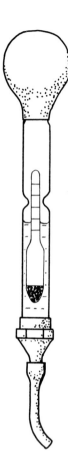

Figure 3.9 A battery hydrometer

The float of a battery hydrometer is inside a glass tube, which has a piece of rubber tubing at the bottom and a rubber bulb at the top. When using a battery hydrometer, the bulb is squeezed, the rubber tubing is dipped into the acid in the battery cell and the bulb is released. This causes some acid to enter the body of the hydrometer and the density of the acid can be read against the scale of the float.

3.3. Water pressure

Investigation 3h. Water pressure and depth

Drill four small holes of equal size along one side of a tin can at different heights from the bottom. Make a larger hole near the top of the opposite side. Into this larger hole, fit a cork and an overflow tube. Place the can so that the holes are facing a sink and the overflow tube is in the sink. Fill the can with water and adjust the tap so that there is a small, steady stream of water coming from the overflow tube, thus maintaining a constant water level in the can. Feel

58

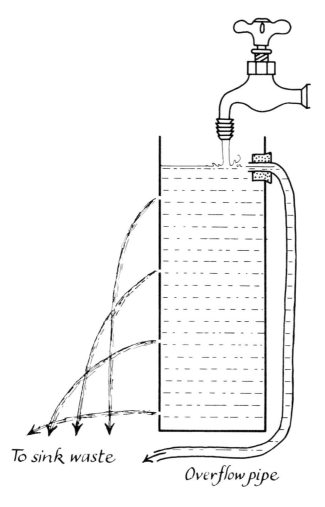

To sink waste

Overflow pipe

Figure 3.10 The pressure
of water at different depths

the force of each of the jets of water with your finger. Figure 3.10
shows the apparatus.

Block each of the holes in turn with a finger, while maintaining a
constant level of water in the can. What effect does this have on the
jets of water from each of the other holes?

$$\text{PRESSURE} = \frac{\text{FORCE}}{\text{AREA}}$$

Since the area of each of the small holes is the same, the pressure
of water emerging from them is proportional to the force exerted by
the water.

Using a stop-clock and a measuring cylinder, find the rate of flow
from each of the holes. What does your result tell you about the relationship between pressure and depth?

The implications of this relationship are many and varied. The hull of a submarine must be built to withstand a much greater pressure than the hull of a surface ship. The bottom of a dam must be much thicker than the top to withstand the greater pressure (see Figure 3.11).

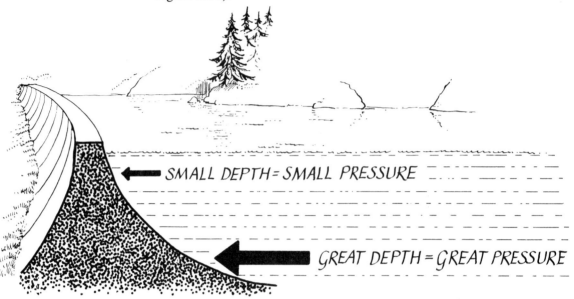

Figure 3.11 The cross-section of a dam

Investigation 3i. The direction of water pressure

Cut off the head of a thistle funnel, leaving a stem about 2 cm long. Stretch a thin piece of rubber sheet (a piece cut from a toy rubber balloon is suitable) over the mouth of the thistle funnel and secure it with rubber bands. Pour some water into a manometer (a U-tube) and connect it with glass tubing and rubber sleeving to the thistle funnel. Note any difference in the levels of the water in the limbs of the manometer. Now, lower the thistle funnel into some water, measure the depth from the surface to the mouth of the thistle funnel and note any change in the difference in levels in the manometer. Repeat this twice more, once with the mouth of the thistle funnel facing sideways and once facing upwards, as shown in Figure 3.12. With the mouth of the thistle funnel facing sideways, it is important to measure the depth to the *centre* of its mouth.

The water used for this investigation should be at about room temperature. If it is not, expansion or contraction of the air in the thistle funnel and the tubing connecting it to the manometer will affect the manometer readings.

Does water exert a greater pressure in any particular direction, or is the pressure equal in all directions?

The information obtained from Investigations 3h and 3i makes it possible to explain the upthrust on an object immersed in a liquid (see Figure 3.13).

60

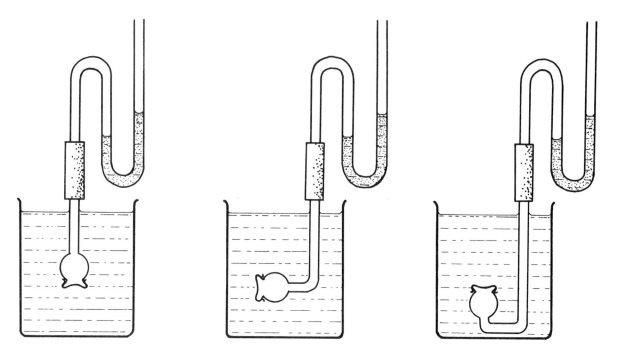

The pressure exerted by the liquid is proportional to the depth: one unit of depth exerts one unit of pressure, two units of depth exert two units of pressure, etc.

The pressures exerted on the sides of the block cancel each other out because they are equal and in opposite directions. The pressures on the top and bottom, however, do not cancel out, because the pressure on the bottom is two units greater than the pressure on the top in this example. You will notice that this difference between the pressures on the top and bottom of the block remains the same, no matter how deep the block is immersed in the liquid. Because the areas of the top and bottom surfaces are equal, the total force on the

Figure 3.12 Apparatus for Investigation 3i

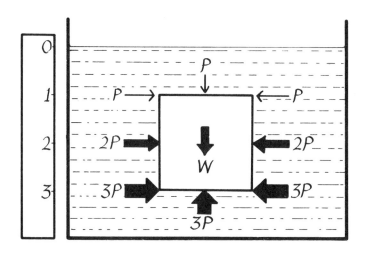

Figure 3.13 The explanation of upthrust

P = 1 UNIT OF PRESSURE

2P = 2 UNITS OF PRESSURE

3P = 3 UNITS OF PRESSURE

W = WEIGHT OF BLOCK

bottom is two units greater than the total force on the top. The difference between the upward force on the bottom and the downward force on the top causes upthrust.

You will realize that if this force of upthrust is greater than the force of gravity acting on the block (its weight), the block will float; if the force of upthrust is less than the weight of the block, it will sink.

3.4. The effect of water pressure

Investigation 3j. Can water be compressed?

Fill a syringe with air, block up the nozzle with a finger, and push the plunger in. How far does the plunger move? Can you feel any increase in pressure with your finger? Release the plunger and note what happens. Can air be compressed? Now, fill the syringe with water and repeat these tests. Can water be compressed?

Investigation 3k. Transmitting pressure

Fit a short length of rubber (or plastic) tubing to the nozzle of a small-diameter syringe and fill it with water. Fill, and then empty, a large-diameter syringe with water. Keeping the plunger depressed, connect it to the water-filled tubing on the other syringe. You will now have two syringes with the space between their plungers filled with water. (The filling and emptying of the large-diameter syringe was necessary to ensure that all air had been removed.) Press the plunger of the small syringe, measure how far it moves and, at the same time, measure the movement of the plunger of the large syringe. Is there any relationship between the movement of the plungers and the diameters of the syringes?

Hold one syringe in each hand and, with your thumbs, move the plungers to and fro. Which plunger exerts a greater force when the other plunger is pushed in? Is there any relationship between the force on the plungers and the diameters of the syringes?

This principle is used in the operation of a hydraulic lift (often found in garages for lifting cars) and, on a smaller scale, in a hydraulic jack. In these devices, a fluid is pumped from a small-diameter pump into a large-diameter cylinder. The action of a hydraulic lift can be compared with the action of a lever. This comparison is shown in Figure 3.14.

You will notice that the ratio between the load and the effort is the same as the ratio between the area of the load cylinder and the area of the effort cylinder.

In practice, an oil is used in hydraulic lifts and jacks. This over-

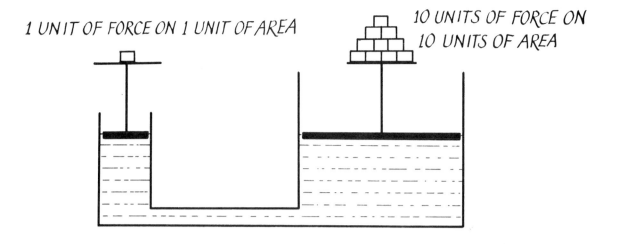

1 UNIT OF FORCE ON 1 UNIT OF AREA

10 UNITS OF FORCE ON 10 UNITS OF AREA

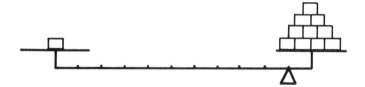

Figure 3.14 The hydraulic lift compared with a lever

comes the disadvantages of water: in winter water would freeze, while in summer it would evaporate. By using oil, rusting is also prevented.

Another instance of the incompressibility of water is shown in the operation of the **Cartesian diver** (see Figure 3.15). The diver is a hollow figure made of thin glass, having an open stem. It floats because the mass of water displaced by the diver is more than the

Figure 3.15 The Cartesian diver

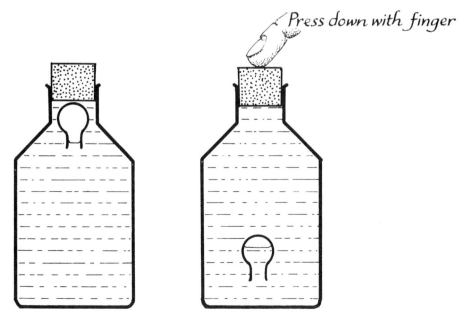

Press down with finger

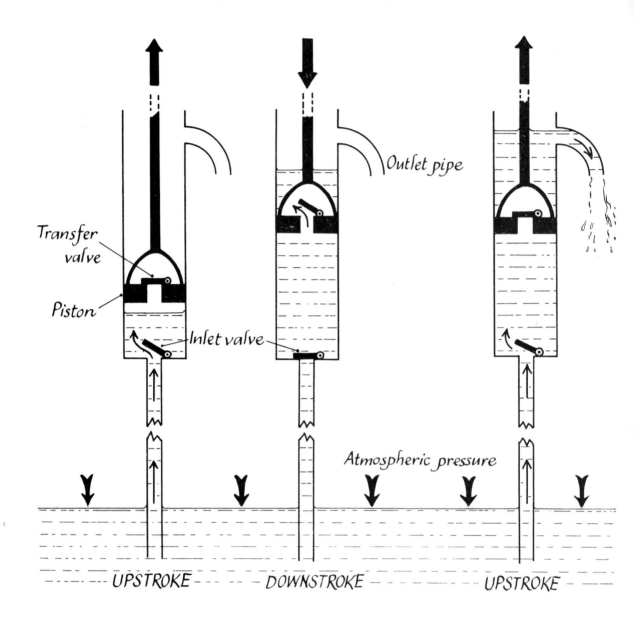

Figure 3.16 The action of a lift pump

mass of the glass (denser than water), air (less dense than water) and a small volume of water in the stem. When the stopper of the bottle full of water is pressed down, the air in the diver, being the only compressible substance in the bottle, becomes compressed, and water rises in the stem of the diver. This increases the overall density of the diver, and when this overall density exceeds the density of water, the diver sinks. When the stopper is released, the air in the diver expands, forcing some of the water out of the stem. This reduces the density of the diver, and it floats to the surface. Can you explain the importance of having the bottle completely full of water, with no air space between the surface and the stopper?

3.5. Making water move

In order to make anything move, a force must be applied to it. The force with which you are most familiar is the force of gravity. It is the force of gravity that is responsible for the obvious fact that water flows downhill. If we are to make water flow against the force of gravity, we must pump it. Although there are many types of pump, we shall only consider three of them.

a. **The lift pump** may be used to raise water from a depth not exceeding about 9 m, because it relies on atmospheric pressure (see Chapter 4). On the first upstroke, the transfer valve closes, the air pressure in the cylinder becomes less and atmospheric pressure on the surface of the water forces it past the inlet valve into the cylinder. On the downstroke, the inlet valve closes and water passes through the transfer valve. On the next upstroke, the water above the piston is raised and flows through the outlet pipe while more water passes through the inlet valve into the cylinder (see Figure 3.16).

When this type of pump becomes worn, and the piston is no longer a good fit in the cylinder, it is sometimes necessary to 'prime' the pump by pouring some water into the cylinder above the piston. This enables sufficient reduction in pressure to be achieved in order to raise water past the inlet valve. In the old-fashioned village pump, the transfer valve was often made of leather. In order to keep this closed during the first few upstrokes, priming was necessary.

Figure 3.17 The action of a force pump

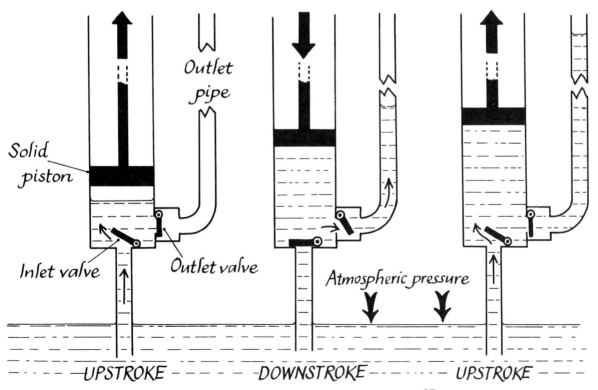

Outlet pipe

Solid piston

Inlet valve

Outlet valve

Atmospheric pressure

UPSTROKE — DOWNSTROKE — UPSTROKE

b. **The force pump** is used for raising water from a depth greater than would be possible with a lift pump. Figure 3.17 shows the action of a force pump. The 'works' of a force pump are placed deep in a well, sometimes in the water. Leading from the pump to the surface, there is a solid rod (to operate the piston) and an outlet pipe. The upstroke action of the force pump is similar to the upstroke action of the lift pump. The downstroke closes the inlet valve and forces water through the outlet valve and up the outlet pipe to the surface. In many modern wells, water is raised by means of a rotary pump, situated at the bottom of the well.

c. **The peristaltic pump** operates on the same principle as peristalsis in the alimentary canal. It forces a liquid through a flexible tube by squeezing the tube with revolving rollers, as shown in Figure 3.18. With this type of pump, the rate of flow can be controlled by

Figure 3.18 The peristaltic pump

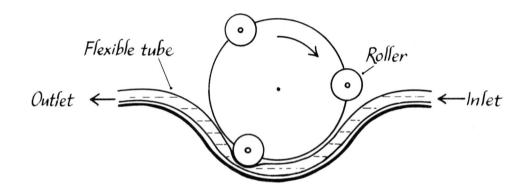

altering the speed at which the rotor turns. The flow is more even than it is with the lift and force pumps, since there are no valves and the rotor (the only moving part) produces a continuous pumping action. One use of the peristaltic pump is in the heart–lung machines in hospitals.

A **syphon** is not a pump because it only transfers a liquid from one level to a lower level but, in one part of a syphon, the liquid flows uphill.

Investigation 3l. The syphon

Place a bowl of water on the bench and an empty bowl on the floor. Fill a long piece of rubber tubing with water by lowering it slowly into the bowl of water. Pinch one end of the tubing and, while holding the open end under the surface of the water in the upper bowl, lift the pinched end out of the water and lower it over the side, so that it is above the bowl on the floor. With the pinched end lower than the surface of the water in the upper bowl, release it and note what happens.

The action of a syphon can be compared with a piece of flexible chain running through a tube, as shown in Figure 3.19. Once the finger is removed from the lower end of the tube containing the chain,

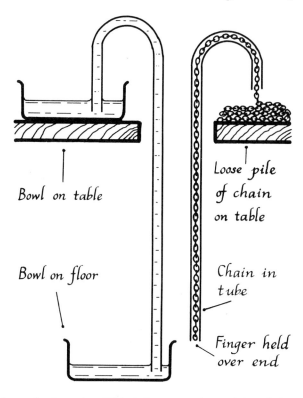

Bowl on table

Bowl on floor

Loose pile
of chain
on table

Chain in
tube

Finger held
over end

Figure 3.19 The action of a syphon

the chain will run through the tube. This is because the weight of the chain in the longer limb is greater than the weight of the chain in the shorter limb.

3.6. Harnessing water power

Moving water has energy. This energy can be converted into useful work when the water makes a wheel rotate, as a rotating wheel can be made to drive machinery. Many early corn mills and cotton looms were driven by water-wheels. Where it was possible to dam a stream, thus raising the water level, an **overshot wheel** was used. Where the damming of a stream was difficult or impossible, the stream was artificially narrowed to increase the rate of flow, and an **undershot wheel** was used. These, together with a turbine, are shown in Figure 3.20.

Nowadays, we use water power to generate electricity. In **hydro-electric generators,** water flowing at high speed turns the rotor of a

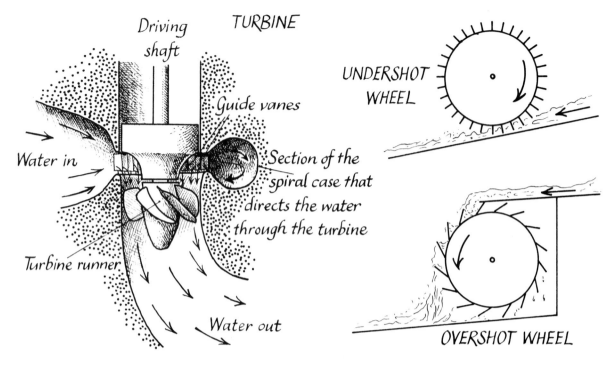

TURBINE

Driving shaft

Guide vanes

Water in

Section of the spiral case that directs the water through the turbine

Turbine runner

Water out

UNDERSHOT WHEEL

OVERSHOT WHEEL

Figure 3.20 Harnessing water power

turbine, which is coupled to a generator. For maximum output, the water feeding a hydro-electric generator must be at high pressure. This is achieved by siting the generating station as low as possible on the downstream side of a dam. In mountainous regions, such as the Swiss Alps and the Canadian Rockies, water is piped from melting glaciers high in the mountains to hydro-electric generating stations in the valleys.

The volume of water moved by the tides in oceans and seas is very great indeed but, in harnessing this source of power, there are difficulties. Consider the following:

a. The difference in depth of water is limited to the difference between sea-levels at low and high tide. This limits the pressure (remember that pressure depends on depth).

b. Because the depth of water is constantly changing, the pressure is also constantly changing, and this affects the speed of the turbines.

c. To maintain a constant depth and pressure, extensive damming is necessary.

d. Where parts of the sea are dammed, there might be a danger of flooding the land.

Fairly recently, the French have succeeded in harnessing the tidal flow in the English Channel by damming, in spite of the difficulties.

1. Steel is denser than water. Explain how it is possible for a steel ship to float in water.
2. Why is a pipette more accurate than a measuring cylinder?
3. What is the volume of a 6 cm diameter sphere? (Take $\pi = \frac{22}{7}$.)
4. A piece of material has a mass of 49 g and a volume of 14 cm³. What is its density?
5. A coin is thought to be made of gold. If it has a volume of 2 cm³, what should its mass be?
6. Why is it easier to float in sea water than in fresh water?
7. Figure 3.21 shows a gas jar containing four liquids and four solids. The liquids are water, mercury, petrol and tetrachloromethane. The

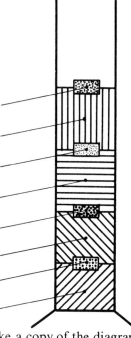

Figure 3.21 Liquids and solids in a gas jar

   solids are copper, cork, ebony and ice. Make a copy of the diagram and, from what you know about density, label the liquids and the solids.
8. If two dams were to be built to hold back the following sizes of reservoirs:
   (a) 15 km long, 1 km wide and 5 m deep
   (b) 2 km long, 1 km wide and 8 m deep
   which dam would need to be thicker at the base? Explain your answer.
9. One hydraulic jack has a safe working load of 1 000 kg; another hydraulic jack has a safe working load of 3 000 kg. What differences would you expect to find in the design of these two jacks?
10. A deep well is fitted with a lift pump. During a drought, the water could not be raised by the pump, even though the water could be seen at the bottom of the well. Explain why this should happen.
11. How could you start a syphon working if you could not put the whole of the syphon tube into the liquid in the upper vessel?

Chapter 4

Air

The surface of the earth is surrounded by a layer of air. This layer of air extends to a height of more than 300 km, and is called the **atmosphere.**

4.1. Air pressure

Investigation 4a. Finding the mass of air

Fit a bicycle valve to a large polythene container. Find the mass of the container. Now, pump more air into the container with a

Figure 4.1 Apparatus for Investigation 4a

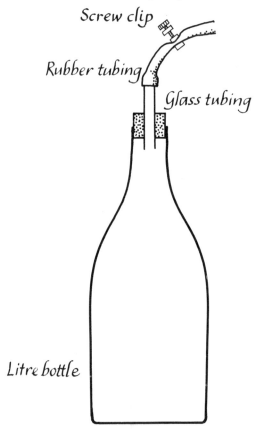

bicycle pump and find its mass again. Is the mass of the container more or less than before? Any difference in mass must have been caused by the increased amount of air in the container, and this increased amount depended on the number of pumpfuls that you put into the container.

To find the mass of a known volume of air at atmospheric pressure, fit a 1 dm³ wine bottle with a single-holed rubber bung. Put a short length of glass tubing through the bung and, over the glass tubing, fit a short length of rubber tubing with a screw clip on it, as shown in Figure 4.1. Wrap a towel round the bottle, so that the glass is entirely covered, and secure it with string. Using as sensitive a balance as is available to you, find the mass of the wrapped bottle with its stopper, tubing and screw clip.

Connect the rubber tubing to a vacuum pump, using thick-walled tubing. Release the screw clip, switch the vacuum pump on and, when as much air as possible has been removed from the bottle, close the screw clip and switch the vacuum pump off. Disconnect the thick-walled tubing and find the mass of the bottle again. Is its mass the same as it was before the air was removed? If not, can you explain the reason for the difference? Place the rubber tubing under water and release the screw clip. Note what happens. Was the bottle really empty? Wrapping the bottle with a towel is a safety precaution. Can you explain what danger it guards against? If not, the next investigation will give you a clue.

★ WARNING. This part must only be done by a science teacher. Use a safety screen.

Investigation 4b. The action of air pressure

Take an empty plastic squeeze bottle (the type in which washing-up liquid is supplied is ideal) and, with thick-walled tubing, connect it to a vacuum pump. Switch the vacuum pump on and watch what happens. Because the plastic squeeze bottle is pliable, there is no danger.

In order to measure air pressure, we must compare it with a known force. An instrument which measures air pressure is called a **barometer**. The simplest type of barometer to understand is the **mercury barometer**.

★ WARNING. When handling mercury, use a mercury tray to prevent spillage, wear a pair of rubber gloves and wash your hands very thoroughly afterwards. Take care not to inhale its vapour, as it is poisonous.

Investigation 4c. Making a simple mercury barometer

Take a strong dish, about 10 cm in diameter and about 5 cm deep, and pour mercury into it to a depth of about 3 cm. Take a barometer tube (a 1 metre length of thick-walled glass tubing, about 1 cm in diameter and closed at one end), place the closed end on a pad of cloth on the bench and fill the tube with mercury. Put one finger over the open end of the barometer tube and invert the tube

Toxic

Clean up any spills as soon as they occur.

several times. This will allow any air bubbles to escape. Top the tube up with more mercury if necessary. Now put the open end (still blocked with your finger) into the mercury in the dish, and remove your finger. Measure the vertical distance between the surface of the mercury in the dish and the top of the mercury in the tube.

(*Note.* If this barometer is to remain set up for any length of time, the mercury in the dish should be covered by a thin layer of oil. This will prevent the mercury from evaporating. Mercury vapour is poisonous.)

Figure 4.2 Making a mercury barometer

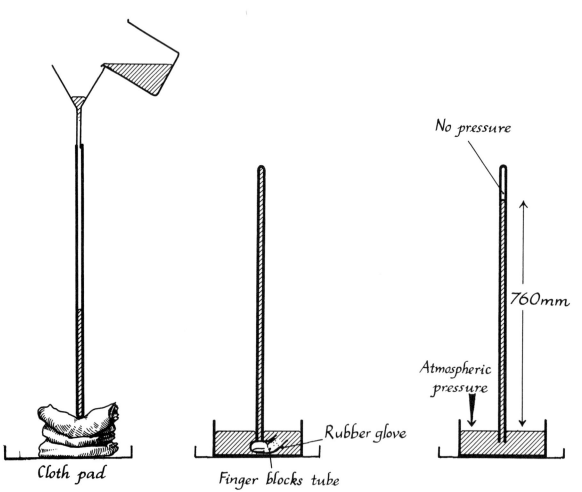

Since there is no air pressure in the space above the mercury in the tube, the column of mercury is being supported by the pressure of the air on the surface of the mercury in the dish. (The space above the mercury in the tube is not a true vacuum, since it will contain traces of mercury vapour. These traces will exert such a small pressure at normal temperatures that, for the purpose of measuring atmospheric pressure, it may be ignored.)

Atmospheric pressure varies considerably. Normal atmospheric pressure will support a column of mercury 760 mm high. This pressure is sometimes used as a standard for comparing pressures, and is called **one atmosphere**.

Figure 4.2 shows the stages in making a mercury barometer. The main reason for using mercury (as opposed to other liquids) in a barometer is that it is a dense liquid. Mercury is 13·6 times as dense as water so, if water was used in a barometer, normal atmospheric pressure would support a column just over 10 metres high. This may help you to understand why a lift pump (see Chapter 3) is limited in the depth from which it can raise water.

When reading a barometer, it is important that the measurement that you take is the *vertical* height of the column of mercury. If the barometer tube is tilted, the mercury will rise up the tube, so that, if the measurement is taken *along* the tube, it will give a false reading. You will notice, however, that the *vertical height remains constant*, as shown in Figure 4.3.

Figure 4.3 The effect of tilting a mercury barometer

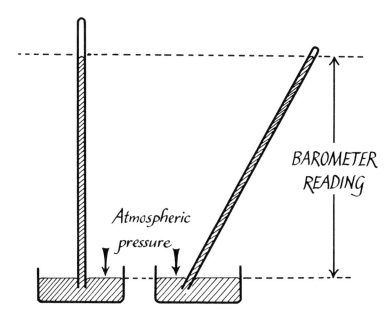

The mercury barometer compares atmospheric pressure with the force of gravity acting on a column of mercury. A more compact, though less accurate, barometer compares atmospheric pressure with the force exerted by a metal spring. This type of barometer is called the **aneroid barometer** ('aneroid' means 'without liquid'). The basis of the aneroid barometer is a circular box made of corrugated metal. Most of the air has been removed from this box so that it contains a partial vacuum. Atmospheric pressure tends to squash the box, but the sides are kept apart by a strong spring. If atmospheric pressure increases, the sides move closer together; if it decreases, the spring pulls the sides farther apart.

If the box contained air at normal atmospheric pressure, any increase in external pressure (which would tend to crush the box) would also increase the pressure of the air inside the box, so that very little movement of the sides of the box would actually occur; the box would also behave as a gas thermometer. If all of the air was removed, the total force on the outside of the box (due to atmospheric pressure) would be so great that the spring would be unable to overcome it and, again, little or no movement would occur.

Any movement of the sides of the box is transmitted through a lever, chain and pulley mechanism to a pointer on a dial, as shown in Figure 4.4.

Figure 4.4 The aneroid barometer

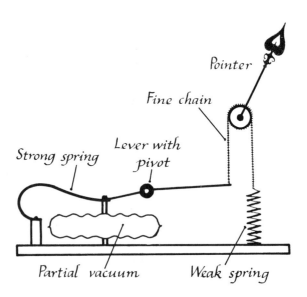

4.2. Some uses of air pressure

Car tyres are filled with air at a pressure of between two and three atmospheres, depending on the type and size of tyre and the weight of the car. Some cars are fitted with extra-broad tyres. These present a larger surface area in contact with the road than normal tyres. Since pressure is force per unit area, these tyres contain air at a lower pressure than normal tyres, in order to support the same load.

If the pressure in a tyre was only one atmosphere, the tyre would be flat, so pressure gauges for checking tyre pressures are calibrated to read pressure *in excess of* normal atmospheric pressure. Many lorries designed to carry heavy loads have tyre pressures in the region of eight atmospheres.

When tunnels are being driven through the ground, there is sometimes a danger of flooding. Where this danger exists, it is overcome by sealing off a space behind the working face and pumping com-

74

pressed air into it. Although this method overcomes the danger of flooding, men working in compressed air are liable to suffer from the 'bends', unless adequate precautions are taken. The 'bends' (more properly known as *caisson disease*) is caused when a man who has been in compressed air emerges too quickly into air at normal atmospheric pressure. When compressed air is breathed, a small amount of nitrogen dissolves in the blood. If compression is rapidly removed, the nitrogen comes out of solution and forms small bubbles, like the bubbles of carbon dioxide that appear when the stopper is removed from a bottle of fizzy drink. When a man leaves the working face, he is decompressed slowly. This slow reduction of air pressure enables the nitrogen to escape from the blood. If, in emergency conditions, a man has to emerge from compressed air quickly, he is put into a decompression chamber, which contains air at high pressure. The pressure is then slowly reduced to normal atmospheric pressure. Similar conditions apply to deep-sea divers.

Two important instruments in an aircraft are the **altimeter**, which indicates the altitude of the plane, and the **air speed indicator**. The altimeter is an aneroid barometer, calibrated to read altitude. Air pressure varies with height, in the same way as water pressure varies with depth. Because air pressure decreases as height increases, this instrument indicates any variation in height, but it has the disadvantage that any change in air pressure will alter the reading on the altimeter and thus make it inaccurate. For low altitudes, modern aircraft use a radio altimeter, which indicates the height of the plane above the ground.

Most early aircraft had a small propeller mounted on one of the wings. This propeller was connected by a flexible cable to an instrument like a speedometer, which measured the speed at which the propeller was rotating. The instrument was calibrated to read air speed. A modern air speed indicator uses a **Pitot tube** (pronounced 'pea-toe' tube), the principle of which is shown in Figure 4.5.

The Pitot tube consists of two vertical tubes, the bottom ends of which face in opposite directions. The top ends are connected by flexible tubes to an instrument which measures the difference between the air pressures in the two tubes, but is calibrated to read air speed. In Figure 4.5, the indicator is shown as a manometer but, in an actual aircraft, the difference in pressure is made to move a pointer on a dial.

The Pitot tube is mounted on an aircraft so that the opening in one tube faces the nose of the plane, while the opening of the other tube faces the tail. When the Pitot tube is in still air, the pressure in the two tubes is the same, so that the indicator reads zero, as illustrated in Figure 4.5(a). As the plane moves forward, the air speed increases and the pressure in the tube facing the nose increases, while the pressure in the tube facing the tail decreases by the same amount. The

75

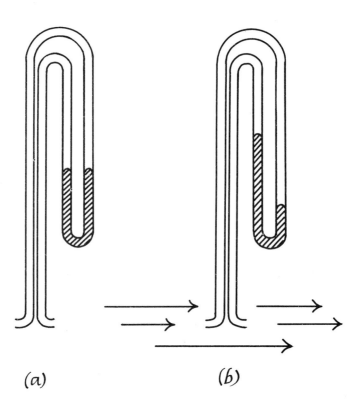

(a)   (b)

Figure 4.5 The principle of
the Pitot tube

effect of this is illustrated in Figure 4.5(b). The faster the air is
moving past the Pitot tube, the greater is the pressure difference,
and this shows on the indicator as an increased air speed.

When a road has to be dug up to lay pipes, the surface is broken
up with a pneumatic drill, the sharp point of which is made to vibrate
rapidly. The energy which causes this vibration is provided by compressed air from a compressor, usually driven by a diesel engine.

Industrial applications of compressed air include its use in power-
ing pneumatic spanners and pneumatic riveting guns (both of which
look rather like pistol drills) and for paint spraying.

Torpedoes are launched from submarines, destroyers and motor-
torpedo boats by compressed air, which enters behind the torpedo
and forces it out of the torpedo tube. Once the torpedo has been
launched, its propellers are driven by a compressed air motor. The
compressed air which powers the motor is stored in strong cylinders
between the war-head and the motor. The escaping air leaves a tell-
tale stream of bubbles which rise to the surface while the torpedo is
running.

A rather novel use of air pressure is the pneumatic postal service
in central Paris, commonly called the 'pneu'. In this system, letters
are enclosed in cylinders which are forced through underground
tubes at a speed of about 60 km h^{-1} by compressed air.

4.3. Flight without wings

In order for anything to rise in the air without the use of wings, it must displace more than its own mass of air (see Archimedes' principle in Section 3.1).

The first attempts to fly in a lighter-than-air craft were made in 1783 in the **Montgolfier balloon** near Paris. The Montgolfier hot-air balloon was a large inverted bag of linen, supported by a frame. When some straw was lit under the balloon, the hot air and smoke inflated the balloon and it rose into the air (see Figure 4.6).

The balloon rose because the hot air inside the balloon was less dense than the cooler air outside. As the air inside the balloon cooled, the balloon slowly fell to the ground. Modern hot-air balloons are kept in the air for greater lengths of time, and rise to greater heights, by suspending a small furnace below the mouth of the balloon to keep the air inside the balloon hot.

A great advance in ballooning came with the introduction of the **gas-filled balloon**. Because of its low density, hydrogen was used to fill the balloon. The balloonists were carried in a basket suspended below the balloon. Before take-off, bags of fine sand were loaded into the basket, and the balloon was inflated with hydrogen until the basket was lifted off the ground. Once the balloon was airborne, its height above the ground was controlled by the balloonists. To make the balloon climb, sand was jettisoned (thrown overboard); this reduced the overall density of the balloon. To lose height, hydrogen was allowed to escape from the balloon through a valve, which dangled from the balloon just above the basket.

The direction and speed of flight of these balloons was entirely dependent on the direction and force of the wind, over which the balloonists had no control. To overcome this disadvantage, **dirigible** (steerable) balloons were developed. These were cigar-shaped balloons made of fabric stretched over a light metal framework, with engine-driven propellers, a rudder and elevators. Several of the later designs of these craft, called **airships,** were made in Great Britain and the United States of America, and many more in Germany, in the early part of the twentieth century. Many commercial flights, including transatlantic flights, were made by these airships before their use was discontinued because of a series of disasters, in which they crashed and burst into flame (remember that hydrogen is highly inflammable). The best-known German airships were the **Zeppelins,** named after their designer, Count Ferdinand von Zeppelin. In addition to commercial flights, these were used in bombing raids during the First World War (1914–18), but were comparatively unsuccessful because they were large targets and were easily destroyed by incendiary bullets. The following figures

Figure 4.6 The Montgolfier
hot-air balloon

78

will give you some idea of the size and performance of an airship:

Length: over 200 m
Diameter: over 20 m
Mass: about 30 000 kg
Payload: about 30 000 kg
Cruising speed: 100 km h^{-1}
Ceiling (maximum height): 5 000 m

4.4. Flight with wings

Man has always envied birds and insects their ability to fly. One of the first accounts of man's attempts to imitate the flight of birds is told in the Greek legend of Icarus, who tried to escape from the island of Crete by strapping large wings to his arms. The wings were made of feathers, stuck together with wax. Unfortunately, like all attempts to achieve man-powered flight, it resulted in disaster. In the legend, Icarus' failure was caused because he flew too close to the sun, which melted the wax. Can you suggest a more likely reason?

Some of the factors which enable birds to fly are:

a. Compared with non-flying animals, their bones are more delicate and less dense.

b. The front limbs of birds (wings) are covered with feathers in such a way as to give them a greater surface area than non-flying animals.

c. The wing feathers overlap each other so that, when the wings beat upward, the feathers twist to allow air to pass between them. When the wings beat downward, the feathers become interlocked, thus preventing air from passing between them.

d. The muscles which move the wings of birds (particularly those which cause the downbeat) are much more powerful than the muscles which move the front limbs of non-flying animals. The breast meat of a chicken is the muscle which causes the downbeat of its wings.

e. Many birds partly fold their wings on the upbeat, to reduce the surface area, and extend them on the downbeat, to increase the surface area.

f. When a bird is flying, its body is shaped in such a way as to allow air to flow past it without disturbing the air to any great extent. A shape which does this is said to be **streamlined**.

g. When a bird glides, it controls its height by altering the angle at which the wings meet the air. A steep angle produces a rapid climb while a smaller angle reduces the rate of climb. Additional control is achieved by slight movements of the bird's tail.

If you watch birds flying, you will notice that some birds have a faster wing-beat than others. In general, which birds have the slower wing-beat, large birds or small birds? Is there any relationship between the rate of wing-beat and the ratio between body-size and wing-span?

A heavier-than-air craft must have a force which will overcome the force of gravity. In a vertical take-off aircraft, this force is produced by the downward thrust supplied by its jet engines. In a conventional aircraft, this force must be produced by the air flowing over the wings.

Investigation 4d. The effect of passing air over a curved surface

Take a piece of paper and fold 2 cm at one end of it back. Place the sheet of paper on a bench, with the folded end towards you. Now, unfold the 2 cm end and stick it to the bench, as shown in Figure 4.7.

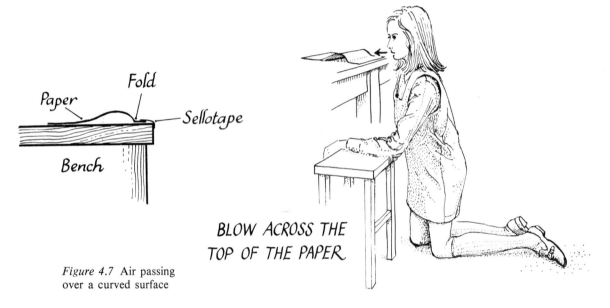

BLOW ACROSS THE
TOP OF THE PAPER

Figure 4.7 Air passing over a curved surface

With your mouth level with the top of the bench, gently blow across the top of the sheet of paper and note what happens. Does the paper rise or fall? What can you deduce about the air pressure above and below the paper?

The shape of the cross-section of the wing of an aircraft is similar to the shape formed by the space between the bench and the sheet of paper. This shape is known as an **aerofoil**. When air flows past an aerofoil, the air is deflected. This deflection causes an *increase* in pressure *below* the aerofoil and a *decrease* in pressure *above* the aero-foil. It is this difference in pressure which produces the upthrust on the wings, resulting in an upward force known as **lift.** When

80

the angle at which the wing meets the airflow increases, the pressure of the air below the wing is further increased. This additional pressure below, combined with a greater reduction in the pressure above, provides an even greater lift. Unfortunately, this also causes greater disturbance of the air, resulting in a braking effect, which tends to slow the aircraft. This braking effect is called **drag.** The effect of a comparatively small angle between the aerofoil and the airstream is shown in Figure 4.8(a), while the effect of increasing this angle is shown in Figure 4.8(b).

Figure 4.8 The effect of the angle of an aerofoil

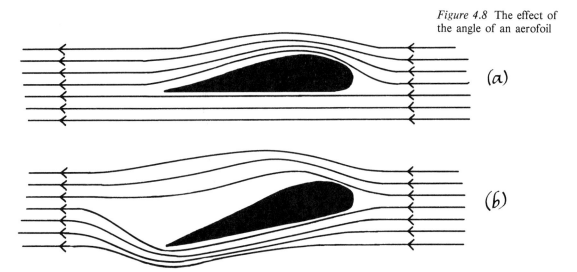

When an aircraft is flying, there are four main forces acting on the aerofoil (see Figure 4.9):

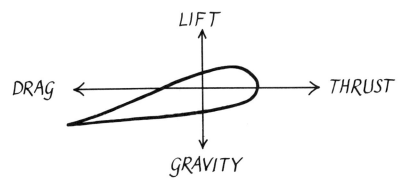

Figure 4.9 The forces on an aerofoil

a. **Thrust** is the force which propels the plane forward. It is provided by the engines.
b. **Drag** is always less than the thrust and is rather similar to the force of friction, being a retarding force.

c. **Lift** is the upward force produced by the flow of air past the aerofoil.

d. **Gravity** is the downward force acting on the mass of the plane.

When an aircraft is in level flight, the forces of lift and gravity exactly balance each other. If the lift is increased by altering the angle of the wing, the plane will climb; if lift is decreased, the plane will lose height.

In order to control the direction, height and attitude (position relative to the horizon) of an aircraft, there are moveable surfaces on the **trailing edges** of the **wings, tailplanes** and **tail fin**. The main control surfaces (**ailerons, flaps, elevators** and **rudder**) are shown in Figure 4.10.

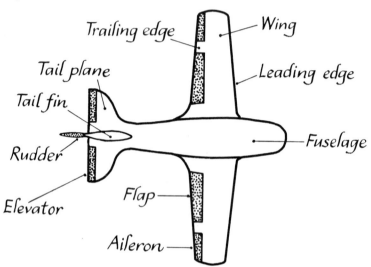

Figure 4.10 The main control surfaces of an aircraft

The ailerons move in opposite directions. They are controlled by moving the 'D-handles' on the control column in the cockpit to the left or to the right. The effect of moving the ailerons is to **bank** the plane, as shown in Figure 4.11. When air passes a raised aileron, the wing drops; when air passes a lowered aileron, the wing rises.

Figure 4.11 The effect of the ailerons

82

The rudder acts in the same way as the rudder on a boat. When it is moved to the right, the increased pressure on the right side of the rudder and the decreased pressure on the left side moves the tail to the left. This has the effect of turning the plane to the right, as shown in Figure 4.12. The rudder is moved by moving the rudder-bar which, in modern planes, is in the form of two pedals.

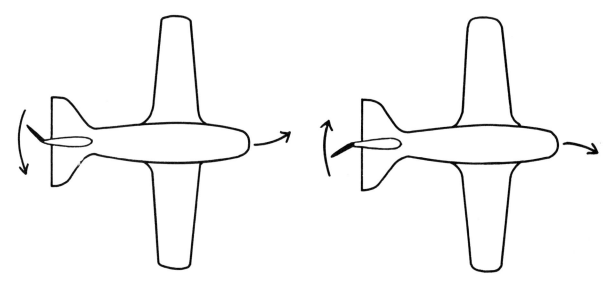

Figure 4.12 The effect of the rudder

The elevators are controlled by moving the control column backward or forward. When the elevators are moved upward, the tail drops. This increases the angle at which the wings enter the airstream, thus increasing the lift, and the plane climbs. When the elevators are moved downward, the tail rises and the plane dives. These effects are shown in Figure 4.13.

Figure 4.13 The effect of the elevators

The flaps, which are controlled by a separate lever in the cockpit, are sometimes called **air brakes**. When the flaps are lowered, the drag increases and the lift increases, thus enabling the plane to land at a slower speed.

4.5. The constituents of air

Air is a mixture of gases, the relative proportions of which are fairly constant.

Investigation 4e. Removing the oxygen from air by burning magnesium

Half fill a sink or a plastic bowl with water. Place three coins on the bottom and rest a bell jar (without its stopper) on the coins. Mark the level of the water in the bell jar. Into the underside of the bell jar stopper, stick a length (about 10 cm) of stiff wire. Make a loop at the free end of the wire and, to this loop, fix a 20 cm length of magnesium ribbon, formed into the shape of a loose coil, so that it will be clear of the water when it is inserted into the bell jar. Holding the stopper, light the end of the magnesium ribbon coil with a bunsen flame. As soon as the magnesium ribbon is burning, insert it through the neck of the bell jar and press the stopper firmly into position. When the magnesium ribbon has stopped burning, wait for the contents of the jar to cool and pour water into the bowl until the levels inside and outside the jar are equal. Mark the new water level.

★WARNING. Do not look directly at the burning magnesium ribbon.

Compare the two levels. Can you estimate the proportion of the air that has been removed by the burning magnesium ribbon? You will realize that the shape of the neck of the bell jar makes it impossible to calculate this proportion exactly. Can you explain the purpose of the three coins?

Investigation 4f. Removing the oxygen from air with iron filings

Wet the inside of a test-tube and sprinkle some iron filings into it. Shake out any loose iron filings and place the open end of the test-tube below the surface of some water in a container, as shown in Figure 4.14.

The iron combines with oxygen to form rust. After a few days, you will notice that the water level inside the test-tube has risen.

Pour water into the container until the levels inside and outside the test-tube are equal. Measure the overall length of the test-tube and the rise in level of the water in the test-tube. From these two measurements, calculate the proportion of oxygen in air.

Investigation 4g. Carbon dioxide in air

Put some fresh lime-water into a flask and connect it to a filter pump, as shown in Figure 4.15.

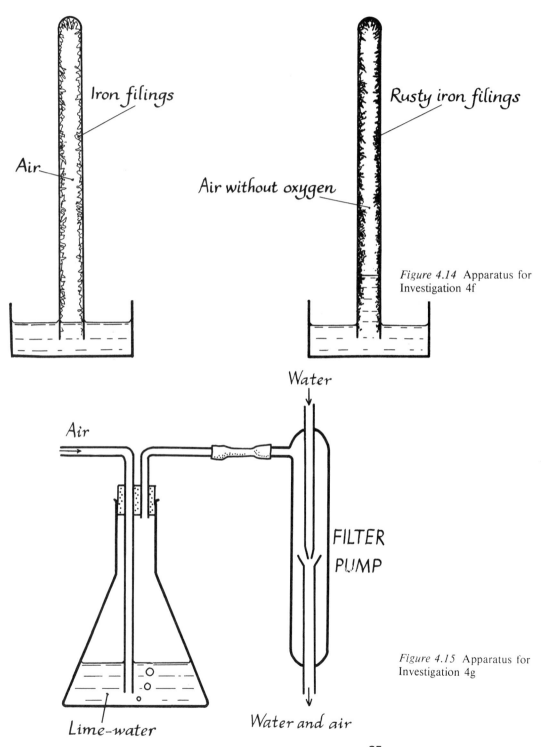

Iron filings

Air

Rusty iron filings

Air without oxygen

Figure 4.14 Apparatus for Investigation 4f

Water

Air

FILTER
PUMP

Lime-water

Figure 4.15 Apparatus for Investigation 4g

Water and air

Pass air through the lime-water for about thirty minutes and note any changes in the appearance of the lime-water. Is the proportion of carbon dioxide in air large or small?

Flammable   Harmful

Investigation 4h. Water vapour in air

Heat about 2 cm³ of water in a test-tube and add a few small crystals of cobalt(II) chloride to it until you have a saturated solution. Soak a piece of filter paper in this solution. What colour is the soaked filter paper? Now, dry the filter paper by waving it above a bunsen flame, being careful to avoid scorching it. What colour is the dry filter paper? Put a drop of water on the dry paper and note any change. Put a drop of propanone on the dry paper. Does the colour change? Mix a little water with some propanone and put a drop of this mixture on the paper. Does the colour change? Does cobalt(II) chloride paper indicate whether a liquid is *pure* water, or whether a liquid *contains* water?

Take a piece of dry cobalt(II) chloride paper and leave it exposed to the air for a short time. Has the colour changed? Does air contain water? Try this test in a steamy bathroom or kitchen.

We have seen, so far, that air contains oxygen (the gas which is removed by burning), carbon dioxide and water vapour. There are other gases in air. By far the greatest proportion of the air is nitrogen (about 78 per cent), a gas which, as a gas, is of little practical use. Nitrogen becomes useful when it combines with other elements to

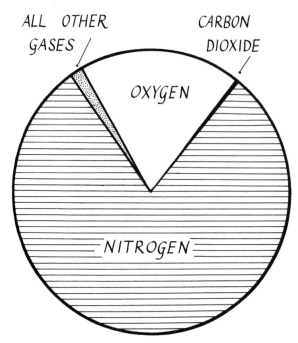

Figure 4.16 The gases in the air

form compounds which are absorbed by plants. All forms of living matter contain proteins, and proteins are compounds of nitrogen.

Air contains about 21 per cent oxygen, about 78 per cent nitrogen and about 0·03 per cent carbon dioxide, by volume. Most of the remaining 1 per cent is made up of a group of gases known as the **noble gases,** because they do not combine with other elements to form compounds. The noble gases are **argon, krypton, neon, xenon** and **helium**. Their main use is in electrical discharge tubes. The proportions of the gases in the air are shown in Figure 4.16. The proportions of oxygen, nitrogen, carbon dioxide and the noble gases in air remain relatively constant, but the amount of water vapour varies considerably.

Investigation 4i. An enclosed world

Into a large, wide-mouthed bottle, put a layer of good garden soil with some worms. Dig up some small plants, each with a ball of soil round the roots, and plant them in the soil in the bottle. Water the soil in the bottle and put the lid on. If possible, find the mass of the bottle and then place it in a warm, sunny position. From time to time, you will see droplets of water on the inside of the bottle. How did the water get from the soil to the inside surface of the glass? Do the plants grow? What is replacing the carbon dioxide that the plants use for photosynthesis? Find the mass of the bottle from time to time. Does the mass vary?

4.6. Pollution of air

In Section 4.5 we considered the constituents of pure air. Unfortunately, in industrial areas and, to a lesser extent, in rural areas, air contains other substances as impurities. The impurities which cause air pollution can be grouped under three main categories:

a. Pollution by solids

Soot from fires burning fuels, other than smokeless fuels, consists of minute particles of carbon. The presence of soot in the air reduces the amount of light and ultraviolet rays that reach the earth from the sun. It also clings to buildings and forms a layer on any horizontal surface. Soot combined with fog produces smog, which reduces visibility and causes great distress to people suffering from respiratory complaints.

b. Pollution by gases

Carbon monoxide, formed by the incomplete oxidation of carbon, is a poisonous gas. Carbon dioxide, although a normal constituent of air, is often present in excessive quantities in industrial areas and in places where large numbers of people gather in badly ventilated conditions. Sulphur dioxide and hydrogen sulphide are also found in air in industrial areas. These gases are soluble in water and form acids; this occurs when rain falls through air polluted by these gases and, under these conditions, fabrics and stonework suffer severe corrosion.

c. Biological pollution

Pollen grains are always present in air, particularly during the summer months, causing distress to sufferers of hay fever. Bacteria and viruses are also present in air and, although we usually have sufficient immunity against their effects, excessive pollution can overcome our natural immunity.

4.7. Air and the weather

Atmospheric conditions determine the weather; changes in atmospheric conditions alter the weather. In order to understand atmospheric conditions and their effect on the weather, we must be able to measure them.

a. **Atmospheric pressure** is measured with a barometer (see Section 4.1). If we are in an area of low pressure, air will move towards us from surrounding areas of higher pressure. If there are clouds between us and the high pressure areas, the clouds will move towards us and, under certain circumstances, could cause rain. Low pressure may be caused by the presence of water vapour (which is less dense than air) and usually brings winds and a deterioration of weather conditions.

If we are in an area of high pressure, air will move away from us. High pressure usually indicates that weather conditions are unlikely to change.

b. **Wind direction and speed.** Wind is a direct consequence of differences in air pressure; the greater the difference, the greater the speed of the wind. The direction of the wind depends on the relative positions of areas of high and low pressure. Wind direction is indicated by weather vanes, wind socks and smoke. Wind speed can be measured by using a Pitot tube (see Section 4.2), or by a 'whirling cup' **anemometer**, as shown in Figure 4.17. Whichever type of anemometer is used, it is mounted well above the ground and is connected to an indicator which is calibrated to read wind speed.

In weather reports, wind speed is usually quoted as a force number on the **Beaufort scale**. Table 4.1 shows the Beaufort scale, together with the approximate speeds and descriptions.

c. **Humidity** is the amount of water vapour which is in the air. This is variable and has a considerable effect on weather. If the air is dry, rain is impossible; if the air is wet, rain is possible but it depends

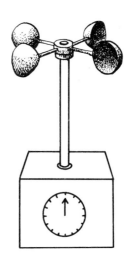

Figure 4.17 A 'whirling cup' anemometer

TABLE 4.1. THE BEAUFORT SCALE

Force	Name	Approximate Speed/km h^{-1}	Description
0	Calm	0	Smoke rises straight up.
1	Light air	3	Smoke drifts gently, wind vanes not affected.
2	Light breeze	8	Leaves rustle, wind felt on face, wind vanes move.
3	Gentle breeze	16	Constant movement of twigs and leaves, light flags blown out from flagpole.
4	Moderate breeze	24	Leaves, twigs and small branches move, dust and paper blown about.
5	Fresh breeze	34	Small trees sway, small waves on water.
6	Strong breeze	45	Large branches move, telegraph wires whistle.
7	Moderate gale	56	Whole trees move, walking against the wind is difficult.
8	Fresh gale	68	Twigs and small branches broken.
9	Strong gale	80	Chimney pots and tiles blown down.
10	Whole gale	95	Buildings damaged, trees uprooted.
11	Storm	110	Buildings severely damaged.
12	Hurricane	Over 120	Whole trees blown about, buildings destroyed.

on other factors. Warm air can contain a greater amount of water vapour than cold air. When warm, wet air rises, it cools and is unable to contain as much water and so rain falls. The humidity of the air can be indicated by a number of methods:

1. A pine cone will open in dry air and close in damp air.
2. A piece of seaweed feels dry and brittle in dry air but feels slimy in damp air.

3. A piece of catgut untwists in damp air and twists in dry air. This is what makes the platform move in a 'weather house'.
4. The petals of the scarlet pimpernel (a small wild flower, sometimes called the 'poor man's weather glass') open in dry air but remain closed in damp air.
5. Paint a piece of cardboard with a saturated solution of cobalt(II) chloride, to which has been added some common salt and a little gum. In dry weather it will be blue; in damp weather it will be pink.

All of these methods merely indicate the presence of water vapour in the air. To measure changes in humidity we use a **hygrometer.** You can make a simple hygrometer by fixing one end of a long hair to a screw in a vertical piece of wood, passing the hair round a spindle and hanging a metal nut from the other end of the hair, as shown in Figure 4.18.

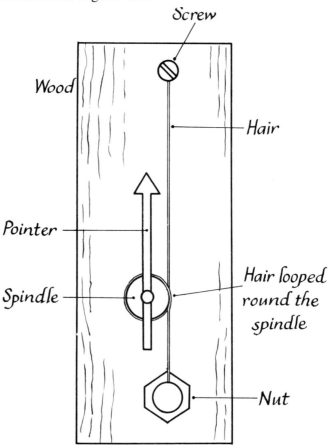

Figure 4.18 A hair hygrometer

If the air is damp, the hair will stretch and the spindle will turn. If the air is dry, the hair will shrink, and the spindle will turn the other way. By fixing a light pointer to the spindle, the movement of the spindle will be made more obvious.

A more accurate method of measuring humidity is to use the

wet and dry bulb thermometer (see Figure 4.19). This consists of two thermometers mounted on a board, one of the bulbs being wrapped with muslin, one end of which is immersed in water. When the air is wet, very little water will evaporate from the muslin, and the two thermometer readings will be almost the same. When the air is dry, water will evaporate from the muslin, causing a drop in the temperature indicated by this thermometer.

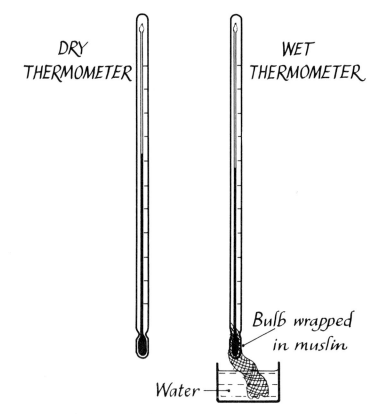

Figure 4.19 The wet and dry bulb thermometer

Because warm air can contain more water vapour than cold air, the relative humidity cannot be read from the wet and dry bulb thermometer directly (e.g. a temperature difference of five Celsius degrees when the air temperature is 30 °C is less humid than the same temperature difference when the air temperature is 20 °C). Once the air temperature and the temperature difference are known, the relative humidity can be found from tables.

Humidity of the air is important to certain industries. Linen and cotton are best spun in damp conditions. Does this explain why cotton is spun and woven in Lancashire and that the centre of the linen industry is in Ulster? Paper manufacture also requires a humid atmosphere and, where the humidity of the air is insufficient, it is artificially increased.

Our physical comfort also depends, to a large extent, on the relative humidity of the air. In a tropical jungle the air is very humid.

This makes life rather uncomfortable because perspiration tends to evaporate very slowly and this, in turn, prevents us from losing heat. In a hot dry climate perspiration evaporates almost immediately.

d. **Air temperature** is, of course, measured with a thermometer.

e. **Rainfall** is quoted as the depth of water which would remain if none was absorbed or evaporated. To measure rainfall, a **rain gauge** is used (see Figure 4.20). This consists of a metal canister, with a funnel-shaped top, leading to a container to catch the water. In order to read a rain gauge, the water is poured from this container into a narrow measuring cylinder, which is calibrated to read the depth of water which fell in the diameter of the funnel.

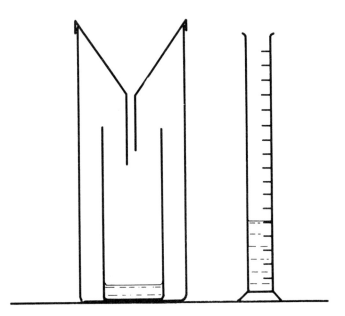

Figure 4.20 A rain gauge

Rainfall has a considerable effect on vegetation. High rainfall promotes rapid growth, particularly if the air temperature is high as well. Low rainfall restricts growth and limits the types of plant that can survive.

4.8. Air and life

Most forms of living organism require oxygen for the process of oxidation, which releases energy. This oxygen is extracted from the air.

Some land animals (e.g. worms) obtain their oxygen by diffusion through the skin. Most land animals use lungs, in which a gas exchange takes place; oxygen diffuses from the air into the blood and carbon dioxide diffuses from the blood into the air. Air can be made to enter and leave the lungs of mammals in two ways:

a. **Abdominal breathing.** Between the chest cavity and the abdomen is a thick sheet of muscle, called the diaphragm. When the diaphragm is lowered, the chest cavity is enlarged. This reduces the pressure around the lungs, causing air at normal atmospheric pressure to enter the lungs through the nose, mouth and trachea (windpipe). When the diaphragm is raised, air is forced from the lungs. The action of abdominal breathing is shown in Figure 4.21.

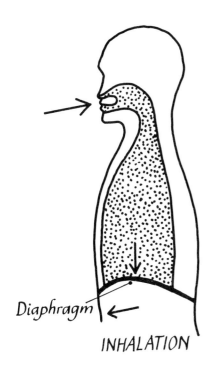

Diaphragm

INHALATION

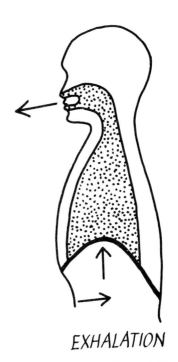

EXHALATION

Figure 4.21 Abdominal breathing

b. **Thoracic breathing.** This method of breathing is so called because it involves movement of the thorax (the chest). When the ribs are raised, thus enlarging the chest cavity, air enters the lungs. When the ribs are lowered, air is forced from the lungs. The action of thoracic breathing is shown in Figure 4.22.

During normal breathing, mammals use both of these methods simultaneously.

Some aquatic animals can only obtain oxygen from the air and need to come to the surface from time to time. Examples of these animals are whales, seals, dolphins and porpoises. Other aquatic animals, including fish, are able to extract oxygen from the air dissolved in the water. When a fish breathes, it closes its gill slits and opens its mouth. Water enters the mouth, which is then closed, and the water is forced over the gills. Blood vessels in the gills absorb oxygen from the water and pass out carbon dioxide into the water, which then passes out through the open gill slits. The passage of water past the gills is shown in Figure 4.23.

If you heat a container of cold water, you will see bubbles appearing long before the water boils. These are bubbles of air. They appear because, unlike most solids, gases are less soluble in warm water than they are in cold water. Try heating some water that has been boiled and allowed to cool again. Do the bubbles of air appear?

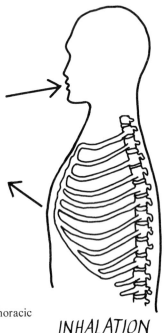
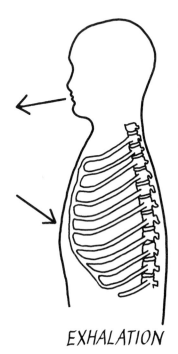

Figure 4.22 Thoracic breathing

INHALATION   EXHALATION

It is interesting to note that, because oxygen is more soluble in water than nitrogen, air which is dissolved in water contains about 30 per cent oxygen, compared with 21 per cent in atmospheric air.

As fish constantly remove the oxygen from the dissolved air in an aquarium, this oxygen must be replaced. Replenishing the dissolved oxygen in an aquarium can be done in several ways:

a. The aquarium can be emptied and refilled with fresh water.
b. Air can be bubbled into the water with an aerator.
c. Oxygenating tablets can be added to the water.
d. Waterweed can be planted in the aquarium to maintain the balance. In daylight, green plants photosynthesize, giving out oxygen. If the right amount of plant life is introduced into the aquarium, the carbon dioxide output from the fish will be balanced by the oxygen output from the plants. If too much

or too little plant life is introduced, the water will turn cloudy and the sides of the aquarium may become covered with algae.

In natural surroundings, this balance is maintained automatically. Where pollution of rivers and streams occurs, plant life is often killed, and the balance is lost.

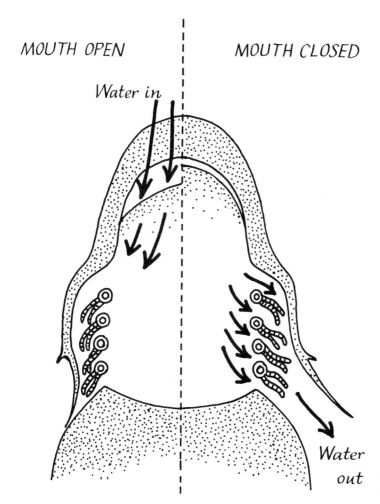

Figure 4.23 The action of the gills

Test your understanding

1. Why do divers sometimes suffer from the 'bends'? How can this be avoided?
2. Why is the aneroid type of altimeter liable to be inaccurate?
3. If an aircraft is stationary, facing east, on an airfield with a 20 km h⁻¹ wind blowing from the east, what will the reading be on the air speed indicator?
4. Why is it necessary for a sparrow to beat its wings faster than a seagull in order to fly?
5. How does a seagull take off from the ground on a windy day by merely opening its wings?

6. If you were flying an aircraft and the starboard (right) wing suddenly dipped, how could you correct it?

7. Which of the moveable control surfaces on an aircraft always move in opposite directions?

8. In most light aircraft the control surfaces are moved by wires connected to the controls in the cockpit. The control surfaces in a heavy aircraft or a high-speed aircraft are moved by motors, which are switched on and off by moving the controls in the cockpit. Why are these motors necessary?

9. When a plane is travelling along the runway at take-off speed, it is made to take off by moving the control column slightly back. What does this movement of the control column do? Why does this make the plane take off?

10. If you used air extracted from water, instead of atmospheric air, in Investigation 4f, what difference would you expect in the results?

11. Why would it be better for a person who suffers from bronchitis to live in the country, rather than in a town?

12. Why is it more comfortable to live in a hot, dry climate than in a hot, humid climate?

13. A boy decides to change the water in his aquarium. Foolishly, he sterilizes the water by boiling it and then allowing it to cool before replacing the fish. The next morning, all of the fish are dead. Can you explain why they died?

Chapter 5

Carbon and its Compounds

All living matter contains compounds of the element carbon. At one time, it was believed that the more complex compounds of carbon could only be produced by living organisms, and for this reason they are called **organic** compounds. Today many so-called organic compounds can be made in the laboratory.

5.1. The element carbon

An atom of carbon possesses six electrons, two of which occupy the innermost shell while the remaining four are in an outer shell. Such an atom may combine with others by sharing electrons. Groups of carbon atoms may combine in two distinctively different ways. These are illustrated in Figure 5.1.

When the tetrahedral pattern is formed, the type of carbon is called **diamond**. The hexagonal pattern gives **graphite**. Diamond and graphite are called **allotropes** of carbon. Allotropes are the same element, but, because they possess different arrangements of atoms, they have different physical properties.

Diamond is transparent and is extremely hard. Small diamonds are used to point drills for cutting very hard substances. Other diamonds are used for jewellery, such diamonds being very carefully cut. Nearly all the world's diamonds come from South Africa. They are found in the craters of extinct volcanoes.

Graphite is black and is extremely soft. Unlike diamond, it is a fairly good conductor of electricity. It is used as a lubricant, for electrodes, for making the 'lead' used in pencils, for making crucibles and for making moderators for nuclear reactors. Graphite is usually made by heating coke to a very high temperature in an electric furnace, but some occurs naturally in Sri Lanka (formerly Ceylon).

Other forms of carbon, such as soot, coke and charcoal, are usually referred to as **amorphous** carbon. The word amorphous means 'without shape', and specimens of these materials do not appear, at first, to have their atoms arranged in any special order. X-ray analysis has shown, however, that they really consist of small fragments of graphite.

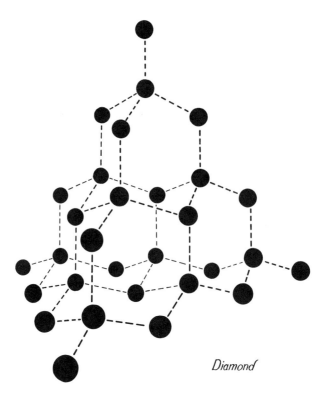

Diamond

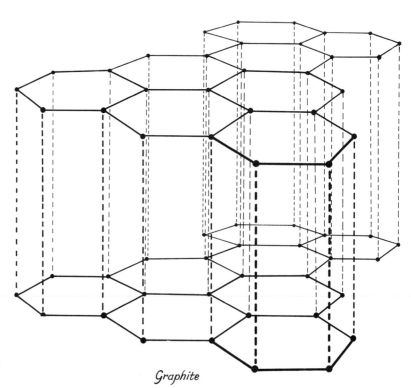

Figure 5.1 The structures
of diamond and graphite

Graphite

5.2. The oxides of carbon

When any form of carbon is burned in a plentiful supply of air or oxygen, carbon dioxide is formed. If, however, the supply of air or oxygen is limited, the carbon dioxide may then be reduced to carbon monoxide. Both of these reactions occur in a coke fire burning normally, as shown in Figure 5.2.

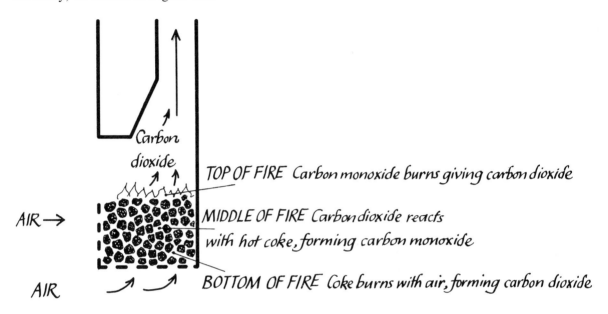

At the bottom of the fire, oxygen from the plentiful supply of air combines with the hot coke to form carbon dioxide. In the middle of the fire, this carbon dioxide reacts with hot coke to form carbon monoxide. At the top of the fire, carbon monoxide burns with a blue flame, producing carbon dioxide.

Figure 5.2 The coke fire

5.3. Carbon dioxide

Investigation 5a. Preparation of carbon dioxide

Set up the gas generation apparatus as shown in Figure 5.3. Obtain four test-tubes and half fill each of them with the following: universal indicator, methyl orange, bromo-thymol blue solution, lime-water. Put two or three marble chips in the flask, fit the bung and pour enough dilute hydrochloric acid (bench reagent) down the thistle funnel to cover the bottom of the funnel tube.

Put the delivery tube into the test-tube containing universal indicator and allow the gas to bubble through until no further colour change takes place. Wash the end of the delivery tube and then pass the gas through the methyl orange. Repeat this, using the bromo-thymol blue solution. Wash the end of the delivery tube and then

Harmful

Corrosive

pass the gas through the lime-water for at least ten minutes. Make a note of all the changes you see.

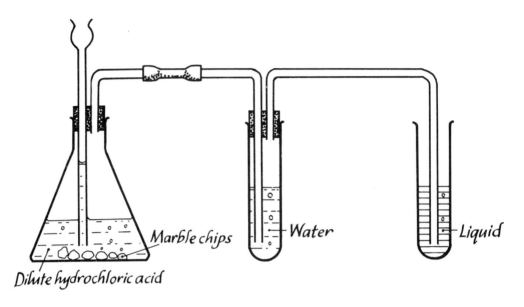

Marble chips — Water — Liquid

Dilute hydrochloric acid

Figure 5.3 Preparation of carbon dioxide

Harmful

Corrosive

Place a little universal indicator in each of two test-tubes. To one, add a few drops of dilute sulphuric(VI) acid and, to the other, add a little sodium hydroxide solution. Make a note of any changes which occur, and then repeat the experiment, using first methyl orange and then bromo-thymol blue solution in place of the universal indicator.

Carbon dioxide dissolves slightly in water to form carbonic acid (a weak acid).

$$H_2O + CO_2 \rightarrow H_2CO_3$$

Do your observations confirm this?

The test for carbon dioxide is that when it is passed through lime-water, the lime-water becomes cloudy due to the formation of small particles of calcium carbonate.

$$Ca(OH)_2 + CO_2 \rightarrow CaCO_3 + H_2O$$

(lime-water)   (carbon dioxide)   (calcium carbonate)   (water)

If more carbon dioxide is passed through this mixture, a clear solution of calcium hydrogencarbonate is formed.

$$CaCO_3 + H_2O + CO_2 \rightarrow Ca(HCO_3)_2$$

(calcium hydrogen-carbonate)

Calcium hydrogencarbonate can only exist in solution, and if the solution is heated it decomposes, forming calcium carbonate, water and carbon dioxide.

100

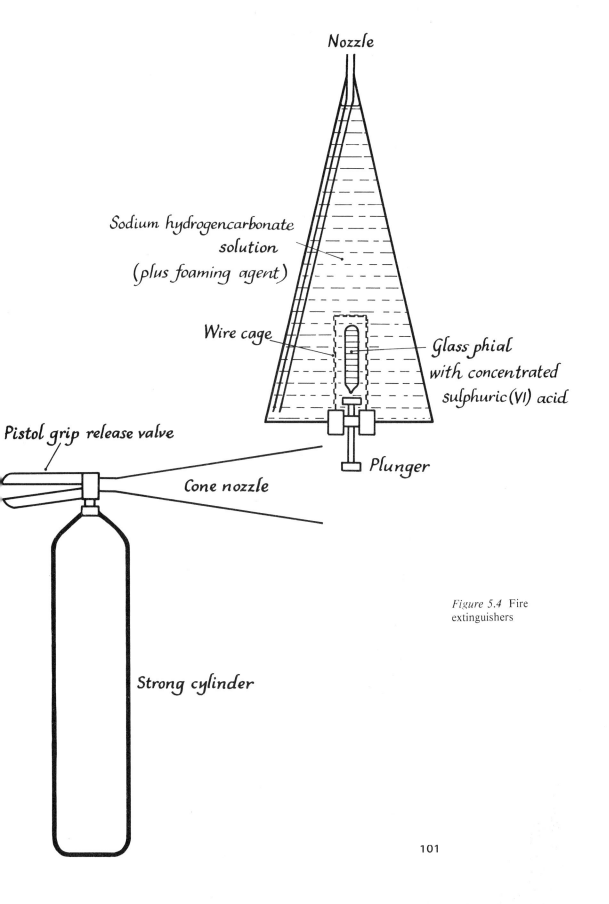

Nozzle

Sodium hydrogencarbonate
solution
(plus foaming agent)

Wire cage

Glass phial
with concentrated
sulphuric(VI) acid

Plunger

Pistol grip release valve

Cone nozzle

Strong cylinder

Figure 5.4 Fire
extinguishers

101

5.4. Uses of carbon dioxide

Carbon dioxide does not usually support combustion and is heavier than air. For these reasons, it can be used to extinguish a fire, by excluding air from it. Some fire extinguishers contain liquid carbon dioxide under pressure. When a valve is opened the pressure is released and a jet of carbon dioxide gas is produced. A more common type of fire extinguisher contains a solution of sodium hydrogencarbonate and some concentrated sulphuric(VI) acid. When the extinguisher is used, the acid is mixed with the sodium hydrogencarbonate solution, producing carbon dioxide. This causes liquid and carbon dioxide to be forced out under pressure. Sometimes, a foaming agent is added to the solution of sodium hydrogencarbonate, so that a thick foam is produced which acts as an effective blanket, preventing the air from coming into contact with the fire. Figure 5.4 shows these two types of fire extinguisher.

A large amount of carbon dioxide is used in the manufacture of 'fizzy' drinks. Carbon dioxide is forced under pressure into the bottle of drink, which is then stoppered. When the stopper is removed, the pressure is released, and the drink effervesces.

Solid carbon dioxide, or 'dry ice' as it is often called, has a temperature much lower than that of ordinary ice. When its temperature increases it changes directly into carbon dioxide gas. 'Dry ice' packs are often used to obtain low temperatures.

Green plants make use of carbon dioxide from the air in the process of photosynthesis. In this process, the plant combines carbon dioxide and water to produce sugar. This process can only be brought about in the presence of sunlight and chlorophyll (the green colouring substance in plants).

$$\text{CARBON DIOXIDE} + \text{WATER} \xrightarrow[\text{chlorophyll}]{\text{sunlight}} \text{SUGAR} + \text{OXYGEN}$$

5.5. Carbon monoxide

This is an extremely poisonous gas. When it is breathed in, it is readily absorbed into the red blood cells. These normally absorb oxygen. Thus oxygen is prevented from reaching the body tissues and death eventually results.

Carbon monoxide is present in the exhaust fumes of internal combustion engines.

Investigation 5b. Preparation of carbon monoxide

Carbon monoxide may be prepared by the action of hot concentrated sulphuric(VI) acid on ethanedioic acid. The sulphuric(VI) acid removes the elements of water from the ethanedioic acid so that a mixture of carbon dioxide and carbon monoxide is given off.

Corrosive

Flammable

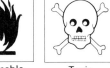
Toxic

★WARNING. *This must only be carried out by an experienced teacher.*

102

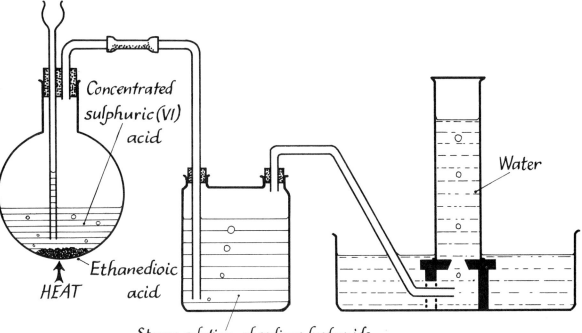

Concentrated sulphuric (VI) acid

Ethanedioic acid

HEAT

Water

Strong solution of sodium hydroxide

Figure 5.5 Preparation of carbon monoxide

If this mixture is passed through a strong solution of sodium hydroxide, the carbon dioxide will react with the sodium hydroxide forming sodium carbonate and water, but the carbon monoxide will be unchanged and may be collected by the displacement of water. Figure 5.5 shows how the apparatus is arranged.

A jar of the gas is collected as described above, the cover is removed and a lighted taper is placed in the mouth of the jar. When the gas has burned, the cover is replaced. From this gas jar some of the gas is extracted using a teat pipette. The contents of the teat pipette are then bubbled through a little lime-water placed in a test-tube.

The equations for the reactions are as follows:

$$H_2C_2O_4 \rightarrow H_2O + CO + CO_2$$

(ethanedioic   (water)   (carbon   (carbon
acid)   monoxide)   dioxide)

$$CO_2 + 2NaOH \rightarrow Na_2CO_3 + H_2O$$

(carbon   (sodium   (sodium   (water)
dioxide)   hydroxide)   carbonate)

Carbon monoxide burns with a blue flame to form carbon dioxide. Do your observations confirm this?

$$2CO + O_2 \rightarrow 2CO_2$$

(carbon   (oxygen)   (carbon
monoxide)   dioxide)

5.6. Chalk

Chalk is a form of calcium carbonate. Although their physical properties are different, limestone and marble are also forms of calcium carbonate and have the same chemical properties.

103

Investigation 5c. Chalk

Put a little powdered chalk in a test-tube and add water until the tube is about half full. Shake the tube vigorously and then place it in a test-tube rack. Leave it to stand for several minutes. Does chalk dissolve in water?

Harmful

Put a little powdered chalk in a test-tube and add a little dilute hydrochloric acid (bench reagent). If there is an effervescence, test to see if carbon dioxide is given off. Place the test-tube in a rack and periodically examine the contents.

Repeat the experiment, using dilute sulphuric(VI) acid in place of dilute hydrochloric acid.

Calcium carbonate is insoluble in water and, like all other carbonates, reacts with acids to form a salt, water and carbon dioxide.

The reaction with hydrochloric acid gives calcium chloride, water and carbon dioxide.

$$CaCO_3 + 2HCl \rightarrow CaCl_2 + H_2O + CO_2$$

(calcium carbonate) (hydrochloric acid) (calcium chloride) (water) (carbon dioxide)

This reaction is the one used in the laboratory for the preparation of carbon dioxide.

Harmful

If sulphuric acid is used in place of hydrochloric acid the salt formed is calcium sulphate(VI). This is almost insoluble in water and coats the marble chips, preventing the reaction from continuing.

When calcium carbonate is strongly heated it breaks down into calcium oxide and carbon dioxide.

$$CaCO_3 \rightarrow CaO + CO_2$$

(calcium carbonate) (calcium oxide) (carbon dioxide)

A very high temperature (900 °C) is required to bring about this reaction.

The common name for calcium oxide is **quicklime**. This is produced commercially by heating limestone in a kiln. Figure 5.6 shows a lime kiln.

When water is added to quicklime, a great deal of heat is produced and calcium hydroxide is formed.

$$CaO + H_2O \rightarrow Ca(OH)_2$$

(calcium oxide) (water) (calcium hydroxide)

The common name for calcium hydroxide is **slaked lime**. When slaked lime is mixed with sand and water a thick paste is formed. This paste is called **mortar**. On exposure to air mortar slowly hardens. Mortar is used in building brick walls.

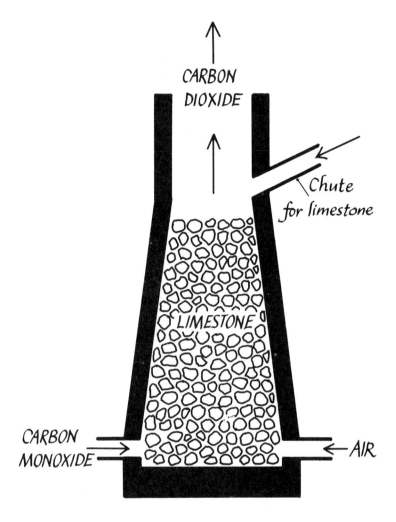

Cement is made by heating a mixture of clay, coke and calcium carbonate. This produces a mixture of calcium aluminate(IV) and calcium silicate(IV). A mixture of cement, sand and water sets hard, forming **concrete**.

Figure 5.6 A lime kiln

5.7. Sodium carbonate and sodium hydrogencarbonate

Sodium carbonate is commonly known as washing soda. It is used to soften water (see Chapter 2). It is also used in the manufacture of sodium hydroxide and in glass-making.

Sodium hydrogencarbonate is commonly called baking soda. If it is heated, it decomposes, forming sodium carbonate, water and carbon dioxide. Baking powder is a mixture of sodium hydrogen-carbonate and tartaric acid. When the powder is moistened, the acid reacts with the sodium hydrogencarbonate forming sodium tartrate, water and carbon dioxide. The carbon dioxide helps dough to rise.

5.8. Hydrocarbons

Hydrocarbons are compounds containing carbon and hydrogen *only*. There are many different hydrocarbons, many of which are valuable as fuels.

5.9. Alkanes

The name **alkane** is given to any hydrocarbon having the general formula C_nH_{2n+2}. The simplest of these is **methane**, which is formed when single carbon atoms combine with four hydrogen atoms (see Figure 5.7).

Figure 5.7 Methane

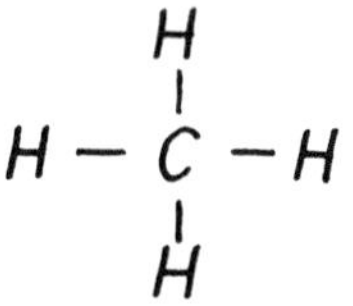

$$H - \overset{\overset{\displaystyle H}{|}}{\underset{\underset{\displaystyle H}{|}}{C}} - H$$

Methane is a light colourless gas which burns with a pale blue flame, forming carbon dioxide and water.

$$CH_4 + 2O_2 \rightarrow CO_2 + 2H_2O$$

Methane is often produced by the decay of vegetable matter under water and, for this reason, is sometimes called 'marsh gas'. The 'natural gas' found under the North Sea is methane. 'Fire damp' which creates a serious hazard in coal mines is also methane.

One of the most important properties of carbon is its ability to form long chains. Figure 5.8 shows the molecular structure of some other alkanes. It should be noted that the correct name for the 'paraffin' used in domestic heaters is kerosene.

Figure 5.8 Some alkanes

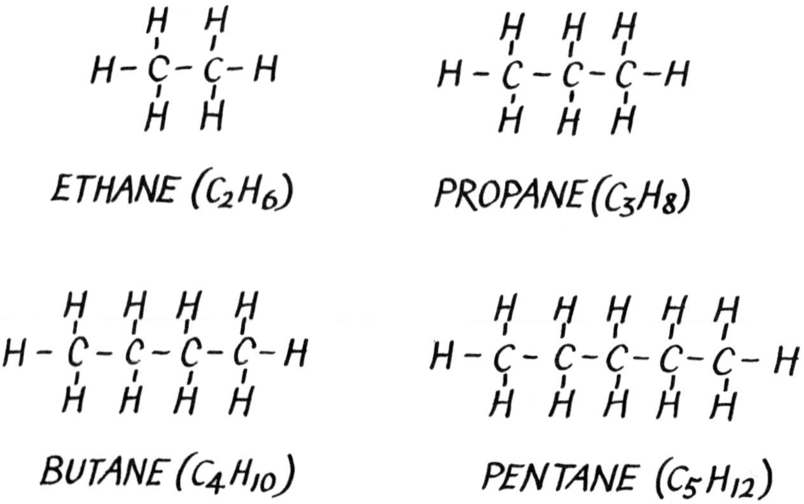

ETHANE (C_2H_6)

PROPANE (C_3H_8)

BUTANE (C_4H_{10})

PENTANE (C_5H_{12})

106

5.10. Ethene

Ethene is the simplest member of a series of hydrocarbons called **alkenes**. The general formula for alkenes is C_nH_{2n}.

Ethene readily combines with bromine to form **1,2-dibromoethane.** This compound is used as an additive to petrol, in order to remove certain impurities from the cylinder. Figure 5.9 represents the structures of ethene and 1,2-dibromoethane.

Figure 5.9 Ethene and 1,2-dibromoethane

ETHENE   1,2-DIBROMOETHANE

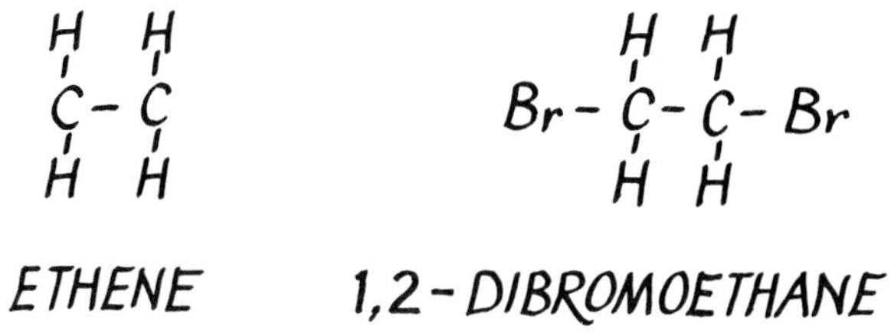

When ethene is compressed, it combines with itself to form long-chain molecules. This process is called **polymerization**, and the name of the polymer produced by the compression of ethene is **polythene**. This is a plastic which is an extremely good electrical insulator. It is also used in the manufacture of bowls, bottles and other containers.

5.11. Benzene

This is a hydrocarbon having the formula C_6H_6. It differs from the other hydrocarbons which we have considered in that the carbon

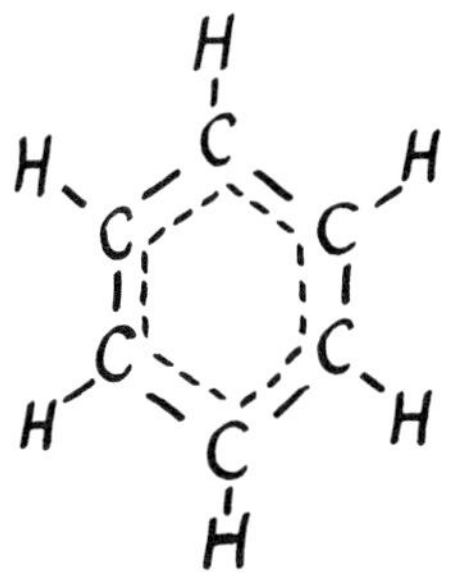

Figure 5.10 The benzene ring

atoms combine in a ring (see Figure 5.10). Benzene is used as an additive to petrol to improve its performance. It is also used as the starting point in the manufacture of many drugs and dyes.

5.12. Carbohydrates

Carbohydrates are compounds containing carbon, hydrogen and oxygen. The hydrogen and oxygen are always in the same proportion as they are in water. Carbohydrates include **sugars, starches**

and **cellulose**. Sugars and starches are an important part of our diet. They are oxidized within the body to form carbon dioxide and water. Heat is produced by this reaction, providing energy and maintaining the body temperature.

5.13. Sugars

Investigation 5d. Dehydration of sugar

A small beaker is half filled with table sugar (sucrose). A few drops of concentrated sulphuric(VI) acid are then added. After a short while a vigorous reaction is seen to take place.

Concentrated sulphuric(VI) acid reacts with the sugar by removing the elements of water. What remains in the beaker at the end of the reaction?

Sucrose is the commonest sugar and is usually obtained from sugar-cane or sugar-beet. The body cannot make direct use of sucrose, but enzymes in the intestine convert it into two simpler sugars, glucose and fructose, which are readily absorbed by the body.

Glucose is a very good source of energy, because it is so readily absorbed into the body. This kind of sugar is found in many fruits, but it may also be prepared from starch.

5.14. Starch

This is a complex carbohydrate which is found in most vegetables and cereals. Potatoes may contain as much as 20 per cent starch while bread contains about 50 per cent starch.

In vegetables, starch grains are enclosed within cellulose cell walls. We cannot digest cellulose and, for this reason, it is necessary to cook vegetables, such as potatoes, in order to break down the cell walls.

Starch is converted into glucose by the action of enzymes. Ptyalin, which is present in saliva, starts this process.

5.15. Cellulose

Cellulose is another complex carbohydrate. It is found in plant fibres and in the cell walls of plants. Human beings are unable to digest cellulose, but animals such as cows and sheep are able to do so because of the presence of certain bacteria and protozoa (single-celled organisms) in their stomachs.

It is possible to dissolve cellulose in sodium hydroxide or carbon disulphide. If the resulting solution is forced through a fine jet into a tank of dilute acid, a thread of artificial silk is produced. Cellophane is made in a similar way.

5.16. Alcohols

These are compounds having formulae similar to the alkanes, except that one of the hydrogen atoms is replaced by the hydroxyl radical (see Figure 5.11). In this chapter we shall discuss two of the commonest alcohols, **methanol** and **ethanol.**

$$H-\overset{\displaystyle H}{\underset{\displaystyle H}{C}}-H$$

METHANE (CH_4)

$$H-\overset{\displaystyle H}{\underset{\displaystyle H}{C}}-OH$$

METHANOL (CH_3OH)

$$H-\overset{\displaystyle H}{\underset{\displaystyle H}{C}}-\overset{\displaystyle H}{\underset{\displaystyle H}{C}}-H$$

ETHANE (C_2H_6)

$$H-\overset{\displaystyle H}{\underset{\displaystyle H}{C}}-\overset{\displaystyle H}{\underset{\displaystyle H}{C}}-OH$$

ETHANOL (C_2H_5OH)

Figure 5.11 Methanol and ethanol

Investigation 5e. The action of yeast on sugar

Make a sugar solution by dissolving 50 g of sugar in 400 cm³ of water. The solution is best prepared using boiling water, but it must be allowed to cool before proceeding with the investigation.

Place some of this solution in a flask and add a little yeast to it. Fit the flask with a delivery tube, arranged as shown in Figure 5.12. Leave the apparatus for several days, making sure that during this time the temperature does not fall below 20 °C. A gas will be given off during the reaction. Can you name this gas?

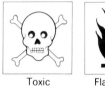

Toxic   Flammable

Figure 5.12 The action of yeast on sugar

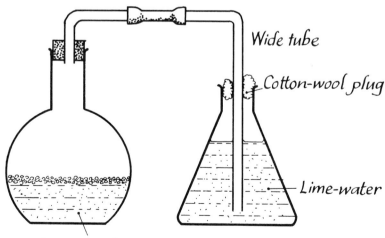

Wide tube

Cotton-wool plug

Lime-water

Sugar solution and yeast

At the end of the investigation, the flask will contain a dilute solution of ethanol, together with a very large number of yeast cells. The liquid may be separated from the yeast by filtering.

Yeast is a very simple form of plant life. When placed in a sugar solution at a suitable temperature, the yeast multiplies and, in doing so, produces several enzymes.

One of these converts sucrose into a mixture of fructose and glucose, while others change these simple sugars into ethanol and carbon dioxide.

$$C_6H_{12}O_6 \rightarrow 2C_2H_5OH + 2CO_2$$
$$\text{(glucose)} \qquad \text{(ethanol)} \qquad \text{(carbon dioxide)}$$

The final solution can contain only a small proportion of ethanol, because if the alcohol concentration becomes too high, the yeast is killed.

This process is used in making beers and wines. If a stronger solution of ethanol is required, this may be obtained by fractional distillation.

In the manufacture of spirits (brandy, gin, rum, etc.), a weak ethanol solution is first produced by means of a process of fermentation. This is then distilled to make a stronger solution. The final product contains about 25 per cent ethanol.

Methanol is not made by fermentation. At one time it was made from an acid (pyroligneous acid) which is obtained when wood is distilled; for this reason it is sometimes called 'wood alcohol'. Methanol is very poisonous.

A heavy duty is payable on ethanol used for drinking. Methylated spirit is duty free and consists of ethanol to which methanol, other unpleasant compounds and a violet dye have been added in order to render it unsuitable for drinking.

5.17. Distillation

There are two distinctly different methods of distillation. One is **destructive distillation**, in which a complex substance is heated without air, in order to decompose it into simpler substances. The other is **fractional distillation,** which is used to separate a mixture of liquids when each has a different boiling point.

Toxic

Flammable

Investigation 5f. Destructive distillation of wood

Set up the apparatus, as shown in Figure 5.13, placing a few wooden splints in the hard-glass test-tube. Heat the test-tube and observe what happens.

110

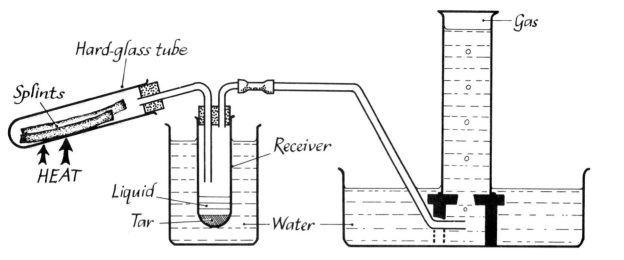

Splints

Hard-glass tube

HEAT

Liquid

Tar

Receiver

Water

Gas

Continue heating until there is no further reaction. The gas collected in the gas jar may be ignited with a taper.

Test the watery liquid in the receiver with red and blue litmus papers and decide whether it is acidic, alkaline or neutral. The watery liquid contains some methanol as well as propanone and ethanoic acid.

At the bottom of the receiver there will be a tarry substance. The residue in the test-tube is charcoal.

All animal and vegetable matter will produce similar substances when subjected to destructive distillation. When coal is distilled the products are coke, gas, tar and an alkaline liquid.

Figure 5.13 Destructive distillation of wood

Investigation 5g. Separating ethanol and water

In this experiment we shall use a **Liebig condenser**. This is connected to a flask which is heated gently until boiling occurs. When this happens, turn down the flame so that just enough heat is provided to keep the liquid boiling. Note the thermometer reading.

Ethanol boils at a temperature below 80 °C. Therefore, when a mixture of ethanol and water is placed in the flask, it is ethanol vapour which is first produced. This condenses to become a liquid as it passes down the condenser. Note that the cooling water enters at the bottom of the condenser and leaves at the top. Why do you think this is?

The same apparatus may be used to obtain pure (distilled) water. In this case, tap water is placed in the flask. The impurities present in tap water will either be given off as gases or will remain in the flask as a solid residue. Distilled water will be collected in the beaker.

Mixtures such as petroleum may be separated by fractional distil-

★ WARNING. *Use a safety screen.*

Toxic

Flammable

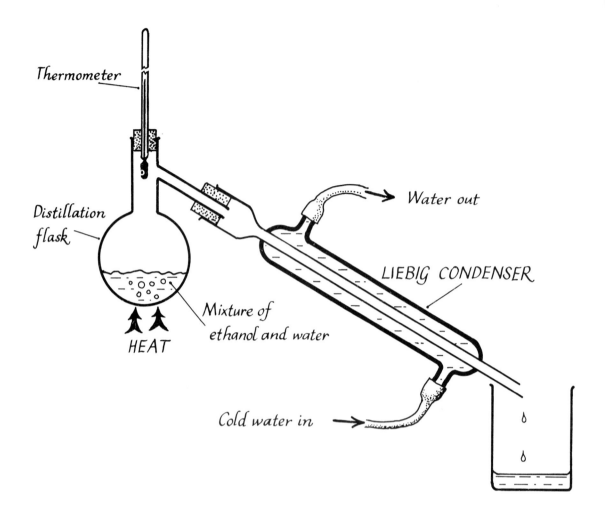

Thermometer

Distillation flask

HEAT

Mixture of ethanol and water

Water out

LIEBIG CONDENSER

Cold water in

Figure 5.14 Distillation using a Liebig condenser

lation, each separate substance (or fraction) condensing at a different temperature.

Commercially, oxygen is obtained from air by fractional distillation. Water vapour and carbon dioxide are first removed from the air and the remaining gases are cooled to about $-200\ °C$ (73 K), at which temperature they are liquids. This mixture is slowly evaporated, the nitrogen boiling at $-196\ °C$ (77 K). Liquid oxygen remains, as this boils at the higher temperature of $-183\ °C$ (90 K).

5.18. Fats and oils

Fats, like carbohydrates, are used by the body as sources of energy. Fats and oils are compounds of certain organic acids and a complex alcohol, called glycerol. The most important fats include glyceryl oleate, glyceryl palmitate and glyceryl stearate. Glyceryl oleate is present in olive oil, glyceryl palmitate is found in palm oil and glyceryl stearate is present in mutton fat. Naturally-occurring fats are mixtures of these and other similar compounds.

Fats are solids at normal temperatures, while oils have a lower melting point, and so are liquid at normal atmospheric temperatures.

Oils may be converted into fats by reacting them with hydrogen. This process is called **hydrogenation**. A catalyst is required to bring the reaction about, and nickel is generally used for this purpose. Margarine and cooking fats are made by this method, vegetable oils and whale oil being used as the raw materials.

Test your understanding

1. What is meant by an 'allotrope'? Name the allotropes of carbon and list their main differences.
2. Sketch the apparatus you would use to prepare carbon dioxide in the laboratory. Describe the test for carbon dioxide.
3. Make a sketch of a normally burning coke fire. Explain the chemical reactions which take place.
4. How is quicklime made? What happens when water is added to quickline?
5. What is a carbohydrate?
6. What is a hydrocarbon?
7. What is polythene?
8. Describe how you could prepare a weak ethanol solution.
9. With the aid of a diagram, explain how you would separate a mixture of ethanol and water.
10. What is meant by 'destructive distillation'? What products are obtained from the destructive distillation of coal?
11. What is hydrogenation? What important foodstuff is made by this process?
12. How is oxygen obtained from air?

Chapter 6

Metals

6.1. What are metals?

For many purposes it is useful to be able to distinguish between the metallic elements and the non-metallic elements. It is usually possible to do this by consideration of the physical and chemical properties of the element, even though many elements do not possess all of the typical properties of one group or the other.

The typical physical properties of metals are as follows:
a. They are good conductors of heat and electricity.
b. When they are freshly cut, they have a glittering appearance, or lustre.
c. They have a high melting point.
d. They are very dense.
e. They are hard.

The chemical properties include the following:
a. The oxides of metals are usually basic, i.e. they react with acids to form a salt and water. If such an oxide dissolves in water it forms an alkaline solution.
b. Atoms of metals tend to lose electrons to become positively charged ions.

Table 6.1 lists some metals and gives some of their properties.

6.2. Sources of metals

A few metals are found in a fairly pure state. These include gold, silver and sometimes copper.

Most metals are found combined with other elements in 'rocky' substances called **ores**. The metal has then to be extracted from the ore. The ores often contain oxygen or sulphur combined with the metallic element.

6.3. Extraction of metals from their ores

Some metals are fairly easy to extract from their ores by a process of **smelting**. Tin is extracted from its ore in this way.

114

TABLE 6.1. METALS

Name	Symbol	Melting Point/°C	Density/ kg m^{-3}	Other Features
Aluminium	Al	660	2 700	Good conductor of heat and electricity. Resistant to corrosion.
Calcium	Ca	850	1 600	Reacts with cold water giving hydrogen gas.
Chromium	Cr	1 800	7 100	Extremely hard. Does not readily corrode.
Cobalt	Co	1 490	8 700	Used in the manufacture of some types of steel.
Copper	Cu	1 083	8 900	Very good electrical conductor.
Gold	Au	1 063	19 300	Very soft. Does not corrode.
Iron	Fe	1 539	7 900	Abundant. With carbon forms steel, the most versatile metal.
Lead	Pb	327	11 300	Very soft. Does not readily corrode. Used in making car batteries.
Magnesium	Mg	650	1 700	Reacts with dilute acids. Reacts with steam giving hydrogen.
Manganese	Mn	1 260	7 400	Used in the manufacture of steel.
Mercury	Hg	−38·9	13 600	Liquid at atmospheric temperature. Vapour very poisonous.
Nickel	Ni	1 453	8 900	Many uses especially in alloys. Plated on to steel before chromium plating.
Platinum	Pt	1 769	21 450	Hard. Does not corrode. Very good electrical conductor. Very expensive.
Potassium	K	63	860	Reacts vigorously with cold water giving off hydrogen gas.
Silver	Ag	961	10 500	Less resistant to corrosion than other noble metals. Reacts with nitric(V) acid.
Sodium	Na	98	970	Reacts vigorously with cold water giving off hydrogen gas. Also used as a heat-conducting fluid in atomic reactors.
Tin	Sn	232	7 300	Expensive. Used largely in tin plating, solder and tinning copper wires.
Zinc	Zn	420	7 100	Used in galvanizing iron and in Leclanché cells.

The tin ore is mixed with powdered coke and heated in a furnace. The ore consists mainly of an oxide of tin and, in the smelting process, carbon from the coke combines with the oxygen from the ore to form carbon dioxide gas. This escapes through a chimney, leaving molten tin which is run off from the bottom of the furnace. Figure 6.1 shows a furnace used for tin smelting.

Figure 6.1 Tin smelting

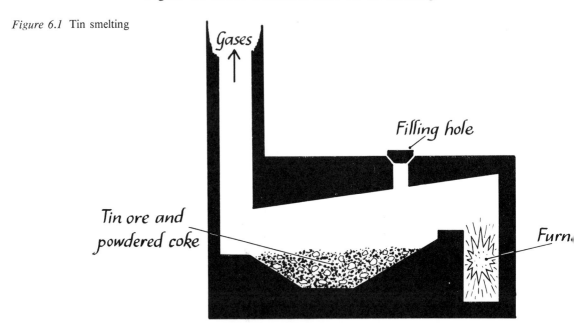

Iron ore consists of iron oxide together with compounds of sulphur, phosphorus, manganese and other elements. Iron ore is smelted in a **blast furnace** (see Figure 6.2).

A mixture of iron ore, coke and limestone (a form of calcium carbonate) is fed into the furnace from the top. As the ore settles lower in the furnace, carbon monoxide coming from the lower part of the furnace reacts with the ore and removes oxygen from it, leaving iron mixed with coke, limestone and other impurities. As it becomes hotter, the limestone is converted into quicklime (calcium oxide) and carbon dioxide. The lime combines with the other impurities to form slag, and carbon monoxide is formed by a reaction between the carbon dioxide and the coke. At a lower level in the furnace, coke burns in a blast of air producing a temperature high enough to melt the iron. As the molten iron is denser than slag, it settles at the bottom of the furnace with the slag floating on top of it. The molten iron and the slag are run off separately. The slag is broken up to be used in road building and the iron is used to make steel. It should be noted that the iron obtained from the blast furnace still contains some impurities, making it unsuitable for use where great strength is required.

116

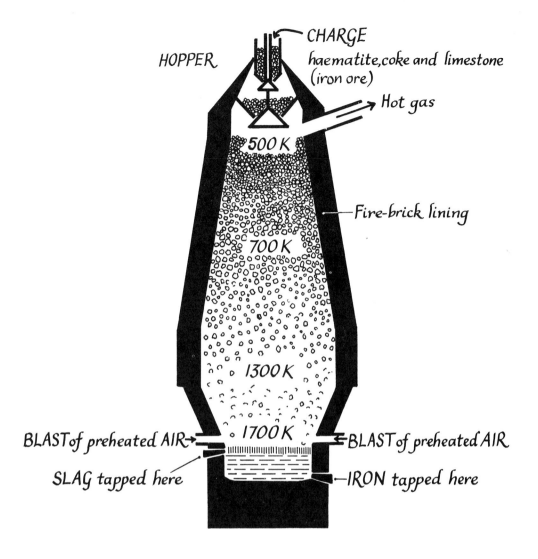

CHARGE
HOPPER
haematite, coke and limestone
(iron ore)

Hot gas

500 K

Fire-brick lining

700 K

1300 K

BLAST of preheated AIR →   1700 K   ⇇ BLAST of preheated AIR

SLAG tapped here

IRON tapped here

Figure 6.2 A blast furnace

Copper is usually found combined with sulphur in an ore called copper pyrites. This is easily converted into copper in a blast furnace, the sulphur combining with oxygen from the air blast to form sulphur dioxide gas. Copper obtained in this way is not pure enough to be used for electrical conductors but it may be further refined by a process of electrolysis.

Aluminium cannot be obtained from its ore by smelting. Bauxite, an aluminium ore, contains aluminium oxide together with other impurities including iron oxide and silica. The first step in the extraction of aluminium is to treat the ore with sodium hydroxide in order to obtain pure aluminium oxide. This oxide is in the form of a white powder known as alumina. Alumina is then dissolved in molten cryolite, a compound containing sodium, aluminium and fluorine, at a temperature of about 1 000 °C (1 273 K). When this molten mass is made to undergo electrolysis, pure aluminium is deposited at the cathode. It is at a sufficiently high temperature to be molten and is removed by suction. Figure 6.3 shows this process.

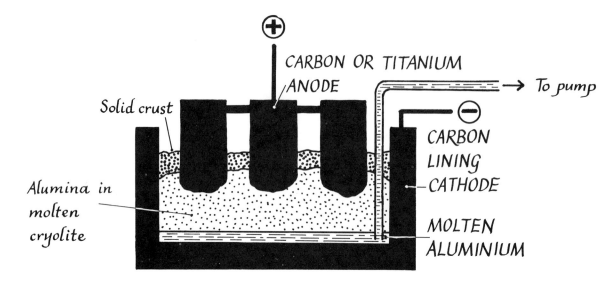

Figure 6.3 Extraction of aluminium

6.4. Steel

Because of its very great strength and its relative cheapness, steel is the most important metal for structural purposes.

The iron obtained from the blast furnace may contain up to 5 per cent carbon and is called **cast iron**. Cast iron is brittle. Steel is iron combined with a much lower percentage of carbon. The lower the percentage of carbon, the easier it is to bend the steel.

Often small quantities of other metals are added to the steel in order to modify its properties. A list of some types of steel is given in Table 6.2.

TABLE 6.2. TYPES OF STEEL

Name	Main Constituents	Uses
Mild steel	Iron and carbon (up to 0.25%)	General structural uses
High carbon steel	Iron and carbon (0.44% to 1.5%)	Machine tools
Nickel steel	Iron, nickel and carbon	Engine parts
Manganese steel	Iron, manganese and carbon	Safes
Vanadium steel	Iron, vanadium and carbon	Springs
Stainless steel	Iron, chromium and carbon	Cutlery, sinks
Tungsten steel	Iron, tungsten and carbon	Magnets, cutting tools
Invar	Iron, nickel (about 35%) and carbon	Gas thermostats

In order to convert cast iron into steel, much of the carbon and other impurities must be removed and any other constituent added. In modern steel-making plants, this is done by the **Linz–Donowitz** process. Figure 6.4 shows two types of converter.

In this process, the converter is a rotating steel container, lined with a special kind of fire-brick called **ganister.** The converter is loaded with scrap steel, iron ore and molten cast iron from the blast furnace. Oxygen is forced into this mixture at high pressure through a water-cooled tube called an **oxygen lance.** This causes the impurities in the iron to be oxidized. The gaseous oxides, such as those of carbon and sulphur, are allowed to escape. Other impurities combine with the fire-brick to make slag. In this way pure iron is formed.

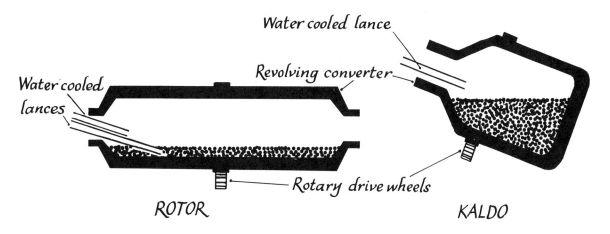

Figure 6.4 Rotor and Kaldo converters

To this, a quantity of Spiegeleisen (pronounced 'shpeegl-eyesn'), a substance containing iron, carbon and manganese, is added. This mixes with the iron to form a mixture of the correct proportions for mild steel. To produce other types of steel, the necessary ingredients are added at this stage.

The Linz–Donowitz process uses about 90 tonnes of oxygen to produce 1 000 tonnes of steel.

6.5. Alloys

An alloy is a mixture of metals made by melting two or more different metals, mixing them and allowing the mixture to solidify. Alloys usually have different physical properties from the metals from which they are made, and special alloys are made for specialist purposes.

The Latin name for iron is 'ferrum', and for this reason any alloy containing iron is called a **ferrous** alloy. Table 6.2 is really a list of ferrous alloys.

119

6.6. Some non-ferrous alloys

These are alloys containing no iron. Table 6.3 lists some non-ferrous alloys, together with their main constituents and uses.

TABLE 6.3. SOME NON-FERROUS ALLOYS

Name	Main Constituents	Uses
Brass	Copper (67%) and zinc (33%)	Electrical components and machine parts
Bronze	Copper (87%) and tin (12%)	
Phosphor bronze	Copper (89%), tin (10%) and phosphorus (0·5%)	Bearings and castings
Tinman's solder	Tin (50%) and lead (50%)	
Plumber's solder	Lead (67%) and tin (33%)	
Typemetal	Lead (86%), antimony (11%) and tin (3%)	Typeface
Wood's metal	Bismuth (50%), lead (25%), tin (12%) and cadmium (12%)	Sprinkler fire extinguisher systems and electrical cut-outs
Duralumin	Aluminium (94%), copper (4%), manganese (1%) and silicon (trace)	Light, strong structures, such as aircraft frames
Cupro-nickel	Copper (75%) and nickel (25%)	Coins

Gold is a very soft metal. For making jewellery, a gold alloy is generally used. This usually contains gold and copper or silver. Pure gold is called 24 carat gold; 18 carat gold is eighteen parts of gold to six parts of copper or silver; 9 carat gold is nine parts of gold to fifteen parts of copper or silver.

6.7. Grouping metals

For practical purposes, it is convenient to divide the metals into groups.

a. The reactive metals

This is a group of metals which react vigorously with water to give hydrogen. These include sodium, potassium and calcium. These metals have little use for mechanical purposes but they form very important compounds.

b. The heavy metals

These metals are extremely important for engineering purposes. In the presence of water, they corrode slowly or not at all. When they are strongly heated in air, they oxidize. This group includes aluminium, chromium, copper, iron, nickel, tin, lead and zinc.

c. The noble metals

Metals in this group may be heated in the presence of air until they are white-hot, without becoming oxidized. They do not react with water, nor with most acids. This group includes gold, platinum and silver.

6.8. Corrosion of metals

Iron and steel will corrode if left exposed to the atmosphere. This corrosion is called **rusting.** Rust flakes off, thus exposing the metal to further corrosion.

Investigation 6a. The rusting of iron

Obtain some iron nails and arrange them in test-tubes as shown in Figure 6.5. Leave the experiment set up and examine the nails at regular intervals over a period of several weeks. Which nails rusted most? Did any of the nails show no sign of rusting?

For rusting to take place, air and water (or water vapour) must be present. In order to prevent iron from rusting, it is necessary to give it a protective coating to prevent it from coming into contact with air and moisture. This may be achieved in many ways:
  a. By greasing or oiling.
  b. By painting. When this is done, it is important to ensure that the surface is free from rust before painting.
  c. By coating with a thin layer of another metal which is more resistant to corrosion. Metals commonly used for this purpose include zinc, tin and chromium.

Investigation 6b. The protective properties of tin and zinc

Obtain small pieces of galvanized iron, tinplate and untreated iron. Make several deep scratches on the tinplate and the galvanized iron and leave the three specimens exposed to the atmosphere for several weeks. Examine them at intervals.

Examination of the tinplate will show that there has been extensive rusting in the region of the scratches, but the galvanized iron will

121

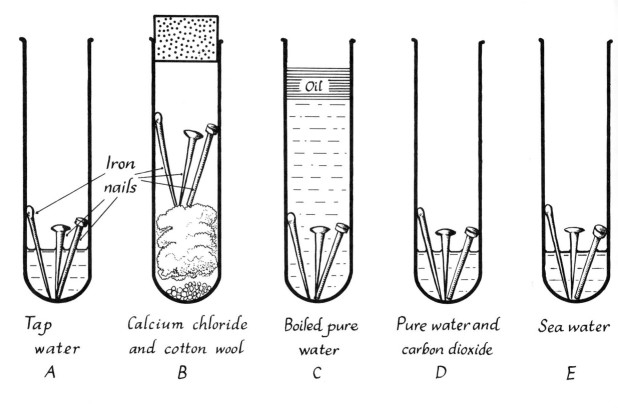

Figure 6.5 The rusting of iron

Tap water	Calcium chloride and cotton wool	Boiled pure water	Pure water and carbon dioxide	Sea water
A	B	C	D	E

show little sign of rusting. The zinc protects the iron, even after the surface has been damaged, but the tin does not. In fact, the tinplate, once it is scratched, rusts even more rapidly than the untreated iron.

The zinc and iron set up a little voltaic cell which opposes corrosion. Some combinations of metals, for example copper and zinc, set up cells which encourage corrosion. For this reason, care must be taken when different metals are used in contact with each other, especially in water systems.

Investigation 6c. Corrosion of copper and aluminium

Repeat Investigation 6a using copper tacks and aluminium rivets in place of the iron nails (one of each in each test-tube). Compare the results with those of Investigation 6a.

When copper is left exposed to the atmosphere, it becomes coated with a green substance called verdigris (pronounced 'ver-dee-gree'). This adheres firmly to the copper and tends to prevent further corrosion. Look around your town for a building with a copper dome.

When aluminium is left exposed to the atmosphere, it becomes coated with a layer of a white substance. This is aluminium oxide

122

and, like verdigris, this sticks firmly to the metal, resisting further corrosion.

6.9. Anodizing

A decorative finish may be given to aluminium by causing a layer of oxide to form on the metal, then dyeing this layer and finally treating the surface to seal it. In order to produce the layer of oxide, the aluminium article is made the anode in an electrolytic cell, and for this reason the process is called **anodizing**.

Test your understanding

1. How is iron obtained from its ore?
2. How is aluminium obtained from bauxite?
3. What is steel? Describe briefly how it is made.
4. What is an alloy? Name two different alloys, stating their main constituents and one use to which each is put.
5. List as many metals as you can under the headings 'reactive', 'heavy' and 'noble'.
6. Under what conditions does iron rust? List as many ways as you can of preventing iron from rusting.
7. Why will a damaged 'tin' can rust more quickly than a piece of scratched galvanized iron?
8. What is anodizing?
9. Steel ships usually have zinc plates attached to their hulls below the waterline. Why do you think this is done?

Chapter 7

Light Energy

7.1. The nature of light

Investigation 7a. Light energy

Place a photographic light meter near a window and note the position of the pointer.

Now place each of the following materials in front of the meter so that the light must pass through them in order to reach the meter: (1) a sheet of clear glass, (2) a piece of greaseproof paper, (3) a sheet of cardboard. In each case note the reading of the pointer.

Investigation 7b. Can you see light?

Switch on a flashlamp in a darkened room so that it throws light on to a wall. Can you see the beam crossing the room?

Now shake a blackboard duster near the flashlamp. Can you see the beam now?

Figure 7.1 Apparatus for Investigation 7c

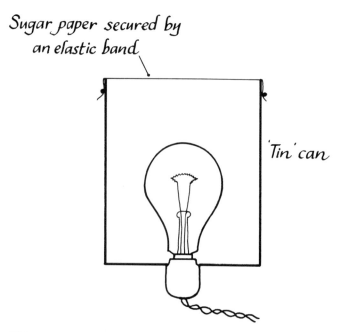

Sugar paper secured by an elastic band

'Tin' can

For this investigation you will need a tin can, fitted with a mains lampholder at the bottom, and a lamp having a clear glass bulb. Cover the open end of the tin with a piece of sugar paper and hold this in place with a strong elastic band, as shown in Figure 7.1.

Now, darken the room and switch on the lamp. With the point of a pair of compasses, make a small hole in the paper and point the tin so that light is cast on the ceiling. Make several other small holes in the paper. Try to explain what you have seen.

Light is a form of energy by means of which we are able to detect the presence of objects. The eye acts as a receiver for light.

A material such as clear glass, which allows light to pass through it without any apparent hindrance, is said to be **transparent**, but a substance such as cardboard, which does not permit light to pass through, is said to be **opaque**. Materials such as greaseproof paper, which allow light to pass through them but do not allow objects to be seen clearly through them, are said to be **translucent**.

Objects which produce light, such as the sun, an electric lamp and a match, are said to be **luminous**. Objects which are not themselves luminous can only be seen when light from some luminous body falls upon them and is then reflected into the eye.

A very narrow parallel beam of light is called a **ray**. Rays of light advance in straight lines at a speed of 300 000 kilometres per second when they are travelling through empty space or through air.

The 'picture' thrown on the ceiling in Investigation 7c is called an **image** of the filament of the lamp. Figure 7.2 shows how it was formed.

Figure 7.2 The image of a lamp filament

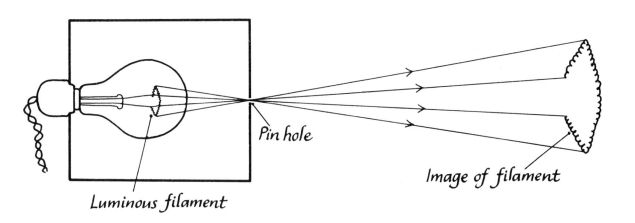

Pin hole

Image of filament

Luminous filament

7.2. Light and shadow

Investigation 7d. Shadow formation

For this investigation you will need a small flashlamp bulb and holder, a piece of white card and some means of holding it vertically, a pencil and a bunsen burner.

Support the card vertically and place the lamp about half a metre away from it. Switch on the lamp and place the pencil between the lamp and the card, so that a shadow of the pencil is cast on the card. Remove the lamp and replace it by the bunsen burner, set to give a large luminous flame. Once more, position the pencil so that it throws its shadow on the screen. Compare the two shadows.

Figure 7.3 Shadows

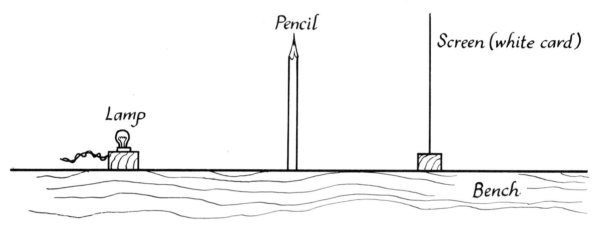

A small source of light casts dark, clearly defined shadows, but a large source of light, which can be regarded as being made up of many separate small sources, tends to cast 'woolly', poorly defined shadows. Figure 7.4 shows why this is so.

Figure 7.4 Formation of shadows

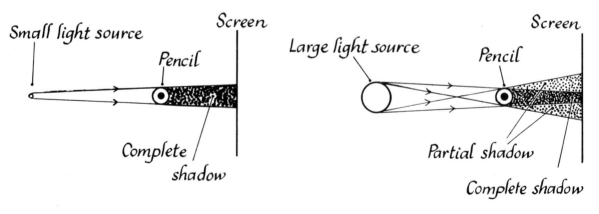

126

7.3. Eclipses

The sun is the only luminous body within the solar system. At night, the moon appears to be a ball of light because it is reflecting light from the sun.

If the earth moves between the sun and the moon, the shadow of the earth is cast on the moon. This is called an **eclipse of the moon**. An **eclipse of the sun** occurs when the moon is positioned between the sun and the earth, so that the shadow of the moon is cast on the earth. Figure 7.5 shows how eclipses occur.

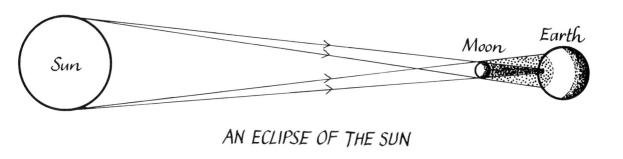

AN ECLIPSE OF THE SUN

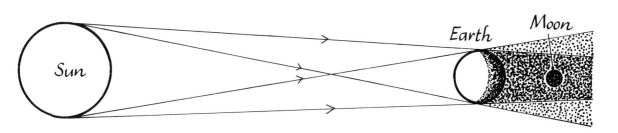

AN ECLIPSE OF THE MOON

Figure 7.5 Eclipses

7.4. Reflection

Investigation 7e. Reflective surfaces

Set up a ray box so that it produces several parallel rays of light. Place a piece of black paper in the rays, as shown in Figure 7.6. What do you see?

Repeat the experiment using: (1) a piece of white paper, (2) a piece of red paper, (3) a piece of blue paper and (4) a small mirror. Make sure that the obstacles are vertical.

The black paper absorbs the light, while the white paper reflects the light. Because the surface of the paper is not smooth, the light is reflected in all directions.

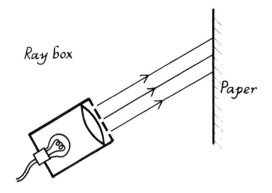

Ray box

Paper

Figure 7.6 Reflection of light rays

The mirror also reflects the light but, because it has a smooth surface, it reflects the light in a particular direction.

Note that the light reflected from the red paper was red and the light reflected from the blue paper was blue.

7.5. Mirror images

Investigation 7f. The image in a plane mirror

Hold a mirror in front of your face and observe your image. Where does it appear to be? Can you see any way in which your image is different from the 'real' you?

You have come to accept the fact that light travels in straight lines. A mirror can cause a ray of light to change direction, but the eye and brain have no way of telling whether a ray has come directly into the eye or whether it has been reflected by a mirror. This explains why the image seen in a mirror appears to be where it is. If you stand in front of a mirror, how far behind the mirror does your image appear to be?

If you hold a page of print in front of a mirror, you will notice that the image appears to be turned from left to right, rather like the impression left on a sheet of blotting paper. This turning from left to right is called **lateral inversion.**

Figure 7.7 represents the image formed by a plane mirror.

7.6. The laws of reflection

Investigation 7g. Laws of reflection

Place a sheet of paper on the bench and support a small mirror vertically on the paper. Carefully mark the position of the *back* of the mirror with a pencil line. Position a ray box so that it sends a single ray of light on to the mirror. This is called the **incident ray.** After reflection, the ray is called the **reflected ray.**

128

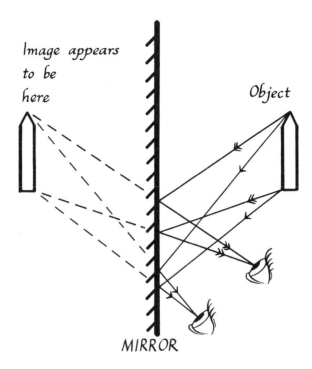

Object

MIRROR

By means of dots, mark the position of the incident and reflected rays. Remove the mirror and join the dots so as to mark the path taken by the light. Where the lines meet, draw a line perpendicular to the mirror. This line is called a **normal**. The angle between the incident ray and the normal is the **angle of incidence**, and that between the reflected ray and the normal is the **angle of reflection**. Measure the angles of incidence and reflection (see Figure 7.8).

Repeat the investigation several times, positioning the ray box to give a different angle of incidence each time. Draw up a table of results, as shown in Table 7.1.

Figure 7.7 The image formed by a plane mirror

TABLE 7.1. RESULTS OF INVESTIGATION 7g

Angle of Incidence	Angle of Reflection

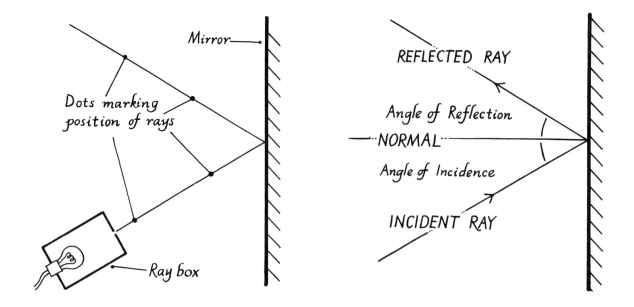

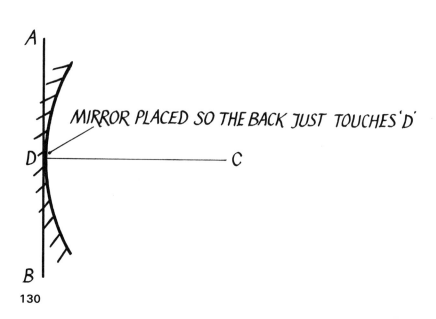

Figure 7.8 Reflection of
rays by a plane mirror

For the next part of this investigation, you will need a cylindrical
concave mirror. Draw two straight lines on a piece of paper, each
line being about 10 cm long and at right angles to each other, as
shown in Figure 7.9. Place the mirror in the position shown in the
figure. Set up a ray box to give a single ray. Direct this ray as
shown in Figure 7.10(a). Where is the reflected ray? What can you
say about the line CD?

Figure 7.9 Positioning
the concave mirror

Now position the ray box to one side of the line CD, as shown in
Figure 7.10(b). Mark the positions of the incident and reflected rays

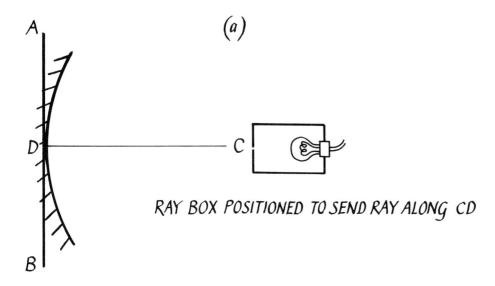

(a)

RAY BOX POSITIONED TO SEND RAY ALONG CD

Figure 7.10 (a) and (b)
Reflection of rays by a
concave mirror

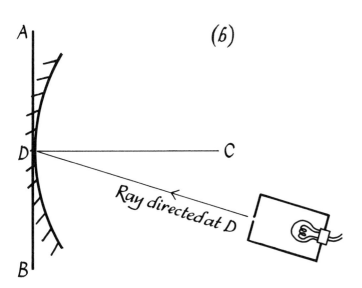

(b)

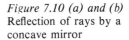

and measure the angles of incidence and reflection. Repeat this for a number of different angles of incidence and tabulate your results.

Place the cylindrical concave mirror on a piece of paper and mark the position of the back by a pencil line. Remove the mirror and draw three straight lines (tangents), each of which just touches the curve at one point. Draw straight lines at right angles to these points, as shown in Figure 7.11. Use a pair of compasses to find out whether the point where these lines cross (marked C in Figure 7.11) is the centre of the curve.

Place the mirror on the curve and use your ray box to find out if the three lines, marked ST, UV and WX in Figure 7.11, are normals. (If a ray travels along a normal before reflection, it will travel back along the normal after reflection.)

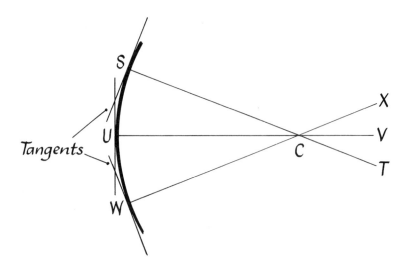

Figure 7.11 Normals to a
concave mirror

In this investigation you have examined the **laws of reflection**:
a. **The angle of incidence is always equal to the angle of reflection.**
b. **The incident ray and the reflected ray lie in the same plane with
the normal but are on opposite sides of the normal.**

These laws apply not only to light but to all reflections. If a
klystron transmitter (3 cm transmitter) is available, you should be
able to verify that they apply to the reflection of radio waves.

7.7. Images

In this chapter you have met two different kinds of image. Images,
such as the one in Investigation 7c, which can be projected on to a
screen are called **real images**. Images, such as those which you saw
in a plane mirror, which cannot be projected on to a screen are called
virtual images.

7.8. Curved mirrors

Investigation 7h. Cylindrical mirrors

Figure 7.12 Reflection of
parallel rays by cylindrical
mirrors

Set up a ray box to produce several parallel rays. Place a cylindrical concave mirror (reflecting surface on inside curve) in the path

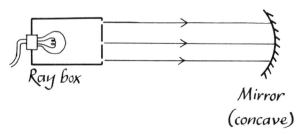

Ray box

Mirror
(concave)

132

of these rays and note how they are reflected. Figure 7.12 shows
the arrangement. Repeat, using a cylindrical convex mirror.

A concave mirror causes parallel rays to converge after reflection.
The point where the converging rays cross is called the **principal focus**
of the mirror. The distance from the centre of the mirror to the
principal focus is the **focal length** of the mirror (see Figure 7.13).

Figure 7.13 The focal
length of a concave mirror

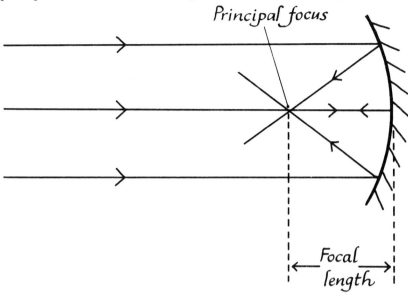

When parallel rays are reflected by a convex surface, they diverge
as if they had originated at a point behind the mirror. This point is
the principal focus of the mirror (see Figure 7.14).

Figure 7.14 The focal
length of a convex mirror

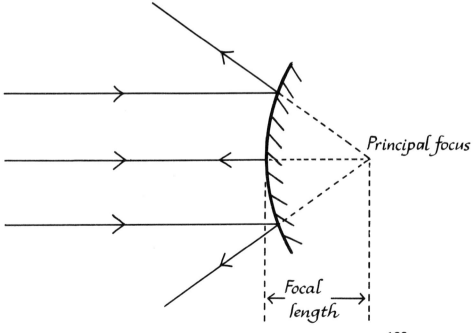

In Investigation 7h, the laws of reflection have been obeyed. The centre of a spherical or cylindrical mirror is called the **centre of curvature**. The distance from the centre of curvature to the mirror surface is the **radius of curvature**. If you wish to draw the normal to a point on such a surface, you simply have to draw a radius.

Investigation 7i. The images produced by concave mirrors

For this investigation you will need a concave spherical mirror, a white screen (a piece of card will do), a festoon lamp, a metre ruler and some means of supporting the mirror and screen vertically. Large corks with slots cut in them would be satisfactory for this purpose.

Figure 7.15 The images produced by a concave mirror

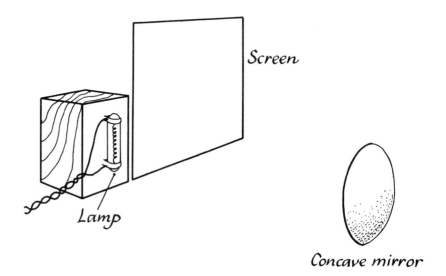

Screen

Lamp

Concave mirror

Place the screen alongside the lamp, as shown in Figure 7.15. Switch on the lamp and adjust the position of the mirror until a sharp image of the lamp filament is produced on the screen. Compare the size of this image with the size of the lamp filament. Is the image the right way up or is it inverted? Measure the distance of the lamp from the mirror. Make a note of all your observations

Now move the mirror away from the lamp and move the screen until an image is formed on it. Measure the distance of the lamp from the mirror and the distance of the screen from the mirror. Again compare the size of the image with the size of the filament and note whether or not the image is inverted. (If you are in doubt about this, place a piece of cardboard so that it covers the bottom of the lamp.)

Repeat the experiment with the mirror in various positions closer to the lamp. Record all your results.

134

Investigation 7j

Take the mirror you used in the previous investigation and hold it close to your eye. Note what you see.

Now move the mirror slowly away from your eye, making a note of any changes which occur in the image you see.

Point the mirror towards a window and, holding a piece of white card in front of the mirror, try to produce an image on it.

The nature of the images produced by a spherical concave mirror are summarized in Table 7.2.

TABLE 7.2. IMAGE FORMATION BY CONCAVE MIRRORS

Position of Object	Position of Image	Nature of Image
Beyond centre of curvature	Between principal focus and centre of curvature	Real, inverted, smaller than object
At centre of curvature	At centre of curvature	Real, inverted, same size as object
Between the centre of curvature and the principal focus	Beyond the centre of curvature	Real, inverted, larger than object
At principal focus	No image formed	
Between principal focus and mirror	No image on screen but an image can be seen on looking into mirror	Virtual, erect, larger than object

Investigation 7k. Convex mirrors

Hold a convex spherical mirror close to your eye. Note what you see.

Now move the mirror slowly away from your eye, noting any changes which you observe.

Point the mirror at a window and, holding a piece of white card in front of the mirror, try to obtain an image on it.

The image produced by a convex mirror is always erect and is virtual, so that it cannot be projected on to a screen. The image is largest when the object is nearest to the mirror.

7.9. Parabolic reflectors

Investigation 7l. The caustic curve

Set up a ray box to produce a large number of parallel rays. (If the design of your ray box does not permit this to be done, use a wide parallel beam of light instead.) Place a concave mirror in the path of the light, as you did in Investigation 7h.

You will notice that, although the rays converge after reflection, they do not all, in fact, pass through the principal focus. The reflected rays form two bright curves of light called **caustic curves**. The bright spot where these curves meet is the principal focus. Figure 7.16 shows the formation of caustics. You may have noticed caustic

Figure 7.16 Caustic curves

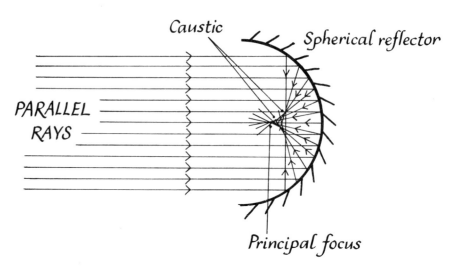

curves formed on the surface of tea in a cup. Parallel rays of light from the sun are reflected by the side of the cup, producing this effect.

Because a concave mirror does not have a point focus, a parallel beam of light cannot be produced by placing a small source of light at the principal focus, unless the radius of curvature of the mirror is very large compared with the diameter of the mirror.

When parallel rays are reflected by a **parabolic** surface, they are made to converge to a point focus (see Figure 7.17). If a point source of light was placed at the focus of such a reflector, a parallel beam would be produced. For this reason, we use parabolic reflectors for car headlamps and searchlights. Even so, it is not possible to obtain

Figure 7.17 The focus of a parabola

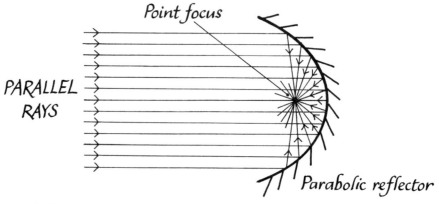

a perfectly parallel beam, because it is impossible to obtain a true point source of light.

The reflecting telescope makes use of a large parabolic reflector. Figure 7.18 shows the principle of the reflecting telescope.

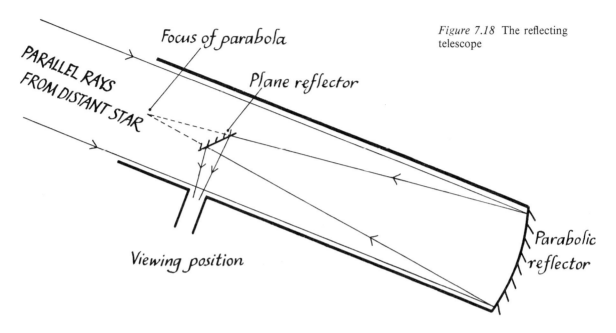

Figure 7.18 The reflecting telescope

Test your understanding

1. Make lists of materials under the headings: 'transparent', 'translucent' and 'opaque'.
2. Make diagrams to show how the following occur: (a) an eclipse of the sun, (b) an eclipse of the moon.
3. Write the word LIGHT as you would see it in a plane mirror.
4. State the laws of reflection.
5. Make diagrams showing clearly what happens to parallel rays of light after reflection by (a) a plane mirror, (b) a concave mirror, (c) a convex mirror.
6. What is the shortest mirror in which a boy 1·6 m tall can see himself 'full length'? (Remember the laws of reflection and draw a diagram.)
7. Driving mirrors may be plane or convex. What are the advantages and disadvantages of each type?
8. Make a diagram showing how a car headlamp produces a beam of light which is nearly parallel. What shape is the reflector? Why is the beam not truly parallel?

Chapter 8

Refraction

8.1. Refraction

If you put a pencil into a beaker of water, you will notice that, if you look into the beaker, the pencil appears to be bent. Of course, the pencil has not really bent; the rays of light from the pencil have changed direction on leaving the water, thus making the pencil appear bent.

For the same reason, a swimming pool always appears to be shallower than it really is. Figure 8.1 shows why this is so.

The bending of light rays is called **refraction**.

Figure 8.1 The bending of light rays

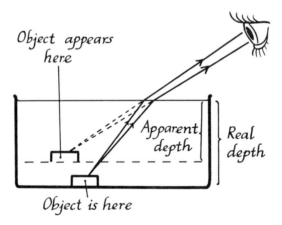

Object appears here

Apparent depth

Real depth

Object is here

Investigation 8a. Refraction by a glass block

Set up a ray box so that it sends a single ray of light into a glass (or 'Perspex') block, as shown in Figure 8.2. Notice that, although some reflection occurs, much of the light passes through the block and, in doing so, changes direction. Rearrange the block so that the light enters it at a different angle. Repeat this several times.

If you imagine a normal drawn at the point where the light enters the block, you will notice that the ray bends *towards* the normal on entering the block. On leaving the block, the refracted ray is bent *away* from the normal at that point.

138

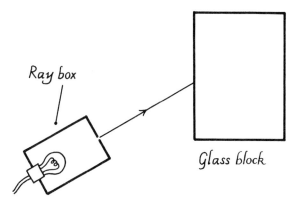

If the ray enters the block at right angles, so that it is travelling along the normal, it does not change direction.

Figure 8.2 Refraction by a glass block

Investigation 8b. Refraction by a triangular prism

Set up a ray box to give a single ray of light. Place a triangular glass (or 'Perspex') prism in the path of the ray, as shown in Figure 8.3. Notice how the ray is refracted *towards* the base of the prism. Make a sketch of the path taken by the light ray and draw in normals where the ray enters and leaves the block.

Move the prism so that the ray enters at a different angle and again sketch what you see. Repeat this several times.

Note that, in every case, the ray bends *towards* the normal when it passes from air to glass and *away* from the normal on passing from glass to air.

Figure 8.3 Refraction by a triangular prism

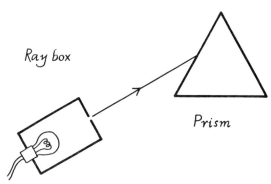

Investigation 8c. Refraction by lenses

Set up a ray box to give several parallel rays of light. Place a cylindrical convex lens in the path of the rays, as shown in Figure 8.4. Make a diagram showing how the rays behave on passing through the lens.

Repeat the investigation, using a cylindrical concave lens.

Figure 8.4 Refraction by lenses

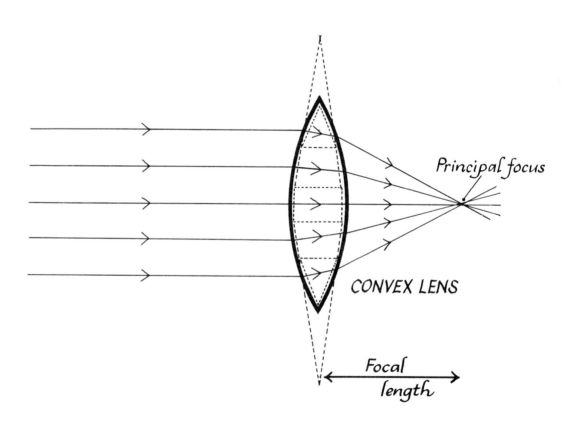

Figure 8.5 Convex lens

A lens behaves as if it is made up of a number of triangular prisms and parts of triangular prisms (see Figure 8.5). When parallel rays of light pass through a **convex lens,** they are refracted so that they *converge*, passing through a point. This point is the **principal focus** of the lens. The distance from the principal focus to the centre of the lens is the focal length of the lens.

When parallel rays of light pass through a **concave lens** they *diverge* as if they had come from a point on the other side of the lens. This point is the principal focus of the lens.

Investigation 8d. The convex lens

Take a spherical convex lens of focal length about 20 cm and carry out each of the following investigations:
1. Take a sheet of paper and try to focus the sun's rays on to it. If you keep the paper in position for several minutes, it will begin to burn. *For this reason, it is very dangerous to attempt to look at the sun through a lens or any instrument using a lens.* (The lens has the effect of concentrating radiant heat in a small area.)
2. Place the lens between a window and a sheet of paper. Move the lens to and fro until you obtain an image of the window frame on the paper. Is the image real or virtual? Is it magnified or diminished? The distance from the paper to the lens is approximately the focal length of the lens.
3. Place a book at arm's length and, holding the lens close to the book, look through it at the print. Now move the lens slowly towards your eye. Make a note of what you see.

Investigation 8e. The images produced by a convex lens

For this investigation you will need a festoon lamp, a metre ruler, a screen (a piece of white card will do), a convex spherical lens (of focal length 5 cm to 20 cm) and some means of supporting the lens and screen vertically.

Place the lamp about a metre from the screen and put the lens between them, very close to the lamp (see Figure 8.6). Move the lens towards the screen until a large image of the lamp filament is produced on the screen. Measure the distances from the lens to the lamp and the lens to the screen, and make a note of them.

Move the lamp closer to the screen until another image of the filament is produced. Again measure the distance from the lens to the lamp and the lens to the screen. Compare these measurements with those you have already made.

Move the lamp 10 cm closer to the screen and repeat the whole experiment. Continue moving the lamp closer to the screen in 10 cm steps, each time repeating the experiment.

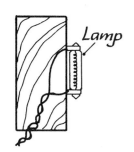

Lamp

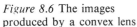

Lens

Screen

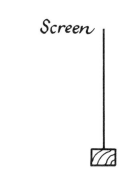

Figure 8.6 The images produced by a convex lens

Investigation 8f. Finding the focal length of a convex lens

For this investigation you will need a convex spherical lens and a holder to support it, a screen, a festoon lamp and a plane mirror.

Place the screen alongside the lamp, as shown in Figure 8.7, and place the lens in front of the lamp. Holding the plane mirror behind it, move the lens backward and forward until a sharp image of the filament is produced on the screen alongside the lamp. Measure the distance from the lens to the screen. This is the focal length of the lens. Figure 8.8 should explain why this is so.

A convex lens may be used to produce either a real or a virtual image. If the object is closer to the lens than the principal focus, the image will be virtual, erect and magnified. Used in this way, the lens acts as a magnifying glass. When the object is farther away from the lens than the principal focus, the image produced will be real and inverted. Whether or not it is magnified, depends on the distance of the object from the lens. Table 8.1 summarizes the relationship between the object distance and the kind of image which is formed.

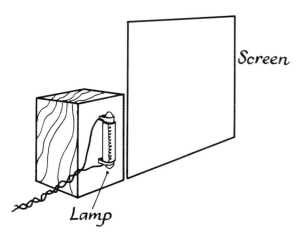

Screen

Lamp

Figure 8.7 Finding the focal length of a convex lens

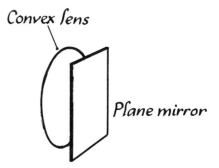

Convex lens

Plane mirror

142

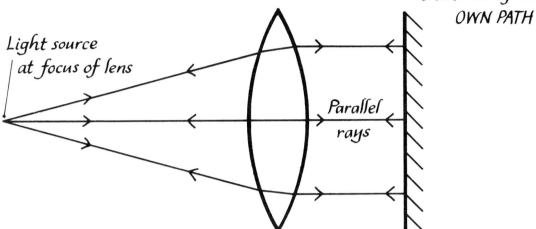

Light source at focus of lens

Parallel rays

Figure 8.8 A ray diagram for Investigation 8f

TABLE 8.1. IMAGE FORMATION BY A CONVEX LENS

Object Distance	Image Distance	Nature of Image
Less than focal length	More than focal length	Virtual, erect, magnified
Focal length	No image produced	—
Greater than focal length but less than twice focal length	More than twice focal length	Real, inverted, magnified
Twice focal length	Twice focal length	Real, inverted, same size as object
More than twice focal length	Less than twice focal length	Real, inverted, diminished

Do your observations in Investigations 8d and 8e agree with Table 8.1?

8.2. Internal reflection

Investigation 8g. Using a right-angled isosceles prism

Set up a ray box to produce a single ray of light. Place a right-angled, triangular glass prism in the path of the ray, as shown in Figure 8.9. Make a sketch of the path taken by the ray.

Now rearrange the prism so that the light enters the longer side, as shown in Figure 8.10. Again sketch the path taken by the ray.

143

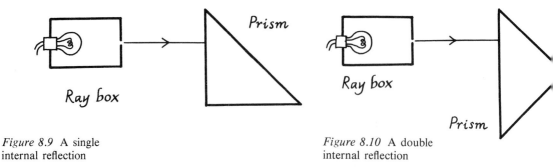

Figure 8.9 A single
internal reflection

Figure 8.10 A double
internal reflection

Investigation 8h. Passing light through water

Place a glass trough on a bench, so that its base projects slightly over the edge of the bench. Pour water into the trough until it is almost full, and add a little fluorescein.

Set up a ray box to give a single ray, holding the ray box so that it sends light through the bottom of the trough. Tilt the ray box so that the light passes through the water at various angles (see Figure 8.11). (It may help if you shake a chalky duster above the trough.)

Notice how the light behaves on leaving the water. Ray A is travelling along a normal and is neither refracted nor reflected. Ray B is refracted away from the normal. Ray C is refracted away from the normal and, in this case, the angle of refraction is a right angle, so that the ray is made to travel along the surface of the water. When this happens, the angle of incidence is called the **critical angle**. Ray D makes an angle of incidence which is greater than the critical angle and is reflected within the water, making an angle of reflection

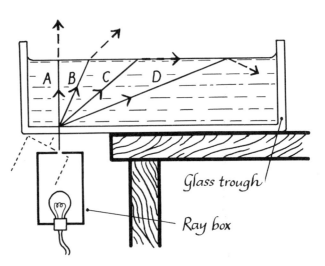

Figure 8.11 Total internal
reflection

144

which is equal to the angle of incidence. (Thus, the usual law of reflection is obeyed.) This is **total internal reflection**, and can only occur when light is travelling from a dense substance towards a less dense substance, making an angle of incidence greater than the critical angle.

Figure 8.12 shows how two prisms may be used to make a periscope.

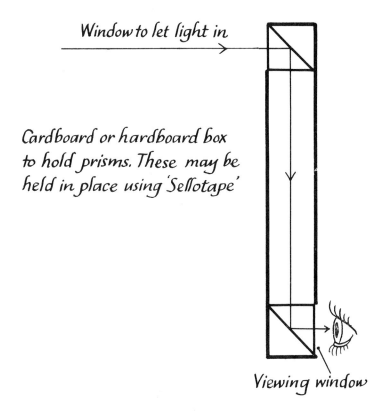

Figure 8.12 A periscope using prisms

8.3. Waves

Light energy is transmitted in the form of electromagnetic waves, advancing at a velocity of 300 000 km s^{-1} when travelling through air. In order to understand this statement, we must consider the nature of waves, generally.

If a rope is fastened to a post, it is a simple matter to produce waves in the rope, by moving the free end up and down. Although the waves can be seen to be travelling along the rope, it is also evident that the only motion of the rope is vertically up and down, in a direction which is at right angles to the direction of motion of the waves (see Figure 8.13).

145

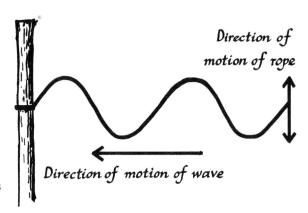

Figure 8.13 Waves produced in a rope

The waves which we see on water are of this form. If you drop a pebble into still water, you will see waves forming at the point where the stone enters the water, and then advancing *along* the surface of the water. If a floating straw is disturbed by the waves, it bobs up and down but does not move across the surface of the water. From this, we may conclude that although the wave moves across the surface the actual water particles move *up and down*. This kind of wave is known as a **transverse wave**.

Water waves may be studied with the aid of a simple ripple tank. By dipping a pencil repeatedly into the water at one place, a set of waves are produced. These are seen to follow one another at regular distances (see Figure 8.14).

Figure 8.14 Water waves

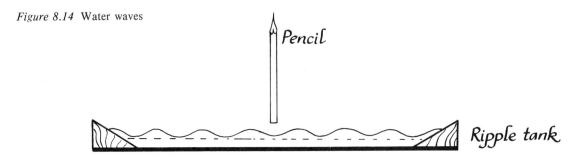

The water waves are a series of crests and troughs, and the distance from one crest to the next is called the **wavelength**. Figure 8.15 shows what is meant by one wavelength. The number of waves produced each second is called the **frequency**.

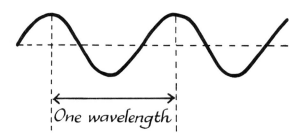

Figure 8.15 Wavelength

146

8.4. Wavelength, frequency and velocity

Suppose that ten complete waves are produced in one second. This is a frequency of ten **Hertz**. If the wavelength is one metre, it will be obvious that the waves are advancing at a velocity of ten metres a second. Figure 8.16 illustrates this.

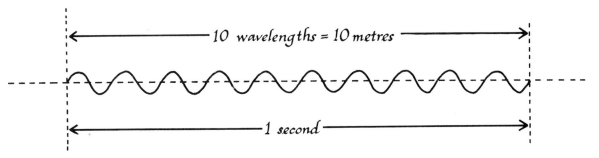

It is seen that wavelength, frequency and velocity are connected by the following relationship:

$$\text{Velocity} = \text{Frequency} \times \text{Wavelength}$$

Figure 8.16 Velocity of waves

This is true for all waves.

8.5. Light waves and rays

All living things depend on light and heat supplied by the sun. Without these supplies of energy, life on earth could not continue.

Both of these forms of energy travel in the form of electromagnetic waves. These are the same kind of waves as those which travel from the transmitter to your radio receiver; they travel at the same velocity, but the wavelengths of light and heat are very much shorter than radio waves.

In order to appreciate the distinction between waves and rays, it is convenient to consider a ray as representing the direction of travel of a point on a wavefront as the wave advances. Figure 8.17 illustrates this. Plane wavefronts are represented by parallel rays, while circular wavefronts are represented by convergent or divergent rays.

When plane wavefronts pass through a convex lens they become curved, so that they tend to converge towards a point. A concave lens imposes a curvature in the opposite direction. Figure 8.18 shows this.

The velocity of light is $300\,000$ km s^{-1} in a vacuum, and in air the velocity is almost the same. The velocity decreases, however, when the light enters relatively dense materials, such as glass or water. It is this change of velocity which causes the characteristic change of direction. Figure 8.19 shows a plane wavefront entering a glass block.

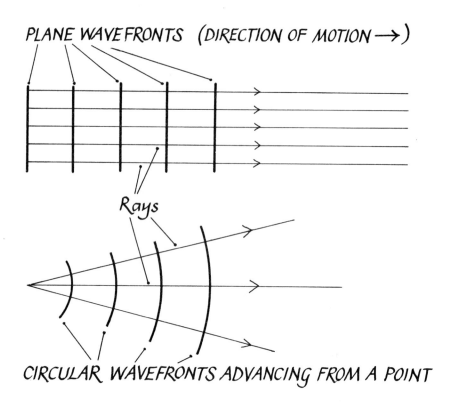

PLANE WAVEFRONTS (DIRECTION OF MOTION →)

Rays

CIRCULAR WAVEFRONTS ADVANCING FROM A POINT

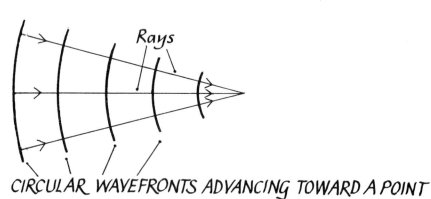

Rays

CIRCULAR WAVEFRONTS ADVANCING TOWARD A POINT

Figure 8.17 Waves and rays

8.6. Coloured light

Investigation 8i. The visible spectrum

Set up a ray box to produce a narrow parallel light beam. Place a green colour filter ('Cinemoid' No. 39 primary green film is excellent for this purpose) in front of the ray box so as to colour the beam green. Now place a triangular glass prism in the path of the ray, as

148

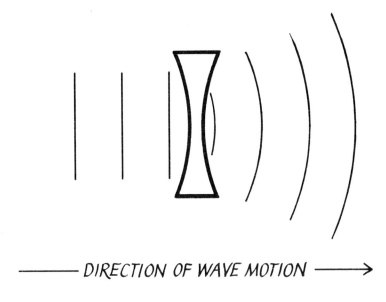

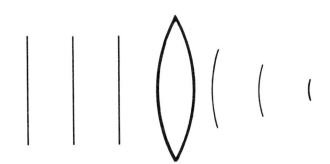

Figure 8.18 The action of lenses on plane wavefronts

shown in Figure 8.20. Rotate the prism until the ray is bent (i.e. deviated) through as large an angle as possible. Now remove the colour filter. What do you see?

Place other colour filters, in turn, in the position which was originally occupied by the green filter. You should use the following colour filters, which will also be needed for Investigations 8k and 8l.

Primary red	('Cinemoid' No. 6)
Primary blue	('Cinemoid' No. 20)
Magenta	('Cinemoid' No. 13)
Yellow	('Cinemoid' No. 1)
Blue green	('Cinemoid' No. 16)

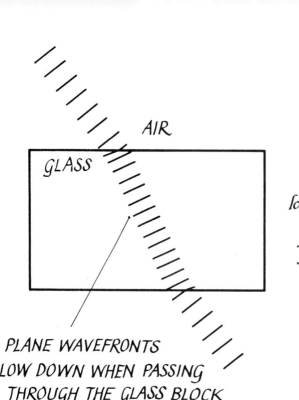

GLASS

AIR

PLANE WAVEFRONTS
SLOW DOWN WHEN PASSING
THROUGH THE GLASS BLOCK

ALTHOUGH THE VELOCITY OF LIGHT
DECREASES IN THE BLOCK, THE FREQUENCY
IS UNCHANGED SO THAT THE WAVELENGTH
BECOMES SHORTER

Figure 8.19 Waves passing
through a glass block

FIRM GROUND

MUD

This track
loses grip on mud

This track
picks up grip first

COMPARE THIS WITH
A TRACTOR CROSSING
A STRIP OF MUD

Narrow beam

Green colour filter

Figure 8.20 Refraction
and colour

('Cinemoid' is a non-inflammable plastic film obtainable from the Strand Electric Company.)

Make a note of what you see to happen in each case. Can you explain these observations?

8.7. The spectral colours

When white light is passed through a triangular prism, it is *deviated* towards the base of the prism but it is also split up, or **dispersed**, into a number of different colours. These are called the spectral colours, and make up the visible spectrum. Sir Isaac Newton listed seven spectral colours, each of which appeared, to him, to be distinctly different colours. They were red, orange, yellow, green, blue, indigo, violet. Most people, however, are unable to see indigo as being distinctly different from blue and violet. Figure 8.21 shows the formation of a spectrum by means of a prism.

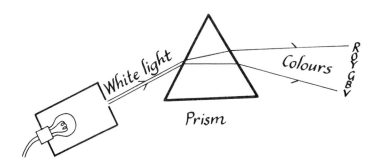

Figure 8.21 Spectrum formation

White light is really a mixture of lights of different colours, each colour being of a different wavelength from the others. Table 8.2 gives the wavelengths of the principal colours.

TABLE 8.2. WAVELENGTHS OF LIGHT

Colour	Wavelength/m
Red	$6 \cdot 6 \times 10^{-7}$
Orange	$6 \cdot 1 \times 10^{-7}$
Yellow	$5 \cdot 8 \times 10^{-7}$
Green	$5 \cdot 4 \times 10^{-7}$
Blue	$5 \cdot 0 \times 10^{-7}$
Violet	$4 \cdot 4 \times 10^{-7}$

When refraction occurs, the colours of longer wavelength are refracted less than those of shorter wavelength. Table 8.3 shows the position of visible light in the electromagnetic spectrum.

TABLE 8.3. THE ELECTROMAGNETIC SPECTRUM

Frequency/Hz	Wavelength/m	Application
10	3×10^7	
10^2	3×10^6	
10^3	3×10^5	
10^4	3×10^4	
10^5	3×10^3	
10^6	3×10^2	
10^7	3×10	Radio
10^8	3	
10^9	3×10^{-1}	
10^{10}	3×10^{-2}	
10^{11}	3×10^{-3}	
10^{12}	3×10^{-4}	
10^{13}	3×10^{-5}	Radiant heat (infrared)
10^{14}	3×10^{-6}	
		Visible light
10^{15}	3×10^{-7}	
10^{16}	3×10^{-8}	Ultraviolet
10^{17}	3×10^{-9}	
10^{18}	3×10^{-10}	
10^{19}	3×10^{-11}	X-rays
10^{20}	3×10^{-12}	
10^{21}	3×10^{-13}	
10^{22}	3×10^{-14}	
10^{23}	3×10^{-15}	Gamma rays
10^{24}	3×10^{-16}	
10^{25}	3×10^{-17}	
10^{26}	3×10^{-18}	

Investigation 8j. Using two triangular prisms

Set up a ray box to produce a parallel beam of white light. Place a triangular glass prism in the path of the beam in order to produce a spectrum. Place a second triangular prism in the path of the rays, as shown in Figure 8.22(a). What effect does this have?

Now, rearrange the second prism, as shown in Figure 8.22(b). By turning this prism, see if you can re-form the spectral colours into white light.

8.8. Mixing coloured lights

Investigation 8k. The effect of mixing primary colours

Set up two ray boxes to produce narrow beams of light. Place the ray boxes so that the beams meet on a screen, as shown in Figure

152

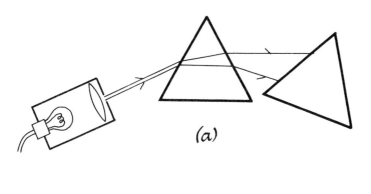

(a)

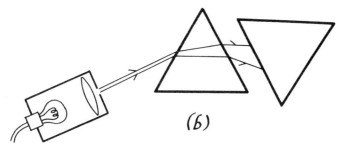

(b)

Figure 8.22 Using two prisms

8.23. Now, place a red filter in front of one ray box and a blue filter in front of the other. What colour is produced on the screen? Repeat the experiment using first red and green filters, and then using blue and green filters.

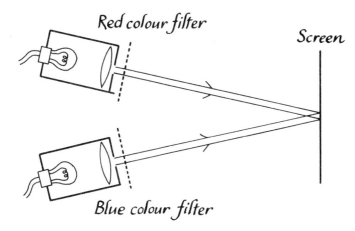

Red colour filter

Screen

Blue colour filter

Figure 8.23 Mixing two colours

Using three ray boxes, as shown in Figure 8.24, find what colour is produced when red, blue and green lights are mixed.

Red, blue and green are called **primary colours**. When two primary colours are mixed the colour produced is called a **secondary colour**. Figure 8.25 shows the colours produced by mixing primary colours.

153

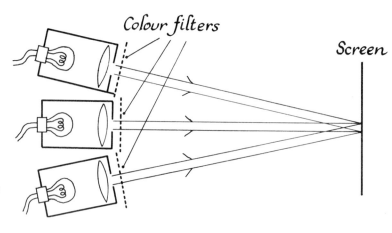

Figure 8.24 Mixing three colours

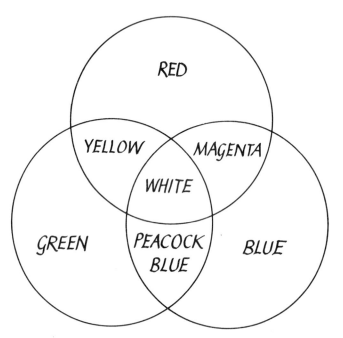

Figure 8.25 Colours produced by mixing primary coloured lights

8.9. Colour filters

Investigation 8I. Examination of colour filters

For this investigation you will need a set of primary and secondary colour filters (red, green, blue, yellow, peacock-blue and magenta). Holding two filters a few centimetres apart, look through them, as shown in Figure 8.26. Note the effect.

Repeat, using every possible combination of two filters in turn.

A colour filter is a material which is transparent to some colours but opaque to others. Thus, a red filter will allow only red light to pass through it. If white light falls upon such a filter, all the colours

154

HOLD THE COLOUR FILTERS
IN FRONT OF A WINDOW

Figure 8.26 Examining colour filters

making up white light are absorbed by the filter except red, which passes through. If magenta light (composed of red and blue) falls on the filter, the blue component is absorbed but the red part passes through. If pure green or pure blue light fall on the filter, they are completely absorbed. Figure 8.27 will help you to check your observations in Investigation 8l.

8.10. Pigments

Opaque materials do not allow light to travel through them. Light falling upon such materials must either be reflected or absorbed. Thus, a red pigment is one which absorbs all other colours except red, which it reflects. For this reason, a red object appears red in white light. If it is illuminated by pure blue or pure green light, it will absorb the light, and so will appear black.

Black objects absorb all light falling upon them while white objects reflect all light falling upon them.

Test your understanding

1. Copy the diagrams at the top of page 157 (Figure 8.28), completing the paths of the light rays.
2. Copy and complete the diagrams at the bottom of page 157 (Figure 8.29). Repeat the diagrams, showing wavefronts instead of rays.
3. How could you use a convex lens as a magnifying glass? In this case, what kind of image does the lens produce?
4. What is meant by (a) 'critical angle', (b) 'total internal reflection'? Use diagrams to assist your answer.

155

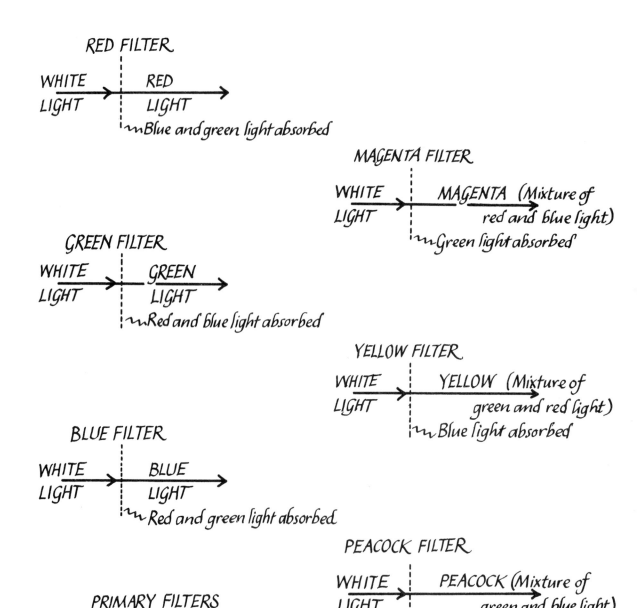

RED FILTER

WHITE LIGHT → RED LIGHT →
Blue and green light absorbed

GREEN FILTER

WHITE LIGHT → GREEN LIGHT →
Red and blue light absorbed

BLUE FILTER

WHITE LIGHT → BLUE LIGHT →
Red and green light absorbed

PRIMARY FILTERS

MAGENTA FILTER

WHITE LIGHT → MAGENTA (Mixture of red and blue light) →
Green light absorbed

YELLOW FILTER

WHITE LIGHT → YELLOW (Mixture of green and red light) →
Blue light absorbed

PEACOCK FILTER

WHITE LIGHT → PEACOCK (Mixture of green and blue light) →
Red light absorbed

SECONDARY FILTERS

Figure 8.27 Absorption by colour filters

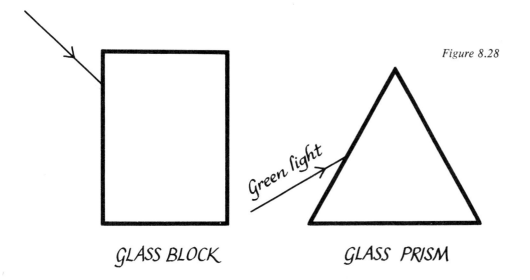

Figure 8.28

GLASS BLOCK

GLASS PRISM

Green light

5. Explain the terms 'frequency' and 'wavelength'. What is the connection between velocity, frequency and wavelength?
6. Draw a diagram showing how a prism may be used to produce a spectrum. Label the spectral colours.
7. List (a) the primary colours, (b) the secondary colours.
8. In a school play, a girl appears on the stage wearing a peacock-blue dress. What colour will it appear to be when the stage is illuminated by (a) red light, (b) blue light, (c) green light, (d) yellow light, (e) magenta light?

Figure 8.29

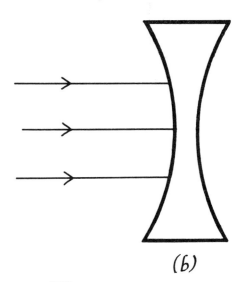

(a)

(b)

Chapter 9

Some Optical Instruments

In Chapters 7 and 8 we studied the behaviour of light. We shall now consider how the laws of optics are used in some everyday optical instruments.

9.1. The camera

Essentially, the camera is an instrument which produces an image, and then makes a permanent record of that image. It is a simple matter to produce an image, even without the use of a lens, but by using a lens, a brighter image may be obtained.

Investigation 9a. The pin-hole camera

Obtain a cardboard box (a chalk box will do) and paint the inside black. Cut a square hole (about 5 cm square) in the lid of the box and stick a piece of tracing paper over this. Using the point of a pair of compasses, make a small hole in the bottom of the box. Figure 9.1 shows the arrangement.

Take the pin-hole camera to a window and point it so that the pin hole is toward a distant, well-illuminated object. Is an image pro-

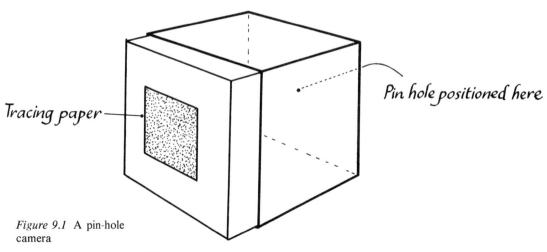

Tracing paper

Pin hole positioned here

Figure 9.1 A pin-hole camera

158

duced on the tracing paper? If so, is it real or virtual? Is it magnified or diminished? Is it erect or inverted? Compare your observations with those obtained with Investigation 7c.

It is possible to take a photograph using a pin-hole camera. In this case, the box must not admit any light, except through the pin hole, and a piece of film must be fitted in the back of the box. It is also necessary to devise some method of covering the pin hole. A small pill box would serve this purpose. Figure 9.2 shows a possible arrangement.

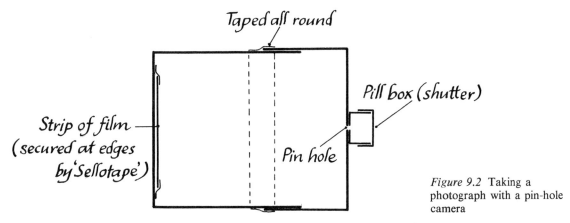

Figure 9.2 Taking a photograph with a pin-hole camera

It is essential to fit the film in a darkroom, using small pieces of 'Sellotape' to hold it in place, and it is advisable to bind black adhesive tape around the gap between the top and bottom parts of the box.

To take the photograph, rest the camera on a solid surface so that it cannot move. Point the camera at the subject, remove the pill-box cap and allow an exposure of a few minutes. It may take several attempts before you find the best exposure to allow.

After exposing the film, replace the pill-box lid and take the camera to the dark-room for the film to be removed. Develop the film while in the dark-room.

The film is developed in a dish containing a proprietary developer solution (e.g. 'Universol') until the latent image is visible. It must then be washed in water, after which it is placed in a dish containing a 'fixer' (e.g. 'Fix-Sol') for ten minutes. Finally, the negative must be thoroughly washed in running water and then allowed to dry.

Investigation 9b. The lens camera

For this investigation you will need the pin-hole camera you made in the first part of Investigation 9a and a convex lens having a focal length of between 5 cm and 10 cm.

Set up the camera to give an image on the tracing paper. Enlarge the pin hole slightly. Does the image change in any way? Continue enlarging the pin hole, a little at a time, until it is about 3 cm in diameter. Each time you increase the size of the hole, notice how the image alters.

When you have cut the large hole, hold the lens just in front of it. Does this produce an image on the tracing paper?

Find the approximate focal length of your lens by the quick method described in Investigation 8d (2). Obtain a piece of postal tubing having an inside diameter slightly larger than that of your lens. Cut this to a length about 2 cm longer than the focal length of your lens. Cover one end of the tube with tracing paper and fit the lens in the other end, using 'Plasticine' to hold it in place. Figure 9.3 shows this arrangement.

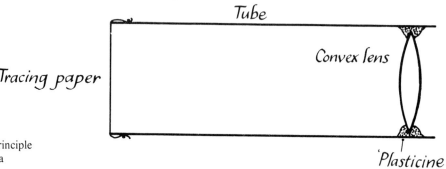

Figure 9.3 The principle of the lens camera

Use the camera to obtain a clear image of an object situated about a metre in front of the lens. Is the background in focus? Now cut a piece of card to fit just in front of the lens, and make a hole about 2 mm in diameter in the middle of the card. Fit the card in place, as shown in Figure 9.4. Is the image as bright as it was before? Is the background in focus?

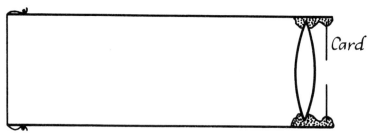

Figure 9.4 Using a diaphragm

You should have found that, by using a lens of fairly large diameter, it was possible to obtain an image very much brighter than the one you obtained with the simple pin-hole camera. You will also have noticed that, with a large diameter lens, it was necessary to adjust the position of the lens in order to bring an object sharply into focus on the screen. When a near object is sharply in focus, it is particularly noticeable that the background is badly out of focus. Matters are considerably improved when the effective diameter of the lens is reduced.

In order to produce a record of the image, photographic film is used. This is simply a strip of transparent plastic, coated with an emulsion containing light-sensitive compounds. These compounds are materials which undergo chemical changes on exposure to light. Generally, silver salts are used for this purpose; in fact, by far the greatest user of silver is the photographic industry.

Investigation 9c. Examination of a light-sensitive salt

Corrosive

Make up a solution of sodium chloride in a test-tube. To this, add a few drops of silver nitrate(V) solution. Observe what happens. Place the test-tube in a rack and put it near a window. Look at this, from time to time, over a period of an hour or so.

When silver nitrate(V) is added to a solution of sodium chloride, a double decomposition reaction takes place in which sodium nitrate(V) and silver chloride are formed.

$$NaCl + AgNO_3 \rightarrow NaNO_3 + AgCl$$

| (sodium chloride) | (silver nitrate(V)) | (sodium nitrate(V)) | (silver chloride) |

The sodium nitrate(V) remains in solution but the silver chloride is insoluble and so precipitates. This is white at first but, on exposure to light, it darkens.

The emulsion used in ordinary photographic film undergoes change when exposed to light, so in order to see what has happened the film must be washed in a chemical bath. This process, which is called **developing**, must be carried out in the dark. Film which has been exposed to light will be opaque when developed, but unexposed film will be transparent. After the film has been developed, it is then treated in another compound in order to prevent any further change taking place. This is called **fixing** the film.

The image on a film of this kind will have rather an odd appearance, because the parts which have been exposed to light will be dark, and the unexposed parts will be light. This is called a **negative** film.

To see the picture properly, a **positive print** must be made. This is done by shining light through the negative on to paper which is coated with an emulsion similar to that used on the film. This is developed and fixed in the same way as the film.

In order to obtain a good negative, it is necessary for the correct amount of light to reach the film. This can be achieved in two ways:

a. By controlling the **shutter** speed. When you press the trigger to take a photograph, the shutter opens and closes, allowing light to enter the camera for a short period of time. In many cameras this period can be controlled between 1 second and $\frac{1}{500}$ of a second. Clearly, it is not only the available light which determines the shutter speed. For example, to take a clear photograph of a fast-moving object, a short exposure must be used. If it is not, a blurred picture will be obtained.

b. Although the camera lens may be of quite large diameter, it is not usual to make use of the whole lens. A device called a **diaphragm** is fitted in front of the lens. This has a small hole, or **aperture**, in the middle. The diaphragm can be adjusted to give apertures of different sizes. The photographer refers to these as **stop** sizes. The stop size controls the amount of light entering the camera during an exposure, and also affects the **depth of field** (i.e. the amount of 'background' which will be reasonably sharply in focus). The stop size is related to the focal length of the lens, so when we talk of a stop of **f8**, we mean that the aperture is of a diameter equal to one-eighth of the focal length of the lens. A stop of **f4** means that the aperture diameter is one-quarter of the focal length of the lens, and so on.

Figure 9.5 shows the relative positions of the lens, film and shutter in a simple camera. Figure 9.6 shows a common type of diaphragm, the **iris diaphragm**.

Figure 9.5 Parts of a simple camera

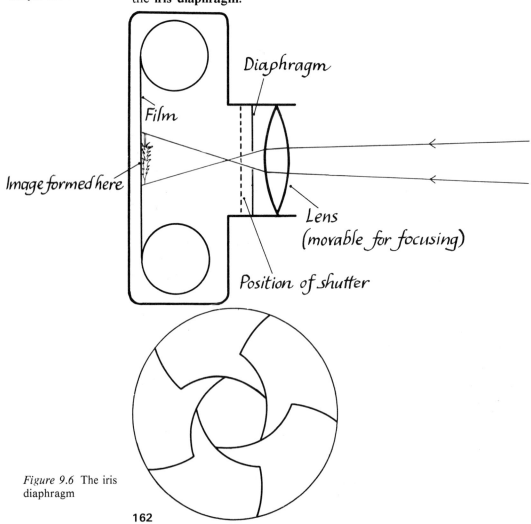

Figure 9.6 The iris diaphragm

162

Figure 9.7 shows the optical arrangement in a modern type of camera. This is a single-lens reflex camera. The main advantage with this type is that there is no separate viewfinder. A prism is used in such a way that the photographer can see in the viewfinder exactly what will be in the final picture. Notice, too, that the lens is not a simple one of the kind you have used in your investigations. One of the problems with a simple lens is that it tends to produce coloured 'fringes', in the same way that a triangular prism produces a spectrum. Compound lenses are designed to overcome this.

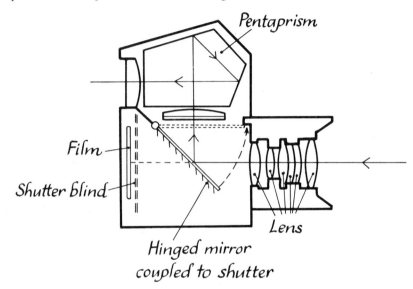

Figure 9.7 A modern camera

9.2. The eye

The human eye is about the size of a table tennis ball, with a bulge at the front (the **cornea**) and a nerve bundle at the back (the **optic nerve**). The cornea is transparent and behind it is the **iris**, which opens and closes to control the amount of light entering the eye through the pupil. Behind the iris is the **crystalline lens**. The space between the cornea and the lens is filled with a watery liquid called **aqueous humour**. The remaining space behind the lens is filled with a transparent jelly called **vitreous humour**. At the back of the eye is a mass of light-sensitive nerve endings forming the **retina** (see Figure 9.8).

Light entering the eye is refracted, first as it enters the eye and again on passing through the lens. In this way, the lens acts as a fine-focusing device, producing a sharp image on the retina. In order to produce a sharp image of objects at different distances from the eye, it is necessary for the lens to be able to alter its focal length. This is brought about by the action of the **ciliary muscle**. When the lens is required to form a sharp image of a distant object, it becomes thinner, in order to have a longer focal length. For near objects, the focal length has to be shorter, and so the lens must become fatter.

163

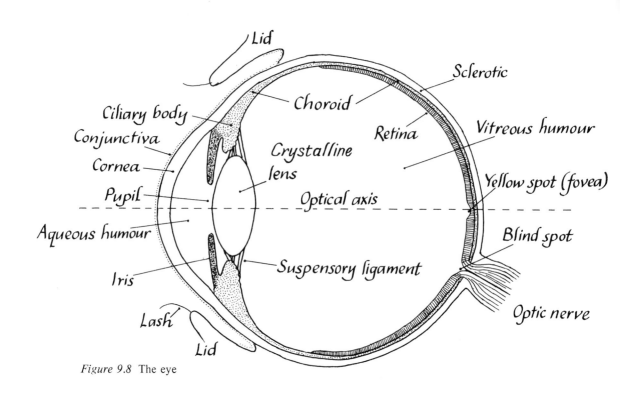

Figure 9.8 The eye

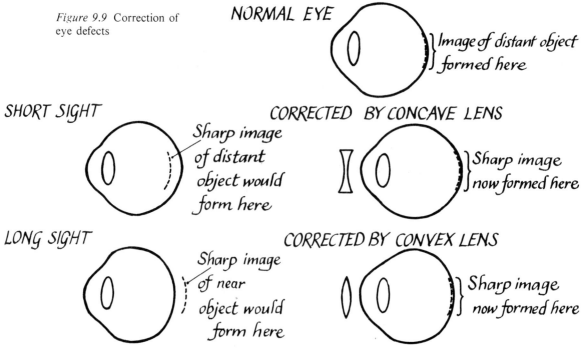

Figure 9.9 Correction of eye defects

NORMAL EYE
} Image of distant object } formed here

SHORT SIGHT
Sharp image of distant object would form here

CORRECTED BY CONCAVE LENS
} Sharp image } now formed here

LONG SIGHT
Sharp image of near object would form here

CORRECTED BY CONVEX LENS
} Sharp image } now formed here

9.3. Long sight and short sight

If a person suffers from **long sight**, the image produced on the retina by a near object is blurred. In this case, the combined focal lengths of the eye and its crystalline lens is too long. This may be corrected by the use of a convex lens.

In the case of **short sight**, the eye is unable to produce a sharp image of distant objects. The focal length is such that a sharp image could form only in front of the position of the retina. A concave lens will correct this condition. Figure 9.9 shows how lenses are used to correct these defects.

It is useful to compare the eye with the camera. In order to prevent colour distortion, the practical camera has a compound lens. This corresponds with the crystalline lens and the aqueous humour. Notice how the pupil of the eye responds to different light intensities. This is similar to the action of the diaphragm of a camera. Notice, too, how the pupil becomes smaller when a person studies a very near object. Compare this with the way in which the stop size used in a camera affects the depth of field and the exposure. In a camera, the lens has to be moved in order to focus at different distances, but the eye achieves this by changing the shape (and therefore the focal length) of the crystalline lens. This is called **accommodation**.

Investigation 9d. Simulation of eye defects

For this investigation you will need a festoon lamp, a screen, a convex lens of focal length 10 cm, another convex lens of longer focal length (20 cm is satisfactory) and a concave lens having a focal length of about 20 cm.

1. **Long sight.** Place the lamp about 50 cm from the convex lens of 10 cm focal length, and position the screen so that a sharp image is produced on it. Now move the screen a few centimetres *closer to* the lens, so that the image is out of focus and blurred. This represents long sight. Position the other convex lens, as shown in Figure 9.10(c), to produce a sharper image on the screen.

2. **Short sight.** Set up the lamp, lens and screen as you did at the start of Investigation 9d (1). Now move the screen a few centimetres *away from* the lens, so that the image becomes blurred. Place the concave lens in position, as shown in Figure 9.11(c), to produce a sharper image.

Before leaving the subject of defective vision, we must mention the subject of colour blindness. This results in a sufferer being unable to distinguish between certain colours in the spectrum. Some degree of colour blindness is quite common in men but is much rarer in

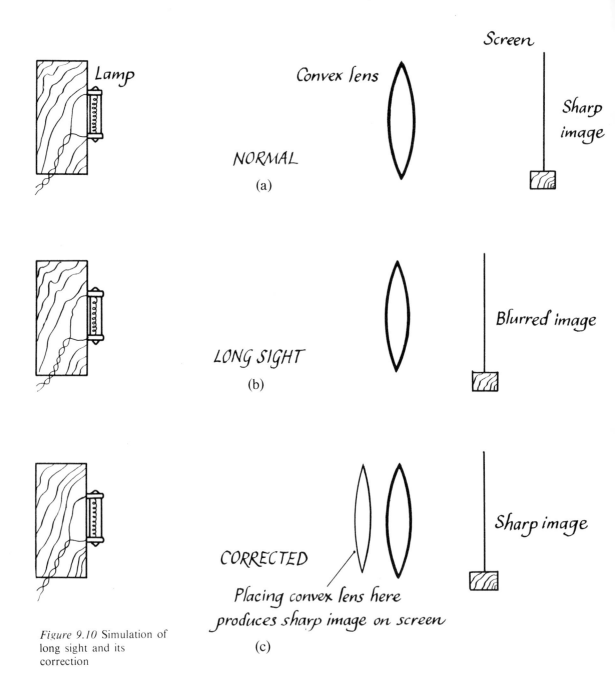

Lamp

Convex lens

Screen

Sharp image

NORMAL

(a)

LONG SIGHT

(b)

Blurred image

CORRECTED

Placing convex lens here produces sharp image on screen

(c)

Sharp image

Figure 9.10 Simulation of long sight and its correction

women. Total colour blindness (i.e. the inability to distinguish any colours at all) is very unusual.

9.4. The projector

Using a convex lens, a magnified real image can be obtained by placing the object at a distance greater than the focal length, but less than twice the focal length, from the lens (see Table 8.1). In the case

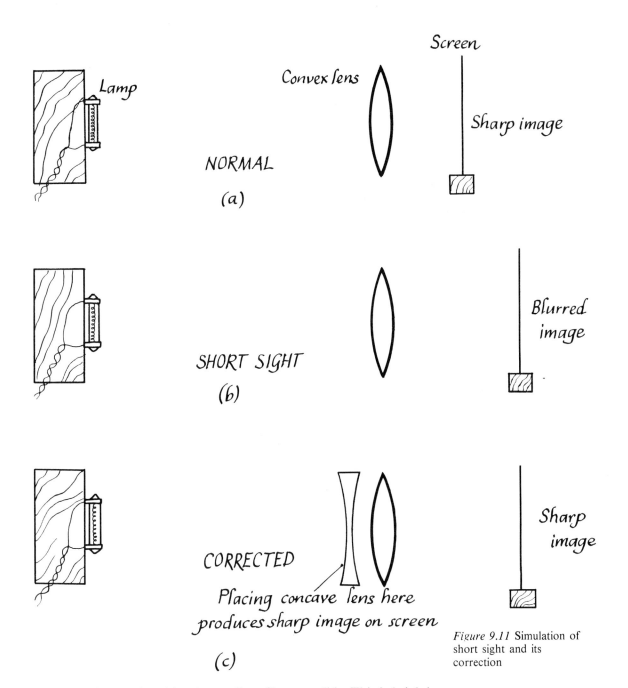

Lamp

Convex lens

Screen

Sharp image

NORMAL

(a)

SHORT SIGHT

(b)

Blurred image

CORRECTED

Placing concave lens here produces sharp image on screen

(c)

Sharp image

Figure 9.11 Simulation of short sight and its correction

of the projector, the object is usually a film or a slide. This is brightly illuminated by means of a lamp having a small filament. A bright parallel beam of light from the lamp is usually produced by means of a convex lens. This is positioned so that the lamp is at its principal focus. The film is positioned on the other side of this lens (called the **condenser** lens), and a second convex lens is required to produce

167

the image on the screen. Figure 9.12 shows the arrangement.

If possible, examine a projector or a photographic enlarger. Notice that, since the image is inverted, the film must be put in place 'upside down' and 'back-to-front'. Notice, too, that the lens systems comprise compound lens arrangements. A typical film-slide projector is shown in Figure 9.13.

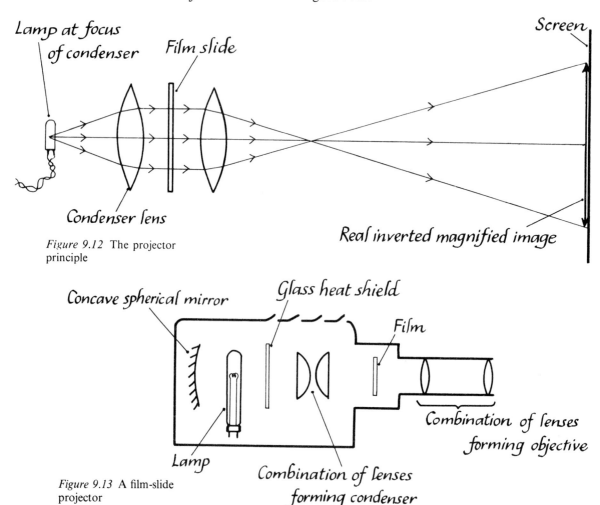

Figure 9.12 The projector principle

Figure 9.13 A film-slide projector

9.5. Telescopes

Investigation 9e. A simple astronomical telescope

For this investigation you will need a metre ruler, some 'Plasticine' and two convex lenses (focal lengths of 5 cm and 20 cm are very suitable, but if these are not available other lengths may be used).

Attach the lens having the shorter focal length to one end of the metre ruler by means of 'Plasticine'. Look through this lens towards

168

a distant object and then position the other lens farther along the ruler, so that you are looking through both lenses. Move the second lens until you obtain a clear image of a distant object. Is the image magnified? Is it erect? Figure 9.14 shows the arrangement.

Measure the distance between the two lenses. Using the quick method, find the approximate focal length of each of the two lenses. Is there any connection between these values and the distance separating the lenses in the telescope?

Figure 9.14 A simple astronomical telescope

Figure 9.15 shows how the astronomical telescope forms its final image. Note how the **objective lens** (the one farther from the eye) forms a real image I_1. The lens nearer to the eye (called the eye lens or the **eyepiece**) causes a magnified virtual image of I_1 to be formed at I_2.

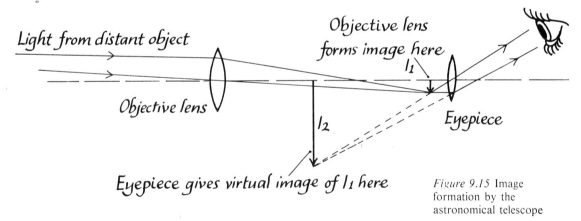

Figure 9.15 Image formation by the astronomical telescope

Investigation 9f. The terrestrial telescope

You will have noticed that the final image produced by the astronomical telescope is inverted. If an erect image is required, this may be obtained by placing a third convex lens between the eyepiece and the objective lens. Try setting up this arrangement, using a third lens of focal length between 5 cm and 20 cm. Figure 9.16 shows the effect of the third lens.

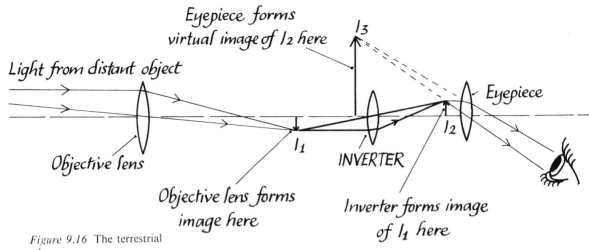

Figure 9.16 The terrestrial telescope

Investigation 9g. Galileo's telescope

This is another type of telescope which gives an erect image. You may set up the instrument by repeating Investigation 9e, but using a concave lens for the eyepiece. Figure 9.17 shows how the image is formed.

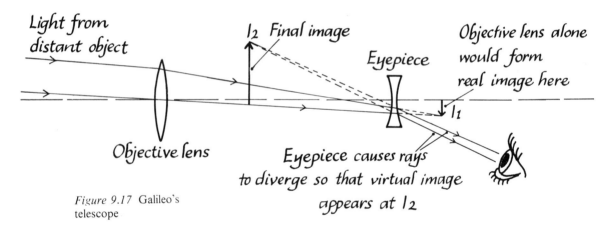

Figure 9.17 Galileo's telescope

9.6. Prismatic binoculars

For viewing distant objects, binoculars have an important advantage over the telescope. By using both eyes, the brain receives two impressions of the same object from two slightly different positions. From these, it is able to compute a three-dimensional 'picture' of the object. This is important in the judgment of distance.

The terrestrial telescope is rather long. The binoculars use what is, essentially, the same optical system except that prisms are used to invert the first image (the objective image). At the same time, the prisms reduce the physical length of the instrument. Figure 9.18 shows the optical system of a pair of binoculars.

170

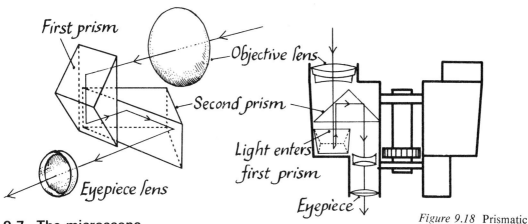

First prism

Objective lens

Second prism

Eyepiece lens

Light enters first prism

Eyepiece

Figure 9.18 Prismatic binoculars

9.7. The microscope

As you already know, a convex lens can be used as a magnifying glass. When an object is placed closer to the lens than its focal length, a virtual image is produced which is erect and magnified. The magnifying glass is sometimes called the **simple microscope**. By using two convex lenses it is possible to produce a large virtual image of a near object. This arrangement is the **compound microscope**. Figure 9.19 compares the simple microscope with the compound microscope.

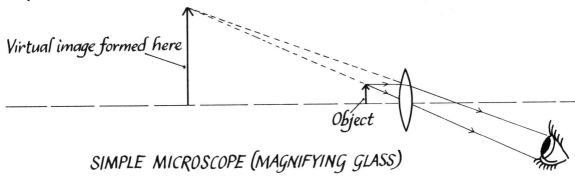

Virtual image formed here

Object

SIMPLE MICROSCOPE (MAGNIFYING GLASS)

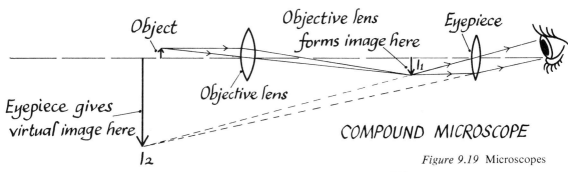

Object

Objective lens forms image here

Eyepiece

Objective lens

Eyepiece gives virtual image here

I_1

I_2

COMPOUND MICROSCOPE

Figure 9.19 Microscopes

171

In the compound microscope, the objective lens is of short focal length and is used to form a real magnified image (I_1) of an object placed just beyond its principal focus. This image is viewed through the eyepiece, which forms a virtual magnified image (I_2) of it.

Test your understanding

1. Sketch a pin-hole camera. Why would the camera not work if the pin hole was enlarged to a diameter of 1 cm?
2. Sketch a simple lens camera, labelling the parts. State the purpose of each part.
3. Make a labelled sketch of the eye.
4. What is short sight? How may it be corrected?
5. Draw a sketch of a film-slide projector, labelling the parts.
6. What are the main differences between the astronomical telescope and the terrestrial telescope?
7. What is the purpose of the prisms in a pair of prismatic binoculars?
8. Make diagrams contrasting the simple microscope and the compound microscope.

Chapter 10

Sound

10.1. Sources of sound

Sounds are produced when objects vibrate.

Investigation 10a. Vibration of a tuning fork

Strike a tuning fork and hold the tang (the pointed end) on the bench. Now fill a beaker with water, strike the tuning fork and allow one of the prongs to touch the surface of the water, as shown in Figure 10.1.

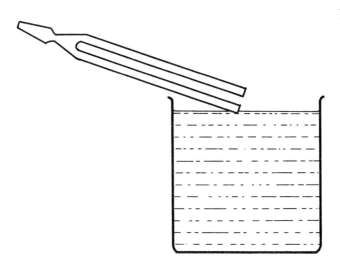

Figure 10.1 Investigations with a tuning fork

Investigation 10b. Vibration of a stretched wire

For this investigation you will need a **sonometer**. This consists of a base-board with a wire fastened to a pillar at one end and a pulley attached to the other. The wire passes over the pulley and a scale pan is attached to the wire, as shown in Figure 10.2.

Set up the sonometer and put a mass of 200 g on the scale pan. Set the movable bridge so that it is 30 cm from the fixed bridge. Now pluck the wire between the bridges. Increase the distance between

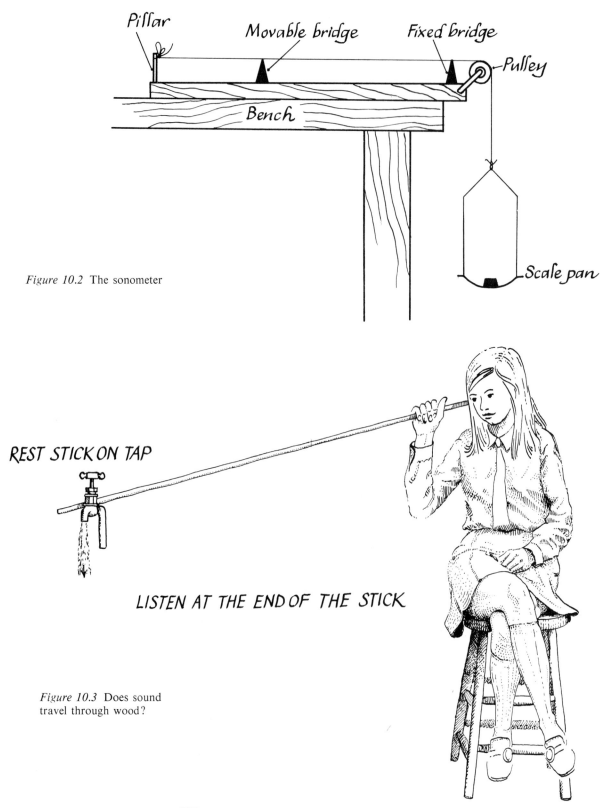

Pillar

Movable bridge

Fixed bridge

Pulley

Bench

Scale pan

Figure 10.2 The sonometer

REST STICK ON TAP

LISTEN AT THE END OF THE STICK

Figure 10.3 Does sound travel through wood?

174

the bridges to 60 cm and pluck the wire again. What difference does this make to the note produced? Can you play a tune on the sonometer?

Now increase the mass on the scale pan to 400 g and repeat the investigation. What effect does increasing the mass have on the note produced?

Change the wire for a thicker one (i.e. one having a larger area of cross-section) and repeat the whole investigation. What effect does increasing the area of cross-section have on the note produced?

10.2. How sound travels

Investigation 10c. Does sound travel through wood?

In this investigation you need to work with a partner. While you stand at one end of a bench, your partner stands at the other end.

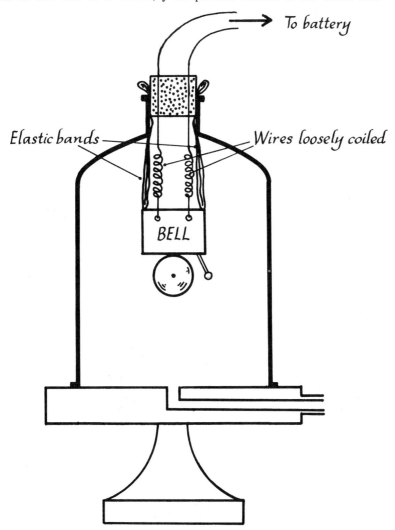

Figure 10.4 Does sound travel through empty space?

To battery

Elastic bands

Wires loosely coiled

BELL

First, ask your partner to sound the tuning fork and place the tang on the bench. Then ask him to do it again, but this time place your ear on the bench. Is there any difference in what you hear?

Turn on a tap so that the water is running slowly. Place one end of a stick on the tap, as shown in Figure 10.3, and put your ear to the other end of the stick. Can you hear the flow of water?

Investigation 10d. Does sound travel through empty space?

An electric bell is suspended in a bell jar which is placed on the platform of a vacuum pump (see Figure 10.4). The bell is then switched on and the vacuum pump started. Does the sound change in any way?

From Investigations 10c and 10d you have probably concluded that sound needs some substance through which to travel, and that some substances seem to allow sound to travel through them better than others.

10.3. Sound waves

Figure 10.5 Longitudinal waves

In Chapter 8 we saw that it was possible to produce transverse waves in a length of rope. Electromagnetic waves are transverse. Sound also travels in the form of waves, but they are **longitudinal** waves.

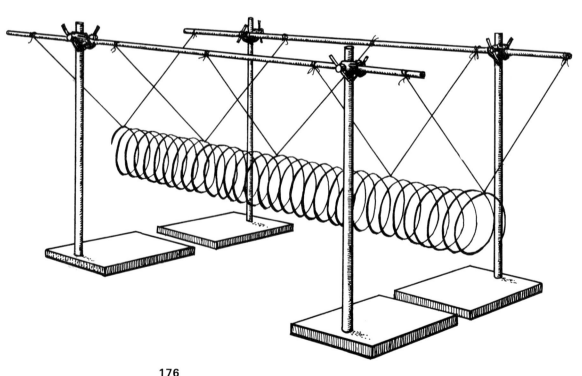

Suspend a 'slinky' spring as shown in Figure 10.5. Give one end of the spring a sharp tug. Notice how the energy travels along the spring. Waves of this kind are called longitudinal waves.

Vibrating objects disturb the surrounding air, producing longitudinal waves. Figure 10.6 shows how the vibrating prong of a tuning

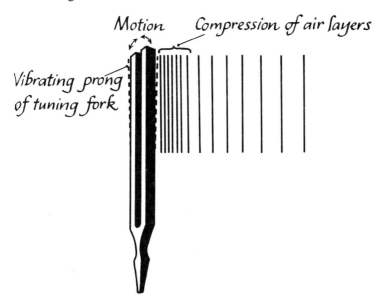

Figure 10.6 A tuning fork produces longitudinal waves in air

fork first compresses layers of air, and then rarefies them. Notice that the effect represented in the figure is much the same as the behaviour of the spring in Investigation 10e.

In a longitudinal wave train, the distance between the beginning of one compression and the beginning of the next is one wavelength (see Figure 10.7).

Figure 10.7 Representation of wavelength

The number of waves produced in one second (the frequency) depends on the frequency with which the prong of the tuning fork vibrates. The rate at which these waves advance depends on the 'springiness' of the substance through which they are travelling. As

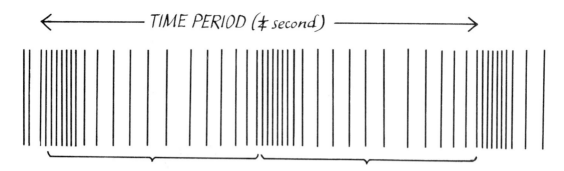

TIME PERIOD ($\frac{1}{4}$ second)

2 WAVELENGTHS (each 40 metres)

FREQUENCY = 8 Hz

WAVELENGTH = 40 m

VELOCITY = FREQUENCY × WAVELENGTH ($8 \times 40 = 320\ m\ s^{-1}$)

Figure 10.8 The connection between velocity, frequency and wavelength

with transverse waves, the velocity is the product of the wavelength and the frequency (see Figure 10.8).

10.4. The ear

Vibrating bodies cause trains of compression waves in the air. When these enter the ear, they cause vibrations similar to those of the vibrating body. The brain interprets these as sound.

The human ear (see Figure 10.9) consists of three main parts: the outer ear, the middle ear and the inner ear.

The outer ear consists of the **pinna** (or lug) and the **meatus**, which is a tube from the pinna to the **tympanum** (or ear-drum). Inside the meatus are glands which produce wax which helps to keep the ear-drum pliable. The ear-drum is a thin skin stretched across the end of the meatus and is very delicate.

The middle ear is a chamber containing three small bones, the **malleus** (hammer), the **incus** (anvil) and the **stapes** (stirrup), which are hinged to each other to form a chain of levers. The malleus is connected to the inner surface of the ear-drum and the stapes is connected to the inner diaphragm (oval window), which connects with the inner ear. The **eustachian tube** connects the middle ear to the junction of the nose and throat (the pharynx).

The inner ear contains a long, coiled tube called the **cochlea**, which is filled with a watery liquid called **endolymph**. Projecting from the walls of the cochlea into the endolymph are nerve endings, connected to the brain by the **auditory nerve**. The inner ear also contains organs associated with our sense of balance.

178

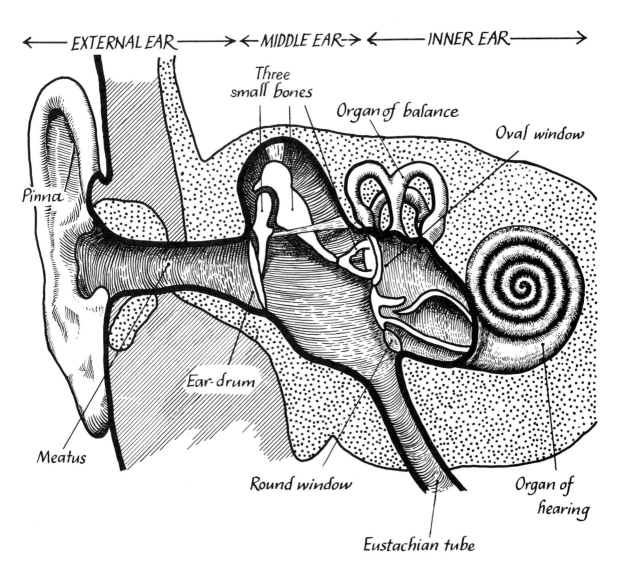

Three small bones

Organ of balance

Oval window

Pinna

Ear-drum

Meatus

Round window

Organ of hearing

Eustachian tube

When compression waves fall on the ear-drum, causing it to vibrate, the movement is transmitted by the bones of the middle ear. Because of the way they are connected together as levers, the movement of the stirrup causes the oval window to vibrate, setting up pressure waves in the endolymph. As these waves travel through the cochlea, the nerve endings sway in sympathy. This movement causes impulses to be transmitted, by the auditory nerve, to the brain. The brain interprets these impulses as sound.

Figure 10.9 The ear

10.5. Musical instruments

Musical instruments are divided into four groups: percussion, strings, woodwind and brass. They are all sources of vibration and the note produced by any instrument depends on the frequency of vibration. Table 10.1 gives the frequencies of notes in a scale beginning with middle C. Notice that the notes of higher pitch have the higher frequencies.

TABLE 10.1. FREQUENCIES OF MUSICAL NOTES

Note	Scientific Frequency/Hz	Musical Frequency/Hz
Middle C	256	262
D	288	294
E	320	330
F	341	349
G	384	392
A	426	440
B	480	494
C	512	523

It is easy to distinguish between two different instruments, even though they may be playing the same note. Middle C on a piano sounds different from the same note played on a guitar, for example. These differences are called the **timbre**, or quality, of the note. The timbre is largely due to the **overtones** which may be present.

The note produced by a stretched string depends on the length of the string, the tautness of the string and the material of which the string is made. The main vibration takes place in the whole length of *Figure 10.10* The the string, as shown in Figure 10.10. The note produced in this way fundamental is called the **fundamental**.

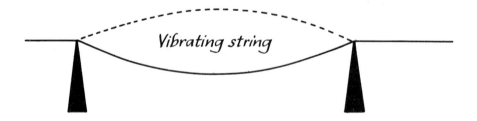

Vibrating string

When a string is plucked or bowed, it usually produces overtones as well as the fundamental. These may have two times, three times or four times the frequency of the fundamental. The sound produced by a string is really a mixture of sounds, comprising the fundamental and some of the possible overtones. Overtones are compared with the fundamental in Figure 10.11.

Many wind instruments produce vibrating columns of air as the source of their sound. In this case the fundamental depends on the length of the air column. Figure 10.12 shows how overtones may be produced in an organ pipe.

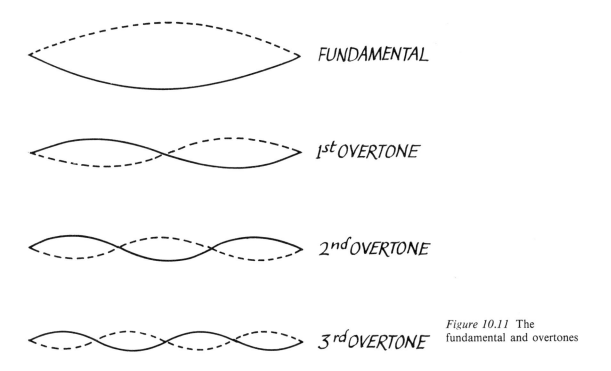

FUNDAMENTAL

1st OVERTONE

2nd OVERTONE

3rd OVERTONE

Figure 10.11 The fundamental and overtones

Figure 10.12 Overtones in organ pipes

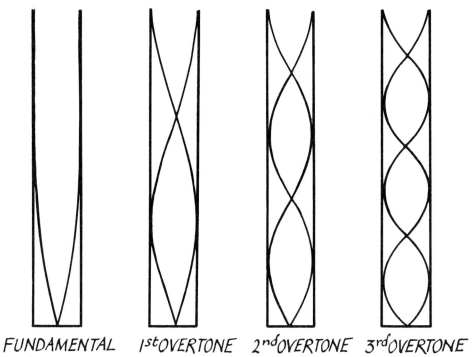

FUNDAMENTAL   1st OVERTONE   2nd OVERTONE   3rd OVERTONE

The differences in quality between different wind instruments also depend on other factors in the design and the method of playing the instrument.

10.6. The velocity of sound

Investigation 10f. A determination of the velocity of sound

For this investigation you will need to find a large open space. One experimenter is provided with a car battery connected to a head-lamp and an electric motor horn. A switch is included in the circuit so that, when it is closed, the lamp lights and, at the same time, the horn sounds. Figure 10.13 shows the arrangement.

Figure 10.13 The horn and headlamp

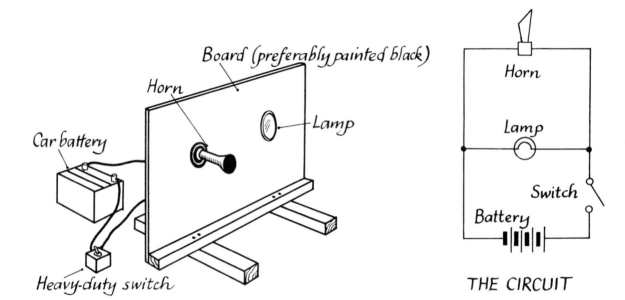

Board (preferably painted black)

Horn

Lamp

Car battery

Heavy-duty switch

Horn

Lamp

Switch

Battery

THE CIRCUIT

A second experimenter is situated at some considerable distance (preferably at least 300 m) from the first. This distance must be measured as accurately as possible.

The second experimenter (the observer) is provided with a stop-watch. The first experimenter closes the switch. When the observer sees the light from the headlamp, he starts the stop-watch and, when he first hears the car horn, he stops the watch.

The velocity of sound is then calculated:

$$\text{Velocity of sound} = \frac{\text{Distance between experimenters}}{\text{Time recorded by observer}}$$

The velocity of sound in air is approximately 330 m s^{-1}. This is very much slower than the speed of light, which is 300 000 000 m s^{-1}. For this reason, the flash of lightning is seen before the clap of thunder is heard, even though they are produced at the same time.

Echoes are produced as a result of the reflection of sound. If a ship 660 m from a cliff sounds its siren, the echo will be heard 4 s later (see Figure 10.14).

Figure 10.14 Echoes

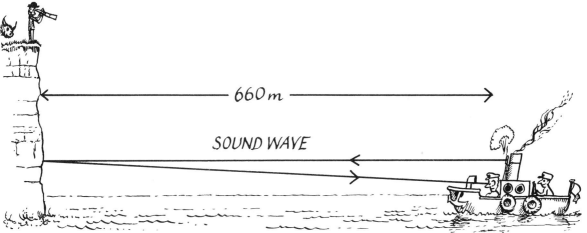

660 m

SOUND WAVE

SOUND TAKES 2 SECONDS TO REACH CLIFF AND 2 SECONDS TO RETURN TO SHIP

Test your understanding

1. In what ways do sound waves differ from light waves?
2. Copy the sketch of the ear (Figure 10.15) and add the labels indicated.
3. What is the velocity of sound in air?
4. A sound wave of frequency 440 Hz is travelling through air. What is the wavelength?

Figure 10.15

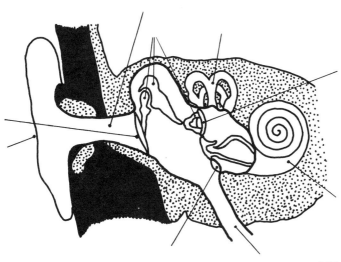

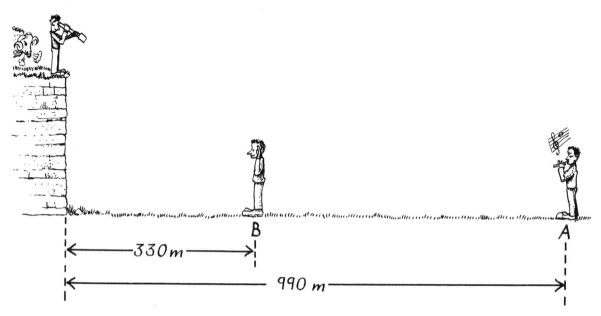

Figure 10.16

5. A man standing in position A in Figure 10.16 blows a whistle. An echo is produced by the cliff face and the man situated at B hears the note twice. How many seconds elapse between the two notes heard by the man at B?

6. Explain why we hear thunder after seeing a flash of lightning. If a clap of thunder is heard 7 s after seeing the lightning flash, how far away is the lightning?

Chapter 11

How the Body Works

In order for a car to function efficiently, each of its systems must be in good working order. Similarly, the human body functions efficiently only if all of its systems are working properly. A decayed tooth can affect the efficiency of several systems, the consequent inefficiency of one leading to the inefficiency of another and so on, rather like a chain reaction. The decayed tooth may lead to insufficient chewing of food, which leads to indigestion, which may cause constipation, which may cause headaches and eye strain. A more serious fault could cause the complete stoppage of all systems; heart failure causes death.

11.1. The skeletal system

The human skeleton consists of just over two hundred bones, connected by joints and held in position by ligaments (see Figure 11.1).

There are four types of joint:

a. **Ball and socket joints**. These allow considerable movement in all directions. Examples are the shoulder and hip joints.

b. **Hinged joints**. These allow considerable movement in one direction only. Examples are the elbow, knee, finger and toe joints.

c. **Gliding joints**. These allow limited movement in all directions. Examples are the wrist and ankle joints, and between the vertebrae of the vertebral column.

d. **Fixed joints**. These allow no movement and are found in the skull and the pelvis.

The bones of the skeleton perform three main functions:

a. **Support**. The bones of the vertebral column, pelvis and legs support the body in its normal posture. The intervertebral discs and the curvature of the vertebral column (see Figure 11.2) make the vertebral column flexible and enable it to act as a shock absorber. As we walk, the curvature alters with each step. If this were not so, the shock of the impact of each foot on the ground would be transmitted through the bones of the legs, pelvis and vertebral column to

185

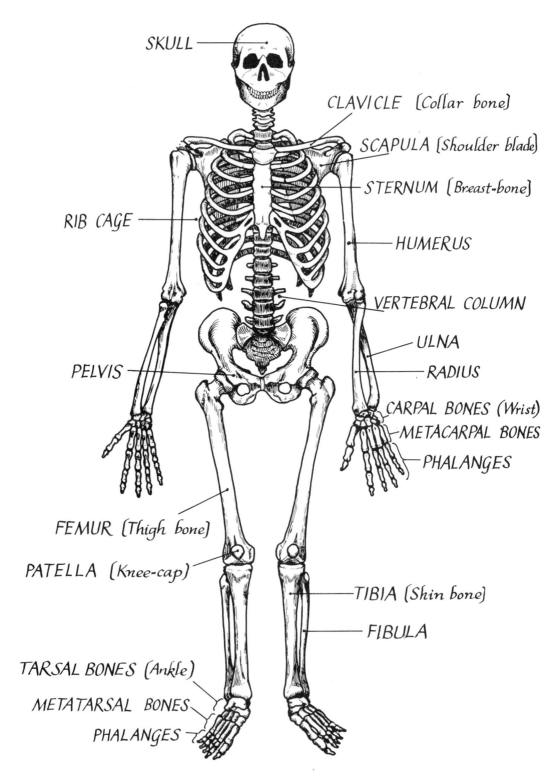

SKULL

CLAVICLE (Collar bone)

SCAPULA (Shoulder blade)

STERNUM (Breast-bone)

RIB CAGE

HUMERUS

VERTEBRAL COLUMN

ULNA

RADIUS

PELVIS

CARPAL BONES (Wrist)

METACARPAL BONES

PHALANGES

FEMUR (Thigh bone)

PATELLA (Knee-cap)

TIBIA (Shin bone)

FIBULA

TARSAL BONES (Ankle)

METATARSAL BONES

PHALANGES

Figure 11.1 The human
skeleton

186

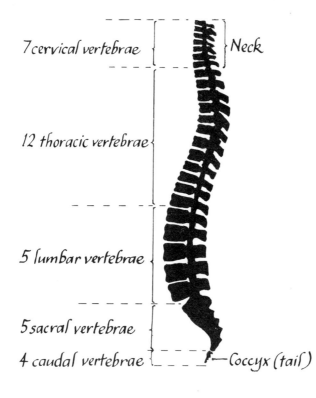

7 cervical vertebrae ⎰ Neck

12 thoracic vertebrae ⎰

5 lumbar vertebrae ⎰

5 sacral vertebrae ⎰

4 caudal vertebrae ⎰ Coccyx (tail)

Figure 11.2 Curvature of the vertebral column

the skull. This would have the effect of repeated blows on the back of the skull. Running would be even more painful and jumping down to the ground from a height might be fatal.

b. **Protection**. Some of the vital organs of the body are protected by bones. The brain is protected by the skull, the spinal cord by the vertebral column, and the heart and lungs by the rib cage.

c. **Movement**. When the body changes its position, the bones are moved by muscles which are attached to them. The bones act as levers, with the joints acting as fulcrums.

11.2. The muscular system

Muscles cause movement. Muscles which move bones are connected to them by **tendons** and always act in pairs. These muscles are called **voluntary muscles** because they are under our control. The way in which a pair of voluntary muscles work is shown in Figure 11.3. The forearm is raised when the biceps muscle contracts while the triceps muscle is relaxed. The forearm is extended when the triceps muscle contracts as the biceps muscle is gradually relaxing.

Muscles over which we have no control are called **involuntary muscles**. Examples of involuntary muscles include the **cardiac muscle** (heart muscle) and the muscles which cause peristalsis.

Semi-voluntary muscles, such as those controlling the bladder and breathing, are under our control to a limited extent. Once this limit

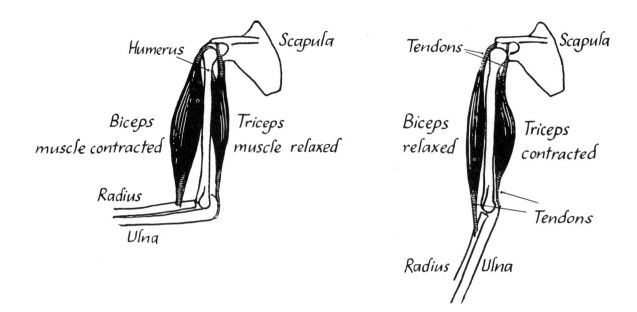

Figure 11.3 The action of a pair of voluntary muscles

is reached, they act automatically, otherwise physical damage could result.

A muscle consists of a large number of muscle fibres, all lying parallel to each other like the strands in a hank of wool. A muscle fibre consists of a large number of muscle cells connected end to end, like a string of beads. A muscle cell has the ability to change its shape; when it is relaxed it is long and thin and when it is contracted it is short and fat. There is no half-way stage; it is either relaxed or contracted. The degree of movement produced by a muscle is determined by the proportion of muscle cells that are contracted.

Investigation 11a. Muscle quiver

Bend your knees so that you are in the half-crouch position. Remain in this position for about a minute. Can you feel a fluttering sensation in the muscles in your thighs? Hold a heavy weight in front of you, or above your head, with your elbows partly bent. Can you feel a fluttering sensation in your biceps and triceps muscles?

A muscle cell cannot remain contracted for very long. After a certain time, it will relax. When a muscle is exerting a force, it maintains this force because the muscle cells contract and relax in relays; as a contracted cell relaxes, an adjacent cell contracts, thus maintaining the force. It is this continuous variation from contraction to relaxation (and vice versa) of the muscle cells which caused the fluttering sensations which you felt in Investigation 11a.

Mechanical energy produces movement; muscles produce movement. Muscle cells are able to produce this movement by converting

188

chemical energy into mechanical energy. As with most energy conversions, some heat energy is also produced. The chemical energy which the muscle cells convert is made available by the action of the digestive system on the food we eat and the extraction of oxygen from the air we breathe.

11.3. The digestive system

The foodstuffs which provide fuel for the muscles are the carbohydrates and, to a lesser extent, the fats and the proteins. These are complex carbon compounds which are converted into somewhat simpler compounds by the action of the digestive system.

The route from mouth to anus is called the **alimentary canal** and is between 8 and 9 metres long in man.

When food is eaten, it is chewed into small pieces by the teeth and mixed to a soft pulpy mass as saliva from the salivary glands is added to it. While in the mouth, cooked starch is converted into maltose by the action of **ptyalin**, an enzyme which is present in saliva.

After being swallowed and passed through the gullet, the food reaches the stomach where dilute hydrochloric acid and gastric juices are added. The gastric juices contain two enzymes: **rennin** and **pepsin**. Rennin reacts with the casein in milk to produce a curd while pepsin converts proteins into soluble peptones. The hydrochloric acid dissolves mineral salts and enables the pepsin to react more effectively. When the food has become thoroughly mixed with the gastric juices in the stomach, it becomes a thick liquid called **chyme**.

When the chyme passes from the stomach to the **duodenum** (the first 30 cm of the small intestine) **liver bile** and **pancreatic juice** are added. Liver bile, which comes from the gall bladder, breaks down fat into small droplets. Pancreatic juice contains three enzymes: **trypsin**, which converts peptones into simpler substances called **proteoses**; **amylase**, which converts any uncooked starch (and any cooked starch which has not already been converted) into maltose; and **lipase**, which converts fat droplets into fatty acids and glycerine. With the addition of these liquids, the chyme is now much thinner and is called **chyle**.

As the chyle passes through the remainder of the small intestine (about 6·5 metres long), four more enzymes are added. These enzymes are **maltase, lactase, sucrase** and **erepsin**. The action of these enzymes is to produce from the chyle, highly soluble substances which are then absorbed through the intestinal wall where some pass directly into the bloodstream while others are carried by lymph vessels which connect with the bloodstream through the thoracic duct.

At the lower end of the small intestine, the chyle passes through

189

a valve to the large intestine (or colon) where most of the excess water and soluble salts are absorbed through the wall into the bloodstream, from which they are removed by the kidneys (see Section 11.11).

11.4. The respiratory system

Respiration can be considered in two stages:

a. External respiration

This is the process by which air enters and leaves the lungs. While the air is in the lungs, a gas exchange takes place; oxygen diffuses from the air into the bloodstream while carbon dioxide diffuses from the bloodstream into the air. The mechanics of external respiration (commonly called breathing) are dealt with in Chapter 4.

b. Internal respiration

This is the process which occurs in the muscle cells. It is a process of oxidation whereby the simple carbon compounds produced by the digestive system combine with the oxygen in the bloodstream, releasing energy and producing carbon dioxide as a waste product. Figure 11.4 shows the energy flow during internal respiration.

Figure 11.4 Internal respiration

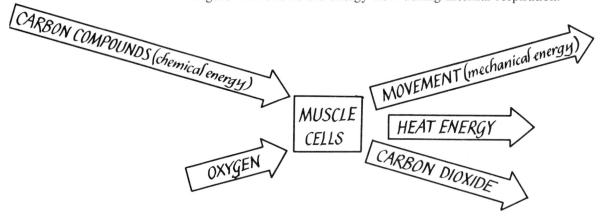

11.5. The blood

The blood can be considered as the main transport medium of the body. Blood is a complicated substance consisting of a liquid called **plasma** with **red cells**, **white cells** and **platelets** floating in it.

Investigation 11b. Looking at blood

Blood cells are very small (too small to be seen clearly with the naked eye) so you will need a microscope. In order to produce a

190

layer of blood thin enough to enable you to distinguish individual cells, you must prepare a **blood smear.**

You will need a sharp needle, a bunsen burner, a piece of string, two clean microscope slides, two teat pipettes, some Leishman's stain and some distilled or de-ionized water. **Sterilize the needle by holding it in the bunsen flame for a few seconds.** Wrap the piece of string tightly round the base of the index finger of your left hand and hold it tight while you bend the finger down towards the palm. This will restrict the flow of blood from the finger, thus increasing the pressure. A quick jab with the point of the sterilized needle about half-way between the base of the nail and the top joint of the finger will produce a small drop of blood (see Figure 11.5).

Biological

Harmful

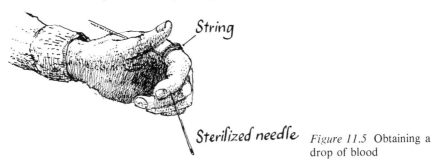

Figure 11.5 Obtaining a drop of blood

Touch this drop of blood with one of the microscope slides and draw it across with the end of the other slide, as shown in Figure 11.6. As soon as you have obtained the slide, unwrap the string around your finger and **dab the needle mark with an antiseptic.**

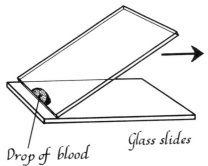

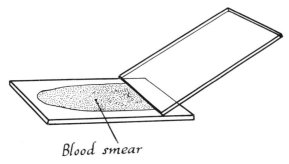

Figure 11.6 Making a blood smear

191

Flammable

Harmful

Place the slide under a low-power microscope (about ×100) and examine it. In order to see the cells more clearly, your blood smear must now be stained. Using one of the teat pipettes, put a few drops of Leishman's stain on the smear and tilt the slide in all directions until the whole smear is covered. Using the other teat pipette, add a few drops of distilled water or de-ionized water to the smear and leave it for about ten minutes. If the smear appears to be drying out during this period, add some more distilled water or de-ionized water. Now wash off the stain with distilled water or de-ionized water and allow the smear to dry.

Alternative stains which may be used instead of Leishman's stain are May–Grunwald's solution or Delafield's haemotoxylin.

Examine your smear under the microscope. Can you distinguish the red cells, the white cells and the platelets? Compare your blood smear with Figure 11.7.

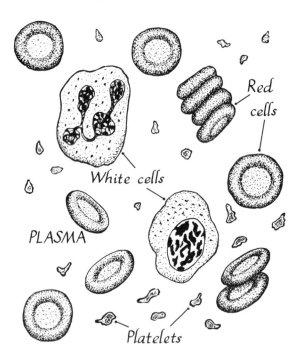

Figure 11.7 Blood, as seen under a microscope

Before you stained your blood smear, you may have been surprised to find that your red blood cells did not appear to be red. Perhaps you may be able to understand why your blood is red, in spite of the apparent lack of colour in the red cells, by considering the following examples:

  a. When you look through a pane of glass, it appears to be colourless, but if you look at the edge of a pane of glass, it is green.
  b. The water in the shallow end of a swimming pool appears to be lighter in colour than the water in the deep end.

192

Red blood cells contain a substance called **haemoglobin**. Haemoglobin is an iron compound which combines with oxygen, forming **oxyhaemoglobin**. Blood which is rich in oxyhaemoglobin is a bright scarlet colour when seen in the mass. When the red cells have given up their oxygen, the colour of the blood is a dark purplish-red. One cubic millimetre of normal healthy human blood contains about 5 000 000 red cells, each being the shape of a circular disc with a depression in each side. A red cell is about 0·008 mm in diameter and about 0·002 mm thick. The red cells are produced in the marrow of the long bones (femur, tibia, humerus, etc.) and are disposed of by the liver (see Section 11.10). Insufficient production of red cells or a shortage of haemoglobin caused by a lack of iron salts in the diet causes **anaemia**. One of the symptoms of anaemia is tiredness. This is a direct result of the inability of the blood to maintain an adequate supply of oxygen to the muscles.

White blood cells are colourless, rather than white, and are called **leucocytes**. They are variable in shape and size, being generally somewhat larger than the red cells and fewer in number. One cubic millimetre of normal healthy human blood contains between 6 000 and 10 000 white cells. The white cells can be compared with a defensive army, killing or neutralizing the harmful effects of invading bacteria. One type of white cell, called **phagocytes**, eats the invading bacteria, as shown in Figure 11.8, while another type produces

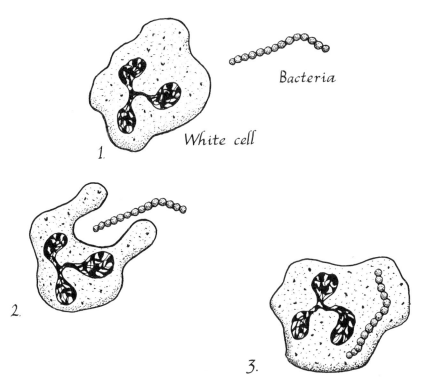

Figure 11.8 The action of a phagocyte

substances called **anti-toxins**, which neutralize the toxins (poisons) produced by the bacteria.

Although the white cells maintain constant patrols throughout the bloodstream, reserves are available in the event of an attack. These reserves are maintained in the **lymphatic glands**, placed in strategic positions throughout the body. When local infection occurs, white cells concentrate in the area to deal with the situation and, while the battle rages, the surrounding tissues become inflamed. When the battle is over, the dead bacteria and the dead white cells form **pus**.

Like any army, the white cells must know what the enemy are like, and must have training in dealing with them. The ability of the white cells in the blood of an individual to deal effectively with certain types of disease-causing organisms is inherited and is called **natural immunity**. Artificial immunity against certain other types can be achieved by **inoculation**, whereby a very mild strain of the particular disease-causing organism is introduced into the blood. Once the white cells have mastered the technique of dealing with the mild strain, they will be able to overcome an attack by a more powerful strain of the same organism.

Blood plasma is a pale, straw-coloured liquid which transports the red cells, white cells, platelets, the dissolved products of digestion, waste products, hormones (see Section 11.9) and a protein substance called **fibrinogen**. Although a small proportion of the carbon dioxide produced by internal respiration in the muscle cells is carried back to the lungs by the red cells, the majority of it is carried by the plasma, either in solution or as sodium hydrogencarbonate. The fibrinogen in the plasma enables the blood to clot. When blood is exposed to air, the fibrinogen forms **fibrin** which produces a tangled network of thin fibres. The red cells and the white cells are trapped in this mesh and form a clot. In the case of a cut or graze, the clot hardens by evaporation to form a scab, which protects the

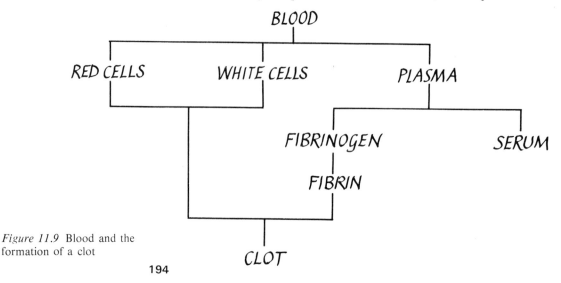

Figure 11.9 Blood and the formation of a clot

wound against further infection. The liquid remaining when the fibrinogen has formed fibrin is called serum. Figure 11.9 shows the constituents of blood and how clotting occurs.

11.6. Blood groups; the A–B–O system

The red cells may contain substances which, for the purpose of blood grouping, are called **A** and **B**. The plasma may contain antibodies which cause the red cells to clump together, thus reducing the fluidity of the blood. The antibody called **anti-A** causes clumping of the red cells containing substance **A** while **anti-B** causes clumping of the red cells containing substance **B**. This gives rise to the **A–B–O** grouping system in which there are four groups: **A, B, AB** and **O** (see Table 11.1).

TABLE 11.1. A–B–O BLOOD GROUPS

Blood Group	Red Cells Contain Substance	Plasma Antibody
A	A	Anti-B
B	B	Anti-A
AB	A and B	Neither
O	Neither	Anti-A and anti-B

When a patient needs a blood transfusion, it is important that the donor's blood is of the same group or a group which will not cause clumping of the red cells (i.e. the recipient's blood and the donor's blood must be compatible). Table 11.2 shows the compatibility of the A–B–O blood groups.

A recipient with group AB blood is known as a universal recipient and can safely accept blood of any group, because AB blood plasma contains no antibodies to cause clumping of the red cells being transfused. The antibodies present in the plasma of groups A, B and O are diluted to such an extent by the recipient's blood plasma that they have little or no clumping effect on the recipient's red cells.

Group O is known as the universal donor group and can be safely transfused into any of the other groups. Since there is nothing in the red cells of group O blood to react with the antibodies, the group O red cells being transfused will not clump together. The antibodies in the plasma of group O blood are sufficiently diluted by the recipient's plasma to reduce the clumping effect on the recipient's red cells to negligible proportions.

In addition to the A–B–O system, there are at least thirteen other blood characteristics, some of which can affect the safety of blood transfusion in spite of A–B–O compatibility.

195

TABLE 11.2. A–B–O BLOOD GROUP COMPATIBILITY

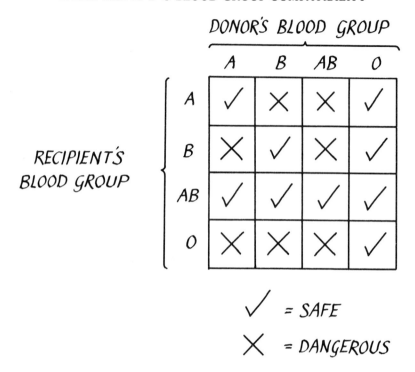

11.7. The heart and circulation

The **heart** is the organ which pumps the blood round the body. The left side of the heart pumps oxygenated blood *from the lungs to the body* while the right side of the heart pumps deoxygenated blood *from the body to the lungs.*

Between the two sides of the heart there is a dividing barrier, so the heart can be considered as a double pump. Circulation of blood round the body is called **systemic circulation.** The circulation of blood through the lungs is called **pulmonary circulation.**

Each side of the heart has two chambers: an upper chamber called an **auricle** (or **atrium**), into which blood flows through valves from the **veins,** and a lower chamber called a **ventricle,** which pumps blood through a valve to the **arteries.** Auricles have comparatively thin walls while ventricles have comparatively thick walls. Between the auricle and the ventricle there is a valve which ensures that the flow of blood is in the right direction, from auricle to ventricle. Figure 11.10 shows the heart and the circulation of the blood.

Investigation 11c. The heart-beat

Listen to your heart-beat with a stethoscope. Can you hear the double thump in each beat? The first thump is caused by the closing

196

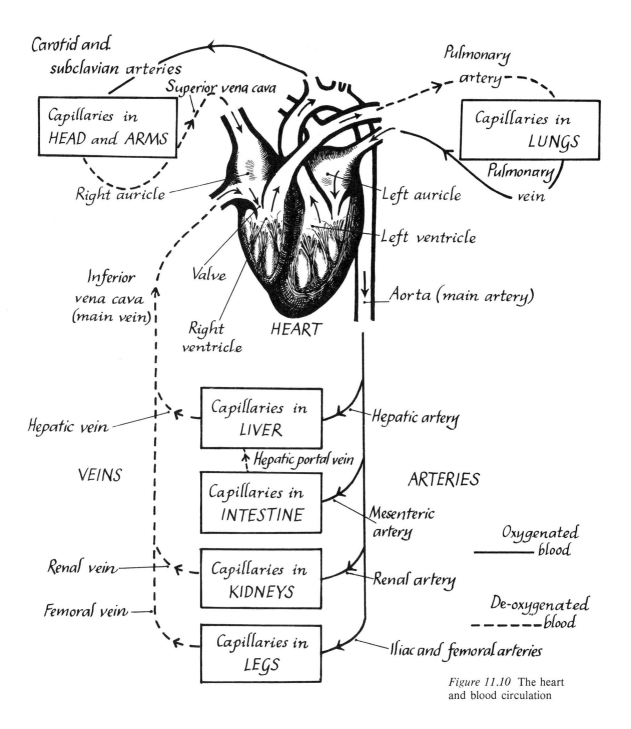

Carotid and subclavian arteries

Capillaries in HEAD and ARMS

Superior vena cava

Pulmonary artery

Capillaries in LUNGS

Pulmonary vein

Right auricle

Left auricle

Left ventricle

Inferior vena cava (main vein)

Valve

Aorta (main artery)

Right ventricle

HEART

Hepatic vein

Capillaries in LIVER

Hepatic artery

VEINS

Hepatic portal vein

ARTERIES

Capillaries in INTESTINE

Mesenteric artery

Oxygenated blood

Renal vein

Capillaries in KIDNEYS

Renal artery

De-oxygenated blood

Femoral vein

Capillaries in LEGS

Iliac and femoral arteries

Figure 11.10 The heart and blood circulation

of the valves and the second thump is caused when the heart contracts, pumping the blood out of the ventricles.

Now, hold your breath while you listen to your heart-beat. Do you notice that your heart beats faster and appears to be labouring? Holding your breath reduces the amount of oxygen available to be

197

transported by the red cells, so the heart beats faster in order to maintain a steady supply of oxygen to the body.

Investigation 11d. Pulse rate and physical fitness

Rest your forearm on a level surface, with the palm of the hand facing downwards. Place the tips of the fingers of the other hand under the wrist, and gently press against the lower end of the radius (the bone which connects with the thumb side of the wrist). You should be able to feel your pulse, although you may have to move your finger-tips to find the position at which it is strongest. Using a stop-watch, or a watch with a sweep seconds hand, count the number of pulses in one minute. This is your normal pulse rate, assuming that you have not recently been doing any strenuous exercise.

Now, step up on a chair and down again twenty times. As soon as you have done this, count your pulse rate during the first minute, the second minute, the third minute, and so on, recording your results until your pulse rate has returned to normal. The fitter you are, the sooner your pulse rate will return to normal after exercise. This test is fairly reliable for comparing your own fitness at different times, but it would be extremely unreliable for comparing the relative fitness of people of different weights. Can you explain why this is so?

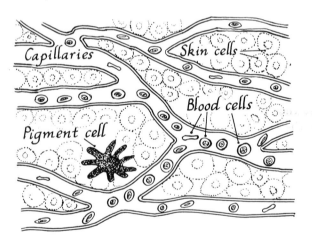

Figure 11.11 Blood flowing through capillaries

Arteries are blood vessels which carry blood from the heart. They have thick walls to withstand the pressure at which the heart pumps blood through them. This pressure is variable because the heart is not a continuous pump but forces the blood into the arteries at regular intervals (there is a pulse every time the heart contracts). To accommodate the variable pressure, the artery walls are elastic. Farther away from the heart the arteries branch off into smaller and smaller vessels until they become so narrow that the variation in pressure reduces to an almost negligible amount.

198

Capillaries are the very small blood vessels through which the arterial blood is forced. The capillaries are so narrow that the blood cells can only pass through them in single file (see Figure 11.11). It is through the walls of the capillaries that oxygen, carbon dioxide, digested nutrients and waste products are transferred. When the capillaries have reached the point where these substances have been transferred, they join together forming larger vessels, rather like tributaries flowing into a river.

Veins are blood vessels which carry blood from the capillaries back to the heart. They have thinner walls than arteries. The pressure of the blood in the veins is practically constant; blood will ooze from a cut vein but it will spurt from a cut artery. The larger veins have valves at intervals along their length. These valves ensure that excessive pressure does not build up in the veins because of the force of gravity acting on the blood. Once blood has passed a valve, it cannot return past it because the valve closes. The action of a valve can be compared with the action of the ratchet and pawl mechanism of a ratchet jack, as shown in Figure 11.12.

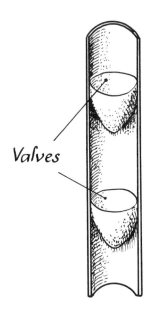

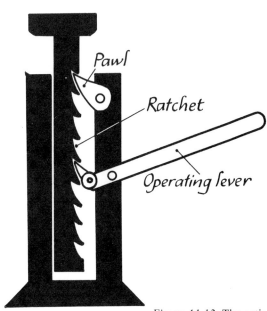

Figure 11.12 The action of valves

The regulation of body temperature is an important function of the blood. If some of the heat energy produced by internal respiration was not removed, body temperature would become excessive. In order that the body may be maintained at its correct working temperature, excess heat is dispersed by the blood in the capillaries, and released through the skin to the surrounding air. Because there are many capillaries, each having a small diameter, the blood is in contact with a comparatively large surface area (see Figure 11.13).

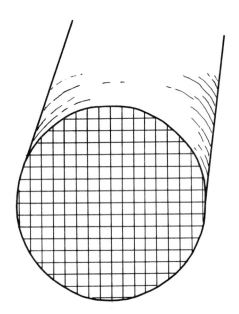

LARGE BLOOD VESSEL

Figure 11.13 Capillaries as cooling tubes

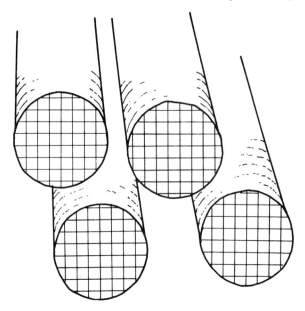

SMALLER BLOOD VESSELS *carrying the same volume of blood but having a much greater surface area*

This method of heat dispersal can be compared with the cooling system of a car, as shown in Table 11.3. When the blood temperature increases, the capillaries close to the skin dilate (become larger in diameter). This allows a relatively greater flow of blood and, consequently, produces a greater cooling effect. This is why the skin reddens during exercise. In cold weather, or when the body is relatively inactive, heat must be conserved in order to maintain body temperature. Under these conditions, the capillaries close to the skin contract, thus reducing the flow of blood and reducing the cooling effect.

TABLE 11.3. COOLING SYSTEMS OF THE BODY AND A CAR

	Body	Car
Heat generated in	Muscle cells	Cylinder
Transporting medium	Blood	Water
Pump	Heart	Water pump
Heat given out by	Capillaries near the surface	Thin tubes in the radiator core
Heat given to	Surrounding air	Air passing through the radiator core

11.8. The nervous system

In order that the body may live, all of its functions must be controlled. In a car, this control is the responsibility of the driver. In the body, it is the brain which exercises control. The control of a car, an aeroplane, a factory, a business firm or anything else, involves a two-way communications system and a controller.

Information entering the nervous system can be considered as being one of five types. Each type of information is detected by a sense organ (see Table 11.4).

TABLE 11.4. THE SENSES AND THEIR ORGANS

Sense	Organ
Sight	Eye
Sound	Ear
Taste	Tongue
Smell	Nose
Touch	Skin

The most important of our senses are sight and sound, because over 90 per cent of our knowledge is received through the eyes and ears. The structure and function of the eye have been dealt with in Chapter 9 and the ear in Chapter 10.

Taste is detected by the tongue, the surface of which is covered with taste buds. There are four basic tastes: sweetness, sourness, bitterness and saltiness. All other tastes are a combination of two or more of the basic tastes in varying proportions. Each of the basic tastes is detected by taste buds in a particular region of the tongue.

Investigation 11e. Making a taste map of the tongue

Obtain the following substances to stimulate the basic tastes:

> Sweetness: sugar solution (saturated)
> Sourness: lemon juice or vinegar
> Bitterness: tincture of quinine (well diluted)
> Saltiness: solution of common salt (saturated).

Using a different glass rod for each of the liquids, to avoid mixing the tastes, touch a drop of each liquid on the tip, centre, back and along the side of the tongue. Note which region responds to each of the four basic tastes. Now, draw a diagram of the tongue and label the taste regions.

Little Johnny, aged five, may be encouraged to take some bitter tasting medicine if he is bribed by the offer of a sweet 'to take the nasty taste away'. He soon discovers, however, that the bitter taste remains, because the sweetness is detected by a different set of taste buds in a different region of his tongue. The best way to take an unpleasant-tasting medicine (not that all medicines are unpleasant) is to numb the tongue with something cold just before taking it. Sucking an ice-cube or eating an ice-cream are excellent methods of numbing the tongue, and thus reducing the sensitivity of the taste buds.

Smell is detected by nerve endings in the lining of the nostrils which respond to the presence of particles in the air passing through the nose. You will know that when you have a cold, food does not taste as good as when you are well.

Investigation 11f. The effect of smell on taste

First, find a volunteer. Blindfold him so that he cannot see what you are giving him to taste. Ask him to hold his nose or, better still, put a padded clothes peg on his nose so that he cannot smell. Now, place a small piece (about 1 cm^3) of apple in his mouth and ask him to identify it. Repeat this with small pieces of foods of similar texture: pear, marrow, raw potato, beetroot, turnip, parsnip, swede, etc. Make a record of the foods and his identification of them. Now, repeat the process with your volunteer's nose free to smell the foods, but alter the order in which you give them to him. Is his identification more accurate when he can smell the food? Can you see the reason for choosing foods of similar texture for this investigation?

A cold reduces the sensitivity of your sense of smell, because the nerve endings in the nostrils are covered with mucus.

Touch is detected by nerve endings in the skin. Different types of nerve endings respond to different stimuli. Some respond to pressure while others respond to heat or coldness (lack of heat). The distribution of the different types varies from one region of the body to another. A region where the nerve endings are close together is more sensitive to a particular stimulus than a region in which they are farther apart.

Investigation 11g. Sensitivity of touch

This investigation must be carried out by two people, an investigator and a subject. Stick three pins into a cork, one in one end and the other two in the other end, so that the heads are level and about 1 cm apart. Blindfold the subject and touch him with either the single pin-head or the two pin-heads on various parts of the body. Ask the subject to tell you each time whether he feels one pin or two. Record your results in a table under three column headings: 'part of body', 'number of pins' and 'subject's reaction'. Which part of the subject's body is most sensitive and which part is least sensitive? The roles of the investigator and the subject should now be reversed. How does this set of results compare with the first set?

Sensory nerves are those which transmit information from the sense organs to the brain, either directly, as in the case of the sensory nerves leading from the sense organs in the skull, or by way of the spinal cord.

The brain receives a mass of information from the sensory nerves and sorts it out into three types. One type of information requires immediate action to ensure the comfort and safety of the body. The second type requires no immediate action but may be of use in the future; this type of information is stored in a part of the brain which we call the memory. The third type is routine information which arrives in the brain at regular intervals to inform the brain that all is well; the brain will only take action if this type of routine information is not received on time.

The brain can be considered in three sections. The **cerebrum** is the largest part, extending from the forehead to the back of the skull. This is the part of the brain which we use while we are conscious to control movement of the voluntary muscles (see Section 11.2) and for conscious thought (i.e. learning and making decisions). When we are asleep or under general anaesthesia, the cerebrum is temporarily out of action. Below the cerebrum, at the back of the skull, is the **cerebellum**, which is smaller than the cerebrum and controls our balance and semi-automatic functions, such as the counter movement

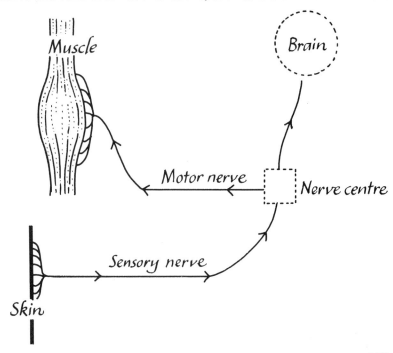

Figure 11.14 A simple reflex action

of the arms when we walk. Below the cerebellum is the **medulla**, which controls vital automatic functions, such as the heart-beat and peristalsis.

Motor nerves are those which transmit orders from the brain to the muscles, controlling their contraction and relaxation.

The spinal cord is a chain of nerve centres in the vertebral column. Both sensory nerves and motor nerves pass through the spinal cord. A nerve centre in the spinal cord is capable of taking immediate action when an emergency signal being transmitted along a sensory nerve to the brain passes through it. The nerve centre short-circuits the signal to the appropriate motor nerve which actuates the muscles while the sensory nerve is still passing the signal to the brain. In this way, the appropriate action is taken at the earliest possible moment while the brain is being informed of the situation and the action that has been taken. This type of action is called a **simple reflex action** (see Figure 11.14).

Investigation 11h. Finding the speed of nervous impulse

For this investigation you will need nine volunteers and a stop-watch. Arrange your volunteers in a circle, holding hands, as shown in Figure 11.15(a), leaving a gap for you. Tell each volunteer that as soon as he feels his left hand being squeezed, he is to pass the

A

Figure 11.15(a) Arrangements for Investigation 11h

squeeze to the volunteer on his right. Hold the stop-watch in your left hand and the hand of the volunteer on your right with your right hand. Start the stop-watch and squeeze your right hand, both at the same time. Quickly, while the squeeze is passing round the circle,

204

transfer the stop-watch to your right hand and hold the hand of the volunteer on your left with your left hand. As soon as you feel your left hand being squeezed, stop the stop-watch and note the time. Repeat this several times until the time taken for the squeeze to pass round the circle remains constant. Now, measure the nerve path. For each person (including yourself), the nerve path will be from the hand to the spine, up the spine to the brain, back down the spine to a point level with the shoulders and along the other arm. Divide the length of the total nerve path by the shortest time taken to pass the squeeze round the circle and you will have some idea of the speed of nervous impulse for your particular group of volunteers.

C

Figure 11.15(b) and (c)
Further steps in
Investigation 11h

Repeat this investigation, using different nerve paths, as shown in Figure 11.15(b) and (c). Calculate the speeds of nervous impulse for these arrangements, and compare them with your original result.

Although this investigation will give you some idea of the speed of nervous impulse, it is not an accurate method. Try to decide where your measurements in this investigation are inaccurate.

Reducing the function of the nervous system into simple terms: the sense organs respond to stimuli; these responses are transmitted through the sensory nerves to the brain (or one of the nerve centres in the spinal cord in the case of a simple reflex action), which considers the situation, decides what action (if any) needs to be taken, and transmits orders for such action, through the motor nerves, to the muscles.

In order for the brain to perform its functions efficiently, it must be supplied with a considerable amount of oxygen. It obtains this oxygen from the blood. Excessive loss of blood or an inadequate supply of blood to the brain are the major causes of fainting.

11.9. The endocrine system

The endocrine system consists of a number of glands, each of which produces a substance called a **hormone**. The endocrine glands are also known as **ductless glands**, to distinguish them from other glands which produce and secrete (give out) fluids through small openings called ducts. Examples of ducted glands include the tear glands, salivary glands and sweat glands, each secreting its product directly to the part of the body for which it is intended—in these examples, the eye, the mouth and the skin. The hormones from the endocrine glands are secreted into the bloodstream, which carries them to all parts of the body. Hormones act as chemical messengers, each hormone having an effect on the rate at which a particular vital function takes place.

Three examples of hormones are **thyroxin, adrenalin** and **insulin**. Thyroxin is produced by the **thyroid gland**, which is situated in the lower part of the neck. A deficiency of thyroxin tends to reduce the normal growth rate (although this can be caused by many other factors), pulse rate, breathing rate and overall mental activity. A person with an over-active thyroid gland has a faster pulse rate, a faster breathing rate, and tends to be more quick-witted and more excitable.

Adrenalin is produced by the **adrenal** (or **supra-renal**) glands, which are situated just above the kidneys. Under normal conditions, a small, steady supply of adrenalin enters the bloodstream. During times of emotional stress caused by fear, excitement or danger, the adrenal glands secrete a much larger amount of adrenalin. The effect of additional adrenalin is to stimulate the heart. This stimulation increases the pulse rate, thereby increasing the blood supply to the muscles. The next time you see a cat cornered by a dog, the cat's back arched and the dog snarling, you may be certain that these effects are the result of an increase in the activity of the adrenal glands.

Insulin is produced by some of the cells in the pancreas, other cells producing pancreatic juice which is secreted into the small intestine. The presence of insulin in the blood enables muscle cells (and others) to utilize the simple sugars which are the products of digestion and are carried, in solution, by the blood. A shortage of insulin causes **diabetes**.

11.10. The liver

The liver weighs about 1·4 kg and is situated just below the diaphragm. The functions of the liver can be compared with the functions of a chemical factory and a storehouse.

Red blood cells perform their oxygen-carrying function for about six weeks and are then destroyed by the liver. The iron from the haemoglobin is extracted, to be used in the marrow of the long bones to make new red cells. The remainder of the red cells is passed to the gall bladder, producing the yellow colour in bile.

Protein foods are converted by the digestive system into amino acids. As blood passes through the liver, any amino acids in excess of the body's growth and repair requirements are converted into **urea**, which is later excreted by the kidneys and, to a lesser extent, by the skin.

The sugar content of the blood is controlled by the liver. Blood flowing from the capillaries of the small intestine contains blood-sugar; it flows through a large vein called the **hepatic portal vein** into the liver. Blood leaving the liver through the **hepatic vein** (and thence, via the inferior vena cava, to the heart) contains a regulated concentration of blood-sugar, depending on the body's energy requirements. In order to perform its functions, the liver must have oxygen. The blood entering the liver through the hepatic portal vein contains very little oxygen, so the liver receives an independent supply of oxygenated blood through the **hepatic artery,** which branches from the aorta (see Figure 11.10).

When a meal has been digested, the amount of blood-sugar flowing into the liver is greatly in excess of the body's energy requirements. The excess is converted and stored in the liver in the form of a starch-like substance called **glycogen**. As time elapses after a meal, the amount of blood-sugar entering the liver decreases until it is less than the body's energy requirements. When this occurs, the liver converts some of the glycogen back into blood-sugar to maintain a steady supply. This function of the liver is illustrated in Figure 11.16.

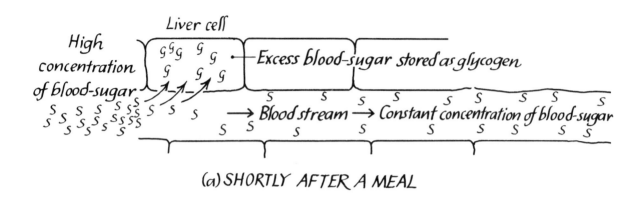

(a) SHORTLY AFTER A MEAL

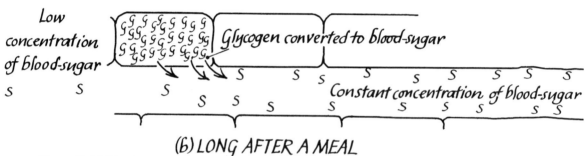

(b) LONG AFTER A MEAL

Figure 11.16 Blood-sugar regulation by the liver

11.11. The excretory system

Many substances enter the body. Waste products which are formed by the chemical processes of the body must be removed. These waste products are mainly water, carbon dioxide, urea and salt. Solid waste, which largely consists of the indigestible parts of our food, is removed by way of the rectum and the anus as faeces. The removal of this solid material is not true excretion, as much of the material has never left the alimentary canal.

There are three excretory organs: the lungs, the skin and the kidneys.

Investigation 11i. Expired air

1. Make a note of the air temperature. Now, breathe on the bulb of a thermometer and note the change in temperature.

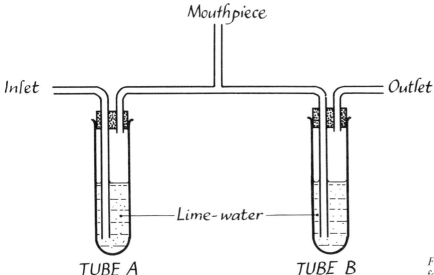

Mouthpiece

Inlet

Outlet

Lime-water

TUBE A

TUBE B

Figure 11.17 Apparatus for Investigation 11i (3)

2. Breathe on a cold, smooth, dry surface (glass or polished metal are ideal). What happens to the surface? Check your answer by touching the surface with a piece of dry cobalt(II) chloride paper.

3. Half fill two boiling tubes with lime-water and connect them with tubing, as shown in Figure 11.17. Breathe in and out through the mouthpiece, blocking the outlet tube when breathing in and blocking the inlet tube when breathing out. By doing this, inspired air will pass through the lime-water in tube A and expired air will pass through the lime-water in tube B.

From the results of the three parts of this investigation, can you name three differences between inspired air and expired air?

The skin performs many functions: it is a barrier between the body and disease bacteria and viruses, the largest sense organ of the body, the major temperature regulator of the body and an excretory organ for the removal of water, salt and traces of urea. The skin consists of two main layers: the **epidermis** and the **dermis**. The epidermis is the upper layer, the surface of which is made up of dead cells. Its thickness is not the same in all parts of the body. Parts of the skin which are constantly subjected to friction will become thick and hard; these pads of hard skin are called **callouses**. When the skin is washed, some of the dead cells are removed from the surface of the epidermis. You may have noticed that a brisk towelling after a long soak in a warm bath often produces 'rolls of dirt'. These are rolls of dead skin cells.

Between the epidermis and the dermis is the **Malpighian layer**. This layer contains deposits of pigments (mainly melanin), which produce our characteristic skin colour.

209

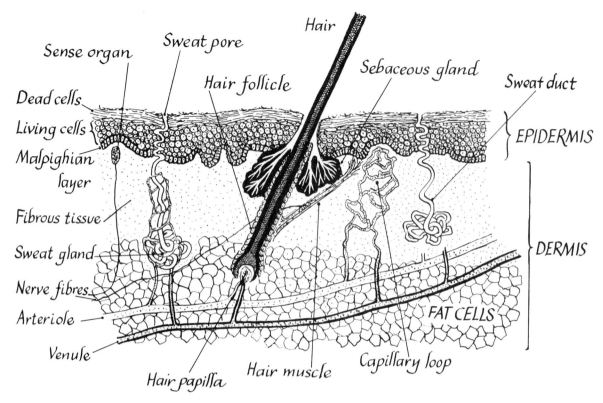

Sense organ
Sweat pore
Hair
Sebaceous gland
Sweat duct

Dead cells
Living cells
Malpighian layer

Hair follicle

EPIDERMIS

Fibrous tissue

DERMIS

Sweat gland

Nerve fibres

Arteriole

FAT CELLS

Venule

Hair papilla
Hair muscle
Capillary loop

Figure 11.18 Cross-section
of the skin (diagrammatic)

The dermis is a somewhat thicker layer of cells. This layer has
nerves and a blood supply. Throughout the dermis there are **sweat
glands**, which are tangled tubes in close contact with the capillaries.
Water, salt and traces of urea are diffused from the blood through
the capillary walls to the sweat glands. This secretion is passed
through ducts (commonly called pores) which emerge through the
epidermis to the surface. Figure 11.18 shows a diagrammatic view of
a cross-section of the skin.

The **sebaceous glands** secrete a greasy substance called **sebum**
which lubricates the skin and keeps it pliable. In the case of sheep,
this natural grease is called **lanolin**, which is the basis of many
cosmetics.

The kidneys, situated one on each side of the vertebral column,
are supplied with blood by the **renal arteries**, which branch off from
the aorta. Inside each kidney, the renal artery branches into many
capillaries which are in close contact with minute 'dead-end' tubes
called **nephrons** or **kidney tubes**. The 'dead-end' of a nephron is
called a **Bowman's capsule** and is shaped rather like the top of a
thistle funnel. The capillary in the Bowman's capsule is convoluted
(twisted like a tangled bundle of string), thus presenting a large surface area. As blood flows through the capillary in the Bowman's

capsule, most of the water, together with the substances dissolved in it, is filtered through into the nephron, leaving the plasma, red and white cells and the platelets. Farther along the nephron, some of the water and the useful dissolved substances, including blood-sugar, are re-absorbed into the blood. The excess water, salt and urea then pass through the remainder of the nephron, which connects with the other nephrons into a tube called the **ureter**. The liquid, which is called **urine**, passes down into the ureter and into the **bladder**, from which it is removed from time to time through the **urethra** (see Figure 11.19).

The blood which has been treated by the nephrons in the kidneys is passed into the **renal vein** and thence, via the inferior vena cava, to the heart.

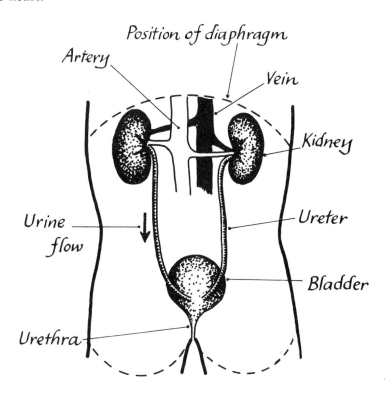

Figure 11.19 The kidneys

Figure 11.20 shows the input of materials into the body, their route from one system to another, and their eventual excretion.

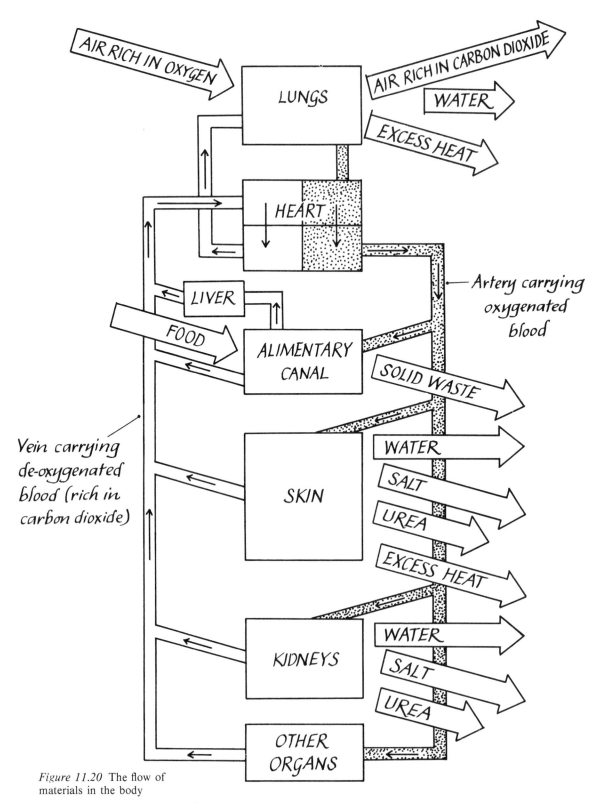

Figure 11.20 The flow of materials in the body

1. Name the types of joint between (a) the humerus and the scapula, (b) the femur and the tibia, (c) the phalanges, (d) the carpal bones.
2. Name the raw materials needed by muscles in order for them to function.
3. What is the difference between external respiration and internal respiration?
4. What are the functions of the red cells, the white cells and fibrinogen?
5. About how many red cells would you expect to find in one cubic milli-metre of normal healthy human blood?
6. Why is it not safe for a patient with blood group A to be given a transfusion of blood group B?
7. How does inoculation protect the body against disease?
8. Describe the route taken by the blood from the vena cava to the aorta.
9. What are the main differences between arteries and veins?
10. Why does holding your nose reduce the unpleasantness of drinking a bitter-tasting liquid?
11. A small piece of grit in your mouth feels much larger than the same piece of grit between your fingers. Can you explain why this is so?
12. Why does injury to the spine sometimes result in paralysis of the lower part of the body?
13. When the driver of a car sees the need to apply his brakes, there is a time lag before he does so. What causes this time lag or reaction time?
14. If you were being chased across a field by a mad bull, you would probably run much faster than you could under normal circumstances. Explain the cause of this temporary athletic ability.
15. How does the liver regulate the supply of blood-sugar?
16. In what ways are the functions of the skin and the kidneys similar?
17. Why does the heart beat faster when you hold your breath?

Chapter 12

Reproduction

All living organisms have a limited life span. In order for a species to survive, it is necessary for new individuals to be produced. This process is called **reproduction.**

12.1. Asexual reproduction

Most very simple organisms reproduce by dividing into two. The amoeba reproduces in this way. When the parent cell has fully grown, the nucleus duplicates itself; the cytoplasm then splits into two halves, each with a nucleus. The parent cell thus ceases to exist, but continues as two identical offspring. This is represented in Figure 12.1. Reproduction of this kind is **asexual** reproduction.

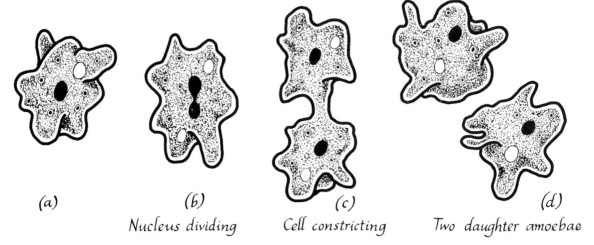

(a)   (b)   (c)   (d)

Nucleus dividing   Cell constricting   Two daughter amoebae

Figure 12.1 Reproduction of an amoeba

Some multicellular organisms also reproduce asexually. This is usually achieved by some part of the parent body becoming detached to form the offspring. This occurs in the vegetative reproduction of plants, such as the potato and the strawberry.

When asexual reproduction takes place, the offspring can be expected to be exactly like the parent.

214

12.2. Sexual reproduction

Most of the higher plants and animals make use of **sexual repro-duction**. In this process, the parents produce special germ cells called **gametes**. There are two kinds of gamete: the **sperm** and the **ovum**. The production of sperm is essentially a male function, while the production of ova, or eggs, is a female function. Figure 12.2 shows typical male and female gametes.

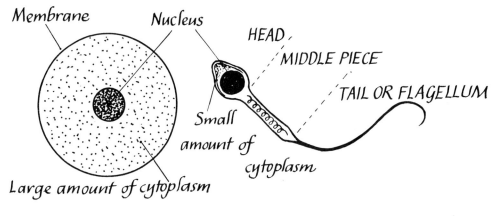

EGG – female gamete   SPERM – male gamete
(not to same scale)

Figure 12.2 Male and female gametes

In order for a new individual to be produced, it is necessary for the nucleus of a sperm cell to join with the nucleus of an ovum. This process is called **fertilization**, and once it has taken place, the new cell, called a **zygote**, can begin to grow.

The fertilized ovum (zygote) then forms many cells by repeated division (see Chapter 13). This many-celled organism is called an **embryo**. At first, the cells of the embryo are all alike, but as the embryo develops, the cells become specialized. These specialized cells will form different parts of the new individual.

12.3. Flowers

In plants, the purpose of the flower is reproduction.

Investigation 12a. Dissection of a flower

For this investigation you will need a hand lens, a piece of white paper, forceps, a needle and a flower (a buttercup or a wallflower would be suitable).

Remove the outermost parts of the flower with the aid of the forceps and needle. Arrange these in a ring near the edge of the white

215

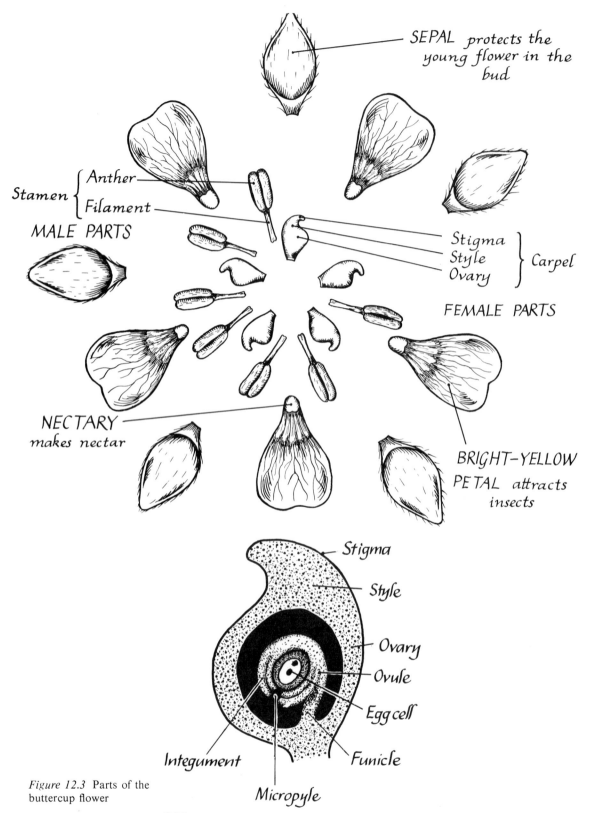

SEPAL *protects the young flower in the bud*

Anther
Filament
Stamen { Anther, Filament }
MALE PARTS

Stigma
Style
Ovary
} Carpel

FEMALE PARTS

NECTARY *makes nectar*

BRIGHT-YELLOW PETAL *attracts insects*

Stigma

Style

Ovary

Ovule

Egg cell

Funicle

Integument

Micropyle

Figure 12.3 Parts of the buttercup flower

paper. The first parts you will remove are green scales called **sepals**. Note how many there are. Can you suggest the purpose of these?

Next, you come to the **petals**. Remove them, count them and arrange them on the white paper. The petals of the buttercup have a scale at their base covering a nectary, which produces a sugary solution called **nectar.**

You should now be able to see the **stamens**. These are the male sex organs of the flower. Each of them consists of a stalk (or filament) with an **anther** at its tip. The anther produces the pollen grains, which contain the male gametes. Remove the stamens and place them on the paper.

You will now be left with the **carpels**. These are the female sex organs of the flower. In the buttercup, there will be a large number of separate carpels, but the wallflower has a single **pistil**. Each carpel consists of a sticky surface called the **stigma**, a **style** and an **ovary**.

Figure 12.3 shows the parts of the buttercup flower.

Investigation 12b. Vertical section of a flower

Take a flower and cut it from its stalk close to the flower. Hold the flower between your thumb and forefinger and cut the flower into halves, using a sharp knife. Make a large, clear drawing of half your flower and label the parts. Write down what each part does.

Figure 12.4 shows a vertical section through a wallflower.

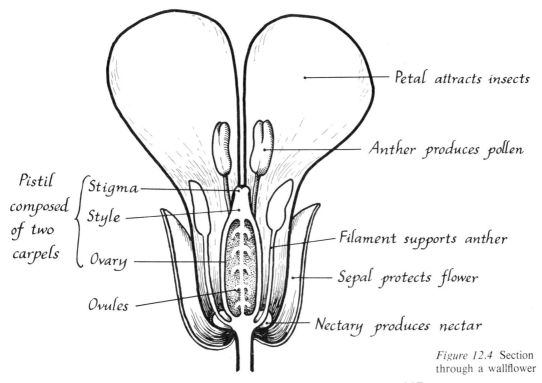

Figure 12.4 Section through a wallflower

217

12.4. Pollination

Flowers form the fruits which contain seeds. Before the flower can begin to form the fruit, it must be pollinated. Pollination occurs when pollen from the stamens of a flower is deposited on the stigma of a flower of the same species. Pollination is mainly brought about by insects or wind (see Figure 12.5).

Figure 12.5 Wind pollination and insect pollination

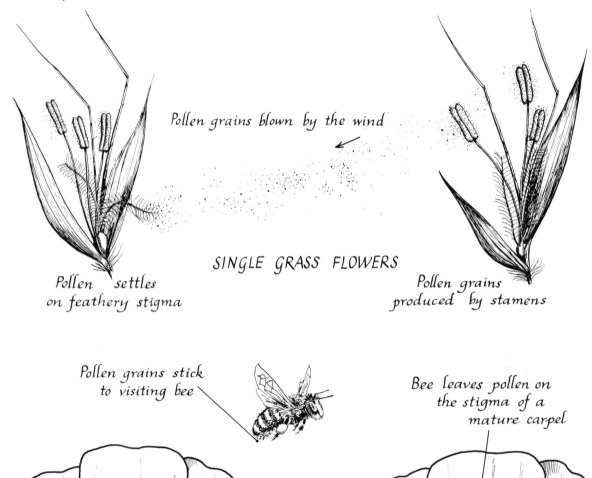

Pollen grains blown by the wind

SINGLE GRASS FLOWERS

Pollen settles on feathery stigma

Pollen grains produced by stamens

Pollen grains stick to visiting bee

Bee leaves pollen on the stigma of a mature carpel

Mature stamens produce pollen

Young carpels

Nectary

Withered stamens

Nectary

a. Pollination by insects

The flowers which are pollinated by insects usually have large colourful petals and produce scent and nectar. Insects, such as bees, are attracted to such flowers. Bees collect nectar in order to make honey and pollen to feed to their young grubs or larvae. As a bee moves from flower to flower, pollen from the stamens of one flower sticks to it and may be brushed off as the bee passes the sticky stigma of the next flower it visits.

b. Pollination by wind

The flowers of grasses and many common trees do not have brightly coloured petals and do not produce nectar and scent. They do, however, produce large quantities of light pollen grains. Their stamens have long filaments which trail out of the flower, so that the wind can carry away the pollen grains. The stigmas of these flowers are branched and feathery, so that they can easily pick up pollen grains being carried in the wind.

12.5. Fertilization in flowers

The pollen grain contains the male gamete, and the ovule, within the ovary of the carpel, contains the egg cell. Before the ovule can develop into a seed, the egg cell inside it must be fertilized by joining with the male cell from the pollen grain.

Figure 12.6 Fertilization in the buttercup

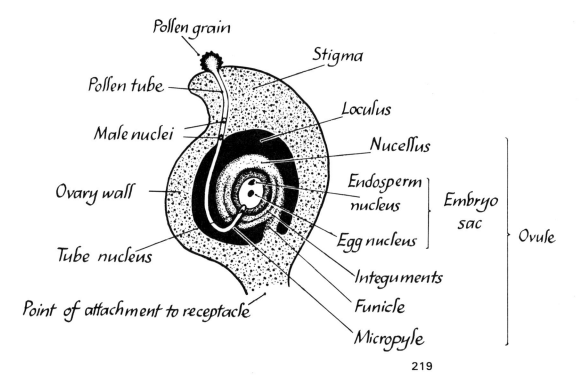

219

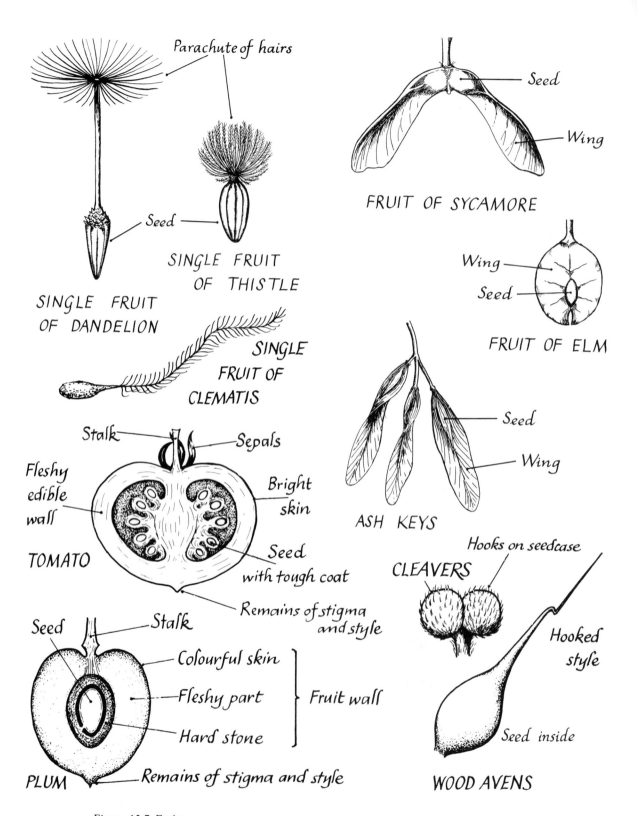

Parachute of hairs

Seed

SINGLE FRUIT
OF THISTLE

SINGLE FRUIT
OF DANDELION

Seed

Wing

FRUIT OF SYCAMORE

Wing

Seed

FRUIT OF ELM

SINGLE
FRUIT OF
CLEMATIS

Seed

Wing

ASH KEYS

Stalk   Sepals

Fleshy
edible
wall

Bright
skin

Seed
with tough coat

TOMATO

Remains of stigma
and style

Hooks on seedcase

CLEAVERS

Seed   Stalk

Colourful skin

Fleshy part   Fruit wall

Hard stone

PLUM   Remains of stigma and style

Hooked
style

Seed inside

WOOD AVENS

Figure 12.7 Fruits

220

A pollen tube grows from the pollen grain down the style to the ovule. The male cell then passes down the tube into the ovule, where it fuses with the egg cell to form a zygote. This zygote grows into an embryo, the ovule becomes the seed, and the whole carpel becomes the fruit.

Figure 12.6 represents the fertilization of the egg cell in a buttercup.

12.6. Fruits

Investigation 12c. Examination of fruits

Obtain as many different fruits as you can. Cut each in half. Make a note of what you find inside each fruit. What do you find in every one?

Figure 12.7 shows the fruits of a number of different plants.

12.7. Fruit and seed dispersal

In order that the new plants should stand a good chance of growing to maturity, it is necessary that they must be scattered as far away from the parent plant as possible. This scattering must be done at the fruit or seed stage. Dispersal of fruits and seeds is done in a number of ways.

a. Wind dispersal

Seeds and fruits scattered in this way are very light. Sometimes a wing-like extension of the pericarp assists in such dispersal. Fruits of the elm, ash and sycamore are of this type. The fruits of the dandelion and thistle have a parachute of fine fibres.

b. Dispersal by animals

Animals help to scatter fruits in two ways. The first method is by the fruit clinging to the fur of a passing animal, and then dropping off at a great distance from the parent plant. Fruits scattered in this way usually have hooks on the pericarp. Examples are wood avens and cleavers (goose grass).

The second method by which animals scatter fruits is by eating them. The plum, for example, has juicy flesh which is pleasant to eat, but the stone is not palatable, so the animal spits it out some distance from the parent plant.

Fruits such as the strawberry, raspberry, gooseberry and tomato have no hard stones like the plum, so the seeds are swallowed. The seeds have a hard coat which resists the digestive juices of the animal, so they pass through the digestive system and are left behind in the droppings, where they can grow into new plants.

c. Dispersal by water

Water helps to scatter the fruits of certain plants which live by the banks of rivers. The fruit of the coconut is light and buoyant. It floats away and may eventually be washed up on a beach where the seed it contains develops into a new tree.

d. Explosive dispersal

The seeds of some plants are scattered violently by explosion. The pea family have pods, or **legumes**, for their fruits. When the seeds are ripe, part of the pod dries more quickly than the rest. This causes tension in the pod wall, which results in the pod bursting open and scattering the seeds that it contains.

12.8. Seeds

A seed develops from a fertilized ovule. It consists of an embryo or baby plant, a supply of food to get it started in life and a protective coat called a **testa**.

Investigation 12d. The structure of a seed

Examine a broad bean seed which has been soaked in water for a day or two. Make two large drawings of it, one from the flat side and the other from the narrow end. Label the pale brown testa, the black scar (called the **hilum**) where it was attached to the pod, and the position of the young root, or **radicle**.

Figure 12.8 The broad bean seed

Squeeze the seed between your thumb and forefinger and observe the tip of the radicle. Did you notice a drop of fluid bubbling out of

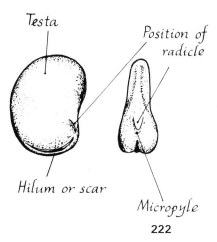

Testa

Position of radicle

Hilum or scar

Micropyle

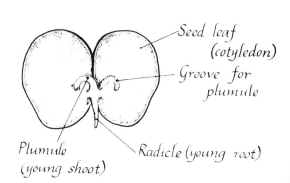

Seed leaf (cotyledon)

Groove for plumule

Plumule (young shoot)

Radicle (young root)

a tiny hole? This hole is called the **micropyle** and it is the place where water first enters the seed.

Carefully remove the testa and look at its inner surface. Look for a pocket with a little hole at the bottom. What do you think fitted into this pocket?

Now open out the seed carefully. Notice the radicle and the young shoot, or **plumule**, which is hooked and fits into a hollow in the seed leaves.

Figure 12.8 shows the broad bean seed. The seed leaves of the broad bean contain stored food. Carry out a test to see if any of this is starch.

12.9. Germination of seeds

A seed contains stored food to provide it with nourishment until it is an independent plant, having green leaves with which it can produce its own food by photosynthesis. The process of changing from a seed into a self-supporting plant is called **germination**.

Investigation 12e. Germination of the broad bean seed

For this investigation you will need a jam-jar, a piece of blotting paper, some sawdust and two or three broad bean seeds which have been soaked in water for twenty-four hours.

Line the jar with blotting paper, trap the seeds between the glass and the blotting paper and pack the jar with sawdust, as shown in Figure 12.9.

Figure 12.9 Germination of broad bean seeds

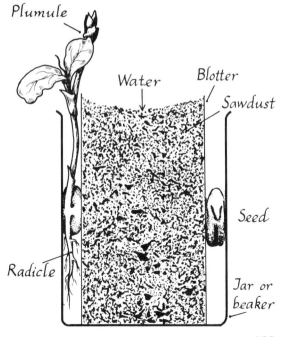

Plumule

Water

Blotter

Sawdust

Seed

Radicle

Jar or beaker

223

Moisten the sawdust and place the apparatus in a light, warm position. Observe the progress every day and draw the apparatus twice a week. Note which appears first, the radicle or the plumule.

12.10. Sexual reproduction in animals

Most of the higher animals reproduce sexually. In the process of fertilization, the sperm are attracted by chemical substances given out by the ova of their own species. The sperm cells surround the ovum and one of the sperm penetrates the outer membrane of the

Figure 12.10 Fertilization

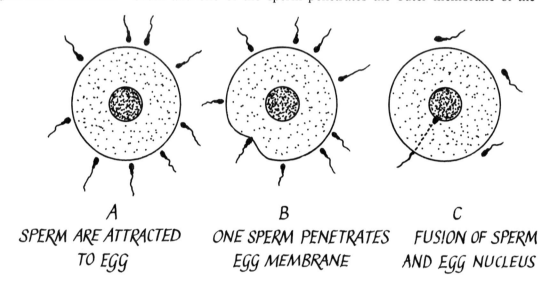

| A | B | C |
| SPERM ARE ATTRACTED TO EGG | ONE SPERM PENETRATES EGG MEMBRANE | FUSION OF SPERM AND EGG NUCLEUS |

ovum. The head of the sperm then breaks off from the tail and fuses with the nucleus of the ovum. Chemical changes occur so that no more sperm may enter the ovum.

In the case of water-dwelling creatures, fertilization of the eggs must take place shortly after the female has laid them, but once fertilized, the eggs will develop in water without any special care being required of the parents. There is a serious risk, however, that the fertilized eggs will be eaten by other creatures.

a. The frog

When frogs mate, the male mounts the back of the female, holding her firmly by means of special pads on his thumbs. The female lays a mass of eggs, and the male ejects sperm on to them. The water causes the eggs to swell, making a jelly-like mass known as frog spawn. The male produces many more sperm than are required to fertilize the eggs, because the sperm do not survive long in water and most of them die before succeeding in fertilizing an egg.

The fertilized eggs develop into tadpoles, which change over a period of weeks into frogs. At the tadpole stage, the young creature is equipped with gills and can live only in water, but the adult frog has a well-developed lung and is an air breather.

It is worthwhile to keep some tadpoles in the laboratory, and to observe their development.

Land-dwelling creatures have a special problem in that neither eggs nor sperm can survive very long in air. The eggs are often prevented from drying up by a shell being developed around them. The egg must be fertilized before this shell forms and so the male often has a specially developed organ for injecting sperm into the body of the female.

b. Mammals

This is the most highly developed group of creatures, and includes man. They all suckle their young (i.e. the female is equipped with special glands which produce milk, on which the offspring live during the early part of their lives). Fertilization occurs internally, the male having a special organ, the **penis**, which enables him to pass sperm into the female.

Figure 12.11 The life cycle of the frog

MALE

Young frog jumps out

External gill stage

Tail absorbed

Sperms shed on to eggs

FEMALE

Internal gill stage

Jelly swells

Limbs develop

The fertilized egg develops into an embryo, which is protected and sustained within the mother's body during the early stages. This period is called the period of **gestation**. In humans the period of gestation is about nine months, but different species have different periods of gestation. At the end of this period, the young creature is born, but is not usually able to fend for itself for some time. During this period its mother's milk is its only food. Table 12.1 compares the gestation periods of various mammals.

TABLE 12.1. GESTATION PERIODS

Mammal	Period of Gestation/days
Mouse	20
Rat	22
Rabbit	32
Cat	56
Dog	65
Sheep	150
Man	280

12.11. Reproduction in human beings

Male sexual organs

The organs reponsible for the production of sperm are two glands called the **testes**. These lie between the legs and are contained in a bag called the **scrotal sac**. Each of these glands consists of a large number of coiled tubes. All these tubes join to form the sperm tube, a long duct which passes upward and enters the abdomen. This duct traverses the prostate gland and then joins the urethra, which passes downward and through the penis (see Figure 12.12).

Female sexual organs

The organs producing ova are the ovaries. There are two of these, each about the size of a large almond. They lie embedded in a mass of supporting tissue in the lower part of the abdomen. At birth, the ovaries contain about 100 000 immature ova, all that will be developed during the life of the woman. When an ovum matures, it breaks through the lining of the ovary to enter the abdominal cavity. Here it lies near to petal-like processes at the end of the **Fallopian tube**. These processes take the ovum into the Fallopian tube, which is lined with cells possessing hair-like structures which move to carry the ovum into the tube and along it to the **uterus**, or womb. The lower part of the uterus leads directly to the vagina. Figure 12.13 shows the female reproductive organs.

226

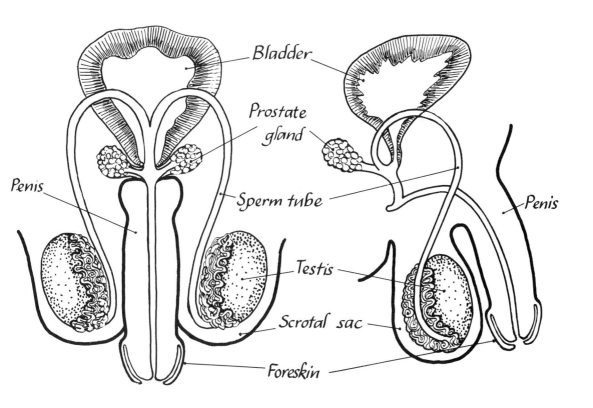

Bladder

Prostate
gland

Penis

Sperm tube

Testis

Scrotal sac

Foreskin

Penis

FRONT VIEW

SIDE VIEW

Figure 12.12 Male
reproductive organs

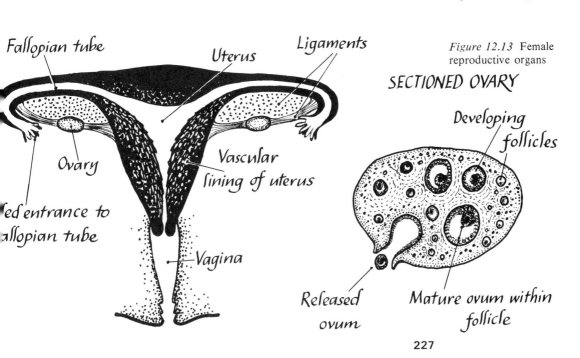

Fallopian tube

Uterus

Ligaments

Ovary

Vascular
lining of uterus

ed entrance to
allopian tube

Vagina

Figure 12.13 Female
reproductive organs

SECTIONED OVARY

Developing
follicles

Released
ovum

Mature ovum within
follicle

227

Fertilization

During sexual intercourse the penis becomes stiffened and erect from a large increase in the volume of blood in the blood vessels in its tissues. It is then inserted into the vagina and, by thrusting movements, the ejaculation of sperm is stimulated. As many as 250 million sperm may be introduced at one time into the vagina in this way.

The sperm propel themselves by lashing movements of their tails and eventually reach the Fallopian tubes. If a mature ovum is present, one of the sperm may succeed in fertilizing it. If no mature ovum is present the sperm will die after several days.

Development of the embryo

If the ovum is fertilized, cell division begins, so that when the egg reaches the uterus, it is an embryo consisting of a number of cells. While the ovum is travelling along the Fallopian tube, the spongy inner lining of the uterus increases in thickness. By the time the tiny embryo reaches the uterus it is not very much larger than a full stop on this page. On arrival at the uterus, it sticks to the lining, which is stimulated to grow around it, completely enclosing it.

The embryo then grows quite rapidly, and becomes enclosed by a double membrane. The innermost membrane, called the **amnion**, encloses a fluid-filled sac which protects the embryo. The outermost membrane, called the **chorion**, together with material tissue with which it is in contact, grows to form an organ, called the **placenta**, which is responsible for all the interchange of materials between the mother and the embryo. At the placenta, the mother's blood system is very close to that of the embryo but there is no mixing of blood, exchanges taking place by diffusion. Oxygen and digestive products, such as glucose and amino acids, pass from the mother to the embryo; waste products, such as carbon dioxide and urea, pass from the embryo to the mother.

As it develops, the unborn child, or **foetus**, floats freely in the enlarged uterus, connected to the placenta by the **umbilical cord**.

Birth

The period of gestation is about nine months, the position of the unborn baby at this time being shown in Figure 12.14. At the end of the period of gestation, the uterus undergoes periodic contractions, which become stronger and more frequent as time goes on. These contractions cause the membranes surrounding the foetus to burst, so that the fluid within them is discharged through the vagina. The neck of the uterus (the **cervix**) and the vagina widen, and the continuing contractions cause the baby to be forced, head first, out of the vagina.

228

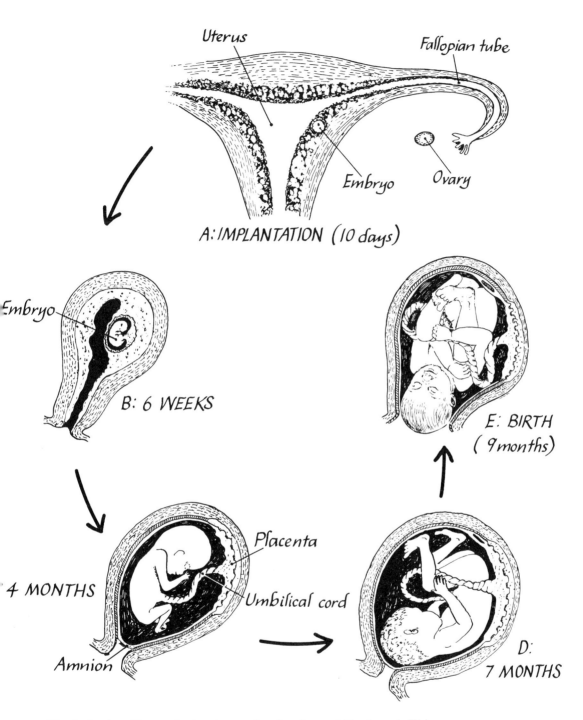

Uterus

Fallopian tube

Embryo

Ovary

A: IMPLANTATION (10 days)

Embryo

B: 6 WEEKS

E: BIRTH (9 months)

Placenta

Umbilical cord

4 MONTHS

Amnion

D: 7 MONTHS

The baby is still attached to its mother by the umbilical cord. This must be tied, to prevent bleeding, and then severed. The short end still attached to the baby is soon absorbed, leaving only the navel to show where it was. Shortly after the birth of the child, the mother's uterus contracts again to discharge the placenta and the remains of the umbilical cord.

Figure 12.14 Growth of the foetus

12.12. Early growth of the baby

For the first few months of its life, the baby feeds on milk. During her pregnancy, the milk glands in the mother's breasts enlarge, and hormones stimulate the secretion of milk. This milk is a complete food for the young baby, containing about 87 per cent water; 3·75 per cent fat; 4·7 per cent lactose (milk-sugar); 3·4 per cent protein; and 0·75 per cent salts. The sucking action of the baby stimulates the continued production of milk at the mother's breasts.

After about six months, the baby is weaned, its milk diet gradually being replaced by more solid food.

12.13. Growing up

Human growth is a rather uneven process, and progresses in spurts, followed by periods of slower growth. The first period of rapid growth is during the first few years of life, the second occurring during adolescence (from about eleven to seventeen years). At about the age of twelve, hormones are released by the pituitary gland, which bring about the maturing of the sex organs, so that they are able to release sperm or ova.

At the same time, the testes and the ovaries secrete their own hormones, which bring about growth changes in other parts of the body. The testes produce the hormone **testosterone** and, as a result, the boy develops hair under the armpits, on the face and in the pubic region, the physique becomes more manly, and the voice deepens. In girls, the ovaries produce the hormone **oestrone**, which results in the growth of hair under the arms and in the pubic region, the development of the breasts, and the widening of the hips.

12.14. Menstruation

When an ovum is released from the ovary, the lining of the uterus thickens in preparation for the embryo. If the ovum is not fertilized, the new tissue breaks down and is discharged through the vagina. This process is called **menstruation**.

The build-up of uterine lining takes about fourteen days, and if, after a period of about five days, an embryo has not been implanted, menstrual discharge begins and continues for about five days. This is followed by a period of repair and renewal of the uterine lining. The whole sequence of events takes about twenty-eight days.

The first menstrual cycle usually occurs at the age of about twelve years, and the cycles continue through life until the age of about fifty, when the release of ova ceases.

1. Explain the terms: gamete, zygote, sperm, ovum, fertilization, embryo.
2. Make a labelled diagram showing the parts of a buttercup flower.
3. What is the difference between a seed and a fruit? List the ways in which seeds or fruits may be dispersed.
4. What is the difference between asexual and sexual reproduction?
5. Write a few lines to explain each of the following terms: placenta, gestation, umbilical cord.
6. Why is it that internal fertilization is necessary for land-dwelling creatures?
7. Write an account of the development of a human ovum from fertilization until the birth of the child.

Chapter 13

Genetics

13.1. What is genetics?

Genetics is the study of heredity, and heredity is the transmission of characteristics from generation to generation.

The number of characteristics in which similarity exists is greatest between parents and their offspring. Members of the same **species** resemble each other more than they resemble members of a different species. Dogs, wolves and hyenas are members of the same **genus** (a group of species which have certain characteristics in common), so they resemble each other more than they resemble cats, which belong to a different genus. Dogs, wolves, hyenas and cats are all mammals, so they resemble each other more than they resemble any organism which is not a mammal. As the groups become larger, the similarities become less.

Investigation 13a. Family characteristics

Compare yourself with your parents, using the following features: eye colour, hair colour, complexion, build, shape of face, nose and mouth, artistic ability and temperament. Make a copy of Table 13.1 and, against each of the features, put a tick where there is a similarity.

You will see from your table that in some of your features you resemble your father, in others you resemble your mother, perhaps in some you resemble both, and possibly some of your features seem to have skipped a generation.

If you have any brothers or sisters, make a table for each of them and compare their tables with yours. In some cases, you will all have inherited one or more of your features from the same side of the family (e.g. you may all have dark hair and brown eyes), but it is probable that in some of your features you will differ; some of you 'taking after' your father and others 'taking after' your mother.

TABLE 13.1. FAMILY CHARACTERISTICS

| | Parents | | Grandparents | | | |
| | | | Father's Parents | | Mother's Parents | |
Feature	Father	Mother	Father	Mother	Father	Mother
Eye colour						
Hair colour						
Complexion						
Build						
Shape of face						
Shape of nose						
Shape of mouth						
Artistic ability						
Temperament						

13.2. The work of Mendel

The first attempt to discover how characteristics are passed on from one generation to the next and subsequent generations was made by an Austrian monk, **Gregor Mendel**, who carried out carefully controlled experiments on garden peas between 1856 and 1865.

Mendel chose the garden pea for his experiments because of the number of variable characteristics which occur in this plant. One of the characteristics that Mendel investigated was the height of the plants, because he had noticed that peas either grew very tall or very short; there were seldom any medium-sized plants.

Before starting the experiment proper, Mendel allowed some tall plants and some dwarf plants to self-pollinate for several generations, discarding all plants which failed to breed true to type. By doing this, he obtained two true-breeding stocks, one which would always produce tall plants and the other which would always produce dwarf plants.

The next stage of the investigation was to cross-pollinate the parent plants. In order to ensure that self-pollination did not occur, the flower buds of the plants intended to be the female parents were carefully opened and the anthers removed. These buds were then covered with bags to protect the stigmas from stray pollen. The pollen from the anthers of dwarf plants was transferred to the stigmas of the tall plants, while the pollen from the anthers of tall plants was transferred to the stigmas of dwarf plants by using a small brush. The resulting seeds were planted and all produced tall plants. These plants are called the F_1 **generation**, or F_1 **hybrids**.

From this result, Mendel deduced the following:
a. The height of a pea plant is the result of the interaction between two factors.
b. These two factors must be carried by the gametes, one by the pollen grain (male gamete) and the other by the ovule (female gamete).
c. Both male and female gametes are capable of carrying either the 'tallness' factor or the 'dwarfness' factor.
d. The 'tallness' factor masks the effect of the 'dwarfness' factor.

Mendel then allowed these tall F_1 hybrids to self-pollinate and collected the seeds. He planted more than a thousand of these seeds, no doubt expecting them all to produce tall plants. He found, however, that the seeds which germinated and grew produced 787 tall plants and 277 dwarf plants. So the characteristic that had disappeared from the F_1 generation had re-appeared in the next (F_2) generation, but only in about a quarter of the plants.

The characteristic which shows in the F_1 generation and which is predominant in the F_2 generation is known as a **dominant** characteristic. The characteristic which disappears in the F_1 generation and reappears in about a quarter of the F_2 generation is known as a **recessive** characteristic. Table 13.2 shows some of Mendel's results.

TABLE 13.2. MENDEL'S RESULTS

Parents	F_1	F_2	Ratio
Yellow seeds × Green seeds	Yellow seeds	6 022 yellow, 2 001 green	3·006 : 1
Smooth seeds × Wrinkled seeds	Smooth seeds	5 474 smooth, 1 850 wrinkled	2·959 : 1
Green pods × Yellow pods	Green pods	428 green, 152 yellow	2·816 : 1
Tall plants × Dwarf plants	Tall plants	787 tall, 277 dwarf	2·841 : 1

From the results of these experiments, which are the dominant characteristics?

The characteristics are carried by **genes**. Figure 13.1 shows the explanation of Mendel's tall × dwarf experiment. The 'tallness' gene (shown as T) is a dominant gene which masks the effect of the 'dwarfness' gene (shown as t), which is a recessive gene.

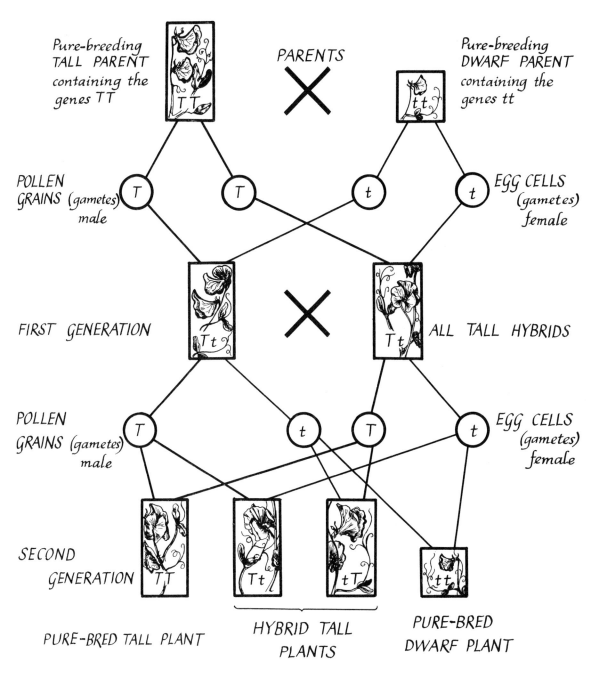

Pure-breeding
TALL PARENT
containing the
genes TT

PARENTS

Pure-breeding
DWARF PARENT
containing the
genes tt

POLLEN
GRAINS (gametes)
male

T T

t t

EGG CELLS
(gametes)
female

FIRST GENERATION

Tt

Tt

ALL TALL HYBRIDS

POLLEN
GRAINS (gametes)
male

T t T t

EGG CELLS
(gametes)
female

SECOND
GENERATION

TT

Tt

tT

tt

PURE-BRED TALL PLANT

HYBRID TALL
PLANTS

PURE-BRED
DWARF PLANT

Figure 13.1 Mendel's
experiment

235

Obtain two bags, a large number of black beads and an equal number of white beads. Put half of the black beads and half of the white beads into one bag and the remainder of the beads into the other bag.

Now, remove the beads in pairs, one bead from each bag and note the colours in each pair. You will notice that there are four possible combinations: black/black, black/white, white/black and white/white. These combinations can be compared with the following types of plants:

Black/black represents a pure-bred dominant plant.

Black/white and white/black both represent hybrids showing the dominant characteristic.

White/white represents a pure-bred recessive plant.

How do your results compare with Mendel's ratio of characteristics in the F_2 generation?

Mendel also carried out experiments to discover if there was any relationship in the distribution of dominant and recessive genes. He found that the distribution of a dominant gene is entirely independent of the distribution of any other dominant gene (i.e. tall plants do not necessarily have smooth yellow seeds and green pods).

13.3. Some terms used in genetics

Corresponding genes which determine a particular characteristic are called **alleles**. An organism in which a characteristic is the result of the combination of two similar alleles is known as a **homozygote** (e.g. two 'tallness' genes or two 'dwarfness' genes in the case of the garden pea). An organism in which a characteristic is the result of the combination of two different alleles is known as a **heterozygote** (e.g. the combination of a 'tallness' gene and a 'dwarfness' gene in the case of the garden pea). The total genes inherited by an organism are known as the organism's **genotype**. The visible effect of an organism's genotype is known as its **phenotype**.

In Figure 13.1, the letters in each rectangle represent the genotype for the 'tallness' characteristic. TT and tt are homozygotes. TT will produce a tall phenotype and tt will produce a dwarf phenotype. Because these phenotypes are the result of homozygotes, they will breed true (for this particular characteristic). The rectangles with the genotype Tt or tT are heterozygotes and will produce tall phenotypes because the 'tallness' allele is dominant over the recessive 'dwarfness' allele. These phenotypes will not breed true and are called **hybrids**.

13.4. The cell

In order to understand how characteristics can be inherited, we must know more about the living cell and, in particular, its nucleus. Animal and plant cells have nuclei and are capable of reproducing themselves (a notable exception being the red blood cells of mammals, which have no nucleus and cannot reproduce). The nucleus of a cell is encased in a **nuclear membrane**, surrounded by **cytoplasm** and a **cell membrane**. Plant cells have an additional layer outside the cell membrane called the **cell wall**. The cell nucleus contains very complicated protein molecules and long-chain molecules of **nucleic acids**, mainly **deoxyribonucleic acid** (commonly called **DNA**).

These substances occur in the cell nucleus in the form of long thread-like structures called **chromosomes**. The number of chromosomes present in the cell nucleus is always the same in any particular species, each chromosome having a similar 'partner' chromosome within the nucleus. A mosquito has three pairs of chromosomes, a fruit fly has four pairs, the garden pea has seven pairs, the bean has eleven pairs, a cat has nineteen pairs, man has twenty-three pairs, a horse has thirty-three pairs, and a shrimp has one hundred and twenty-seven pairs. This list will give you some idea of the variation between the cells of different organisms.

Figure 13.2 An animal cell showing two pairs of chromosomes (diagrammatic)

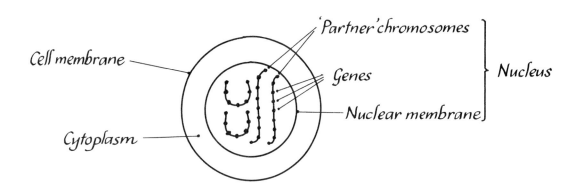

Each chromosome can be considered as being made up of a number of genes arranged in a line, rather like a string of beads (see Figure 13.2). Characteristics are determined by the chemical structure of the genes, some characteristics being determined by a single pair of genes (each situated in the same position on 'partner' chromosomes) and others by several pairs of genes.

237

13.5. Mitosis

Mitosis is the normal growth process by which a cell subdivides into two daughter cells, each identical in every way to the parent cell. Figure 13.3 illustrates a cell dividing by mitosis.

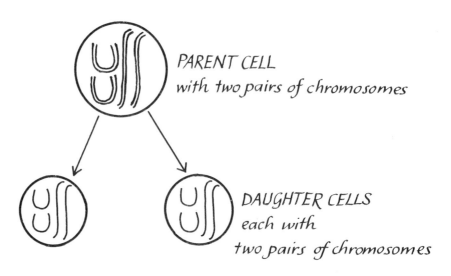

PARENT CELL
with two pairs of chromosomes

DAUGHTER CELLS
each with
two pairs of chromosomes

Figure 13.3 Mitosis

Before a cell divides by mitosis, each chromosome duplicates itself by forming a double structure, each part being called a **chromatid**. When the parent cell divides, one chromatid from each chromosome migrates towards one end of the cell, while the other chromatid from each chromosome migrates towards the other end of the cell. The two ends of the cell then separate. The genes in the original chromosomes are represented in the chromatids, which now become the chromosomes of the daughter cells.

It is very important to realize that in every individual, every body cell except the gametes (see Section 13.6) and red blood cells contains identical sets of chromosomes. In man, for example, each skin cell, bone cell, muscle cell, nerve cell, etc., contains an identical set of twenty-three pairs of chromosomes.

13.6. Meiosis

You will know, from Chapter 12, that sexual reproduction is accomplished by fertilization, which occurs when the nucleus of a male gamete fuses with the nucleus of a female gamete to form a zygote (see Figure 13.4).

Human gametes contain twenty-three single chromosomes. A human zygote contains twenty-three pairs of chromosomes, one of each pair being derived from the male gamete and the other from the female gamete. Reproductive cells in the testes and the ovaries

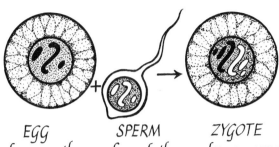

One set from father

One set from mother

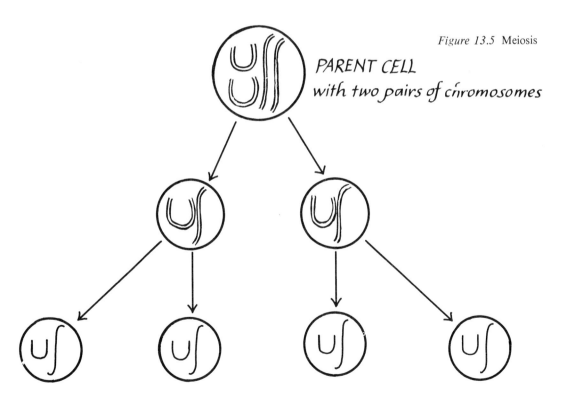

EGG
from mother

SPERM
from father

ZYGOTE
forms young

Figure 13.4 The pairing
of chromosomes in
fertilization

Figure 13.5 Meiosis

PARENT CELL
with two pairs of chromosomes

GAMETES, each with one pair of chromosomes

each have twenty-three pairs of chromosomes. The way in which these reproductive cells divide to produce gametes is called **meiosis,** or **reduction division**. This is shown diagrammatically in Figure 13.5.

Before a reproductive cell divides by meiosis, each chromosome forms two chromatids. The chromosomes line up in matching pairs across the cell, each matching pair consisting of four chromatids. From each group of four chromatids, two migrate towards one end of the cell while the other two migrate towards the other end. The cell then separates into two daughter cells, each having half as many chromosomes as the original reproductive cell. These cells now subdivide by a process similar to mitosis, thus producing four gametes from the original reproductive cell.

13.7. Incomplete dominance

Cross-breeding red-coated cattle with white-coated cattle results in an F_1 generation with roan coats (a mixture of red hairs and white hairs). When a roan cow is mated with a roan bull, the offspring may be red, roan or white, as shown in Figure 13.6.

Some characteristics are caused by genes in which the alleles are neither dominant nor recessive, resulting in a blend of the characteristics carried by the alleles showing in the phenotype. Such a characteristic is known as an example of **incomplete dominance**.

In addition to the coat colour in cattle, the flower colour in many plants shows incomplete dominance. When red antirrhinums (snapdragons) are crossed with white antirrhinums, the F_1 generation is entirely pink. When these F_1 hybrids are crossed, the F_2 generation occurs in approximately the following ratios: 1 red : 2 pink : 1 white.

13.8. The sex chromosomes

Every cell which is capable of subdivision by mitosis has, within its nucleus, a fixed number of chromosomes, a number which is common to all cells of organisms of the same species. Human cells have forty-six chromosomes and, of these, forty-four occur in matching pairs while the remaining two chromosomes may or may not match. These latter two chromosomes are the **sex chromosomes**. There are two types of sex chromosome: the X chromosome and the Y chromosome. The Y chromosome is smaller, contains very few genes and, consequently, does not completely match or balance the X chromosome, in the same way as the letter Y has one limb less than the letter X.

In the human female, every body cell has two X chromosomes. In the human male, every body cell has an X chromosome and a Y chromosome. When female gametes (ova) are produced by meiosis

240

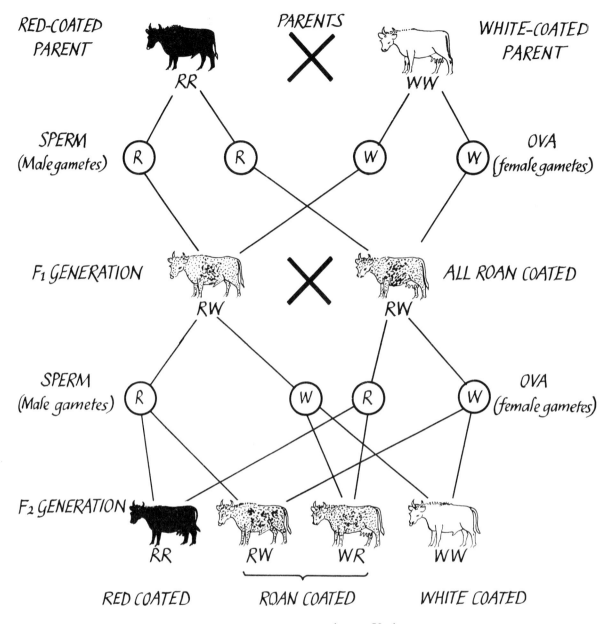

RED-COATED PARENT

PARENTS

WHITE-COATED PARENT

RR

WW

SPERM (Male gametes)

R R W W

OVA (female gametes)

F₁ GENERATION

ALL ROAN COATED

RW RW

SPERM (Male gametes)

R W R W

OVA (female gametes)

F₂ GENERATION

RR RW WR WW

RED COATED

ROAN COATED

WHITE COATED

from a female reproductive cell, each gamete contains an X chromosome. When male gametes (sperm) are produced from a male reproductive cell by meiosis, half of them will contain an X chromosome and the other half will contain a Y chromosome.

If an ovum is fertilized by a sperm carrying an X chromosome, the zygote will contain two X chromosomes and will be female. If an ovum is fertilized by a sperm carrying a Y chromosome, the zygote will contain an X and a Y chromosome and will be male. This determination of the sex of a zygote is a matter of pure chance, depending on which type of sperm fertilizes the ovum (see Figure 13.7).

Figure 13.6 Incomplete dominance

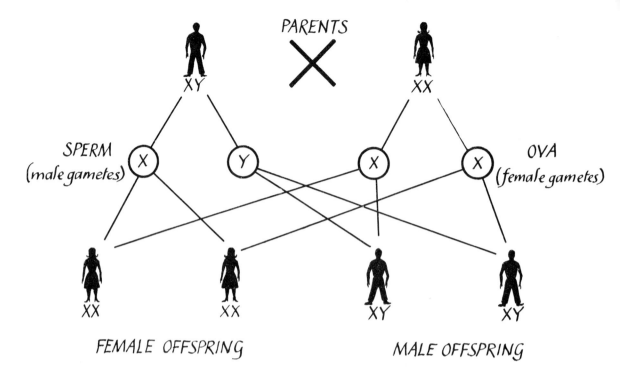

PARENTS

SPERM
(male gametes)

OVA
(female gametes)

FEMALE OFFSPRING

MALE OFFSPRING

Figure 13.7 The determination of sex

13.9. Sex-linkage

The sex chromosomes also carry genes for other characteristics. Because of the difference in the sex chromosomes of males and females, the effects of these genes are different in males and females. These effects are called **sex-linked** characteristics.

Colour vision and the ability of the blood to clot are both controlled by genes on the X chromosome. If one of these genes is faulty, the defect which it causes can be passed on to future generations. Fortunately, both of these faults (colour blindness and haemophilia) are caused by a recessive allele, which is dominated by the normally functioning allele on the matching X chromosome in the female. In the male, however, the Y chromosome carries no corresponding allele to nullify the effects.

In Figures 13.8 and 13.9, XH represents an X chromosome with a normally functioning gene for blood clotting and Xh represents an X chromosome with a faulty gene for blood clotting. You will notice that, in Figure 13.8, the daughters of a female carrier have an even chance of being carriers, while her sons have an even chance of suffering from haemophilia. Figure 13.9 shows that a father suffering from haemophilia cannot pass the disease on to his sons, but that all of his daughters will be carriers. A carrier is a person who does not suffer from a disease but can pass it on to the next generation.

242

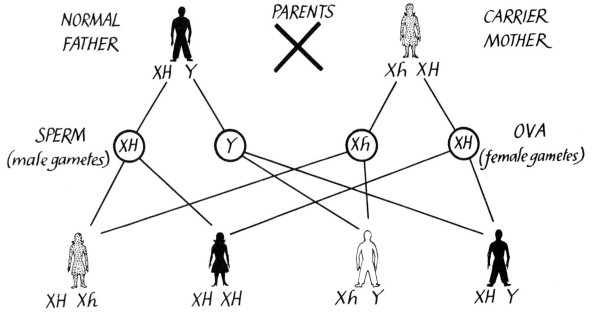

Figure 13.8 The effects of sex-linkage (faulty gene from the mother)

Figure 13.9 The effects of sex-linkage (faulty gene from the father)

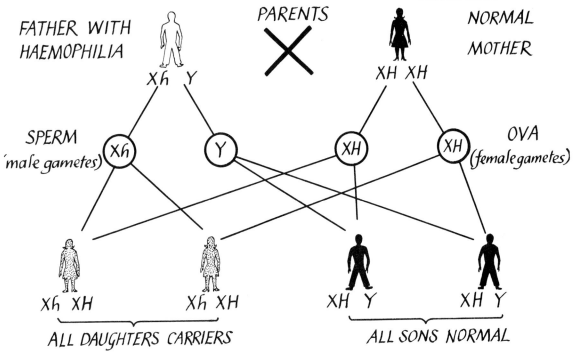

13.10. The functions of the genes

The functions of the genes are many and varied. Some genes are responsible for large-scale characteristics, such as size and shape, while others are responsible for minute detail.

The development of an individual organism from a zygote is similar in many respects to the building of a house, although much more complicated. A house is built from a set of plans (or blueprint) and a specification. The 'blueprint' of an organism is the set of chromosomes in the zygote, instructions for each detail being carried by one or more of the genes in the chromosomes.

When a zygote is formed by the fusion of the nucleus of a male gamete with the nucleus of a female gamete, each gamete contributes a complete set of chromosomes, containing genes capable of determining all the details of the organism. When these two sets of chromosomes meet in the zygote, each detail is decided by the interaction of the alleles.

It is important to realize that the number of possible combinations of the chromosomes in the gametes is very large indeed. Reproductive cells each contain forty-six chromosomes, twenty-three originating from the sperm of the previous generation, and the matching twenty-three from the ovum. During meiosis, it is unlikely that all of the sperm-originated chromosomes will migrate towards one end of the cell, while all of the ovum-originated chromosomes migrate towards the other end. If this were so, then children would resemble their grandparents to a far greater extent than they actually do.

During meiosis, adjacent chromatids of matching chromosomes lie across each other and become entangled. As the chromosomes separate and start to migrate towards opposite ends of the cell, the parts of the chromatids interchange their positions. This interchange may occur in several places along the chromatids. Such an interchange is called **crossing-over** and is responsible for even greater variation between individuals of the same species.

13.11. Heredity and environment

Once a baby is born (and, to a lesser extent, before birth) its development, both mental and physical, is dependent upon parental care, training and environment, although the genes still hold overall control. If a child receives genes for great musical ability from its parents but is given no musical training, the child will not become a great musician. On the other hand, if the genes for great musical talent are lacking, no amount of training will turn the child into a musical virtuoso.

Similarly, in the plant kingdom, seeds which are capable of producing a good crop will only do so if they are planted in a suitable soil (or other medium) and are correctly cultivated.

Genes determine the maximum capability of an individual. The degree to which the individual achieves this maximum is controlled by environment.

13.12. Eye colour and heredity

The eye-colour genes control the amount and distribution of pigment in the iris. 'Brown-eye' genes are dominant over 'blue-eye' genes.

If we use the symbol 'B' for a 'brown-eye' gene and 'b' for a blue-eye' gene, then a person with brown eyes will have a genotype which is either BB or Bb. A blue-eyed person can only have a genotype of bb.

Figure 13.10 Eye-colour inheritance

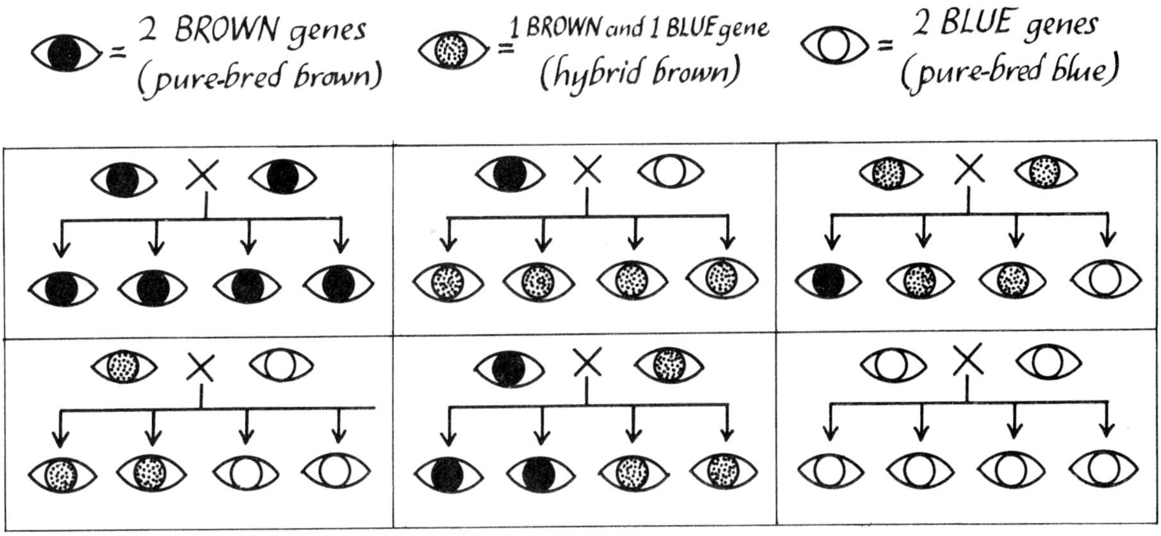

Figure 13.10 shows the effects of eye-colour inheritance, but remember that the resulting eye colours of these crosses only indicate the statistical probabilities. For example: the offspring of a hybrid brown-eyed father and a blue-eyed mother will have an even chance of having brown eyes or blue eyes; the offspring of parents who are both hybrid brown-eyed are three times as likely to have brown eyes as they are to have blue eyes.

It is important to note that it is possible for blue-eyed parents to have a brown-eyed child. This can be caused by a change in the degree of dominance of the genes, brought about by mutation (see Section 13.15).

13.13. Height and heredity

Height is controlled by a group of genes. Let us assume that it is controlled by a group of five pairs of genes, each gene casting a vote for tallness or shortness. If a zygote receives five 'tallness' genes from each parent, it will develop into a very tall individual. If it receives five 'shortness' genes from each parent, it will develop into a very short individual. The majority of zygotes will receive a mixture of 'tallness' and 'shortness' genes and the height of the individual which develops will vary according to the proportion of 'tallness' and 'shortness' genes present in the genotype (see Figure 13.11).

Figure 13.11 Multi-gene action controlling height

'TALL' GENES	10	9	8	7	6	5	4	3	2	1	0
'SHORT' GENES	0	1	2	3	4	5	6	7	8	9	10

13.14. Disease and heredity

The vast majority of diseases are caused by environment and not by heredity, though some people are more susceptible than others to certain diseases. In these cases, what may be passed on by heredity is a reduced resistance, or immunity, to these diseases. A person can only suffer from a bacterial or virus infection if he is subjected to the bacteria or viruses which cause the disease, and his immunity is insufficient to combat the infection. If, however, the bacteria or viruses causing the disease are not present, then he will not suffer from the disease, no matter how little immunity he has inherited. Hereditary susceptibility to a disease is rather like being given a ticket to see a play in a theatre; if you don't go to the theatre, you won't see the play!

Certain functional diseases, however, can be inherited. Two examples of this type of disease are haemophilia (see Section 13.9) and **'sickle-cell' anaemia**. The 'sickle-cell' gene, which occurs chiefly in Negroes, causes the red blood cells to become distorted into sickle-shaped cells, which cannot absorb as much oxygen as the normal red cells. The inheritance of a normal 'red-cell' gene from one parent and a 'sickle-cell' gene from the other causes a condition called **sicklaemia**. This condition produces little or no ill effect, but can be an advantage because it gives a certain amount of immunity against malaria. The inheritance of a 'sickle-cell' gene from both parents causes 'sickle-cell' anaemia, which is usually fatal.

13.15. Mutation

The word **mutation** comes from the Latin word 'mutare' meaning 'to change', and is used to describe an alteration in the function of a gene, or genes, resulting in a variation in an individual which does not appear in the normal population. Most mutations have a relatively minor effect, a mutated gene being recessive, in most cases, to the normal gene. A mutation can only be transmitted to future generations if it occurs in the reproductive cells, or the gametes which they produce. The effect of a mutation is usually only apparent when a zygote is the product of two gametes, each carrying similarly mutated genes.

Some gene mutations have relatively minor effects while others produce radical changes. When mutation produces a radical change from the normal, the resulting individual is usually at a disadvantage (some mutations are lethal) compared with the normal, although advantageous mutations do occur. Such advantageous mutations are used by breeders of plants and animals to improve the quality of their stocks.

Genes mutate from time to time, the frequency of mutation for any particular gene being in the order of one in 40 000. This mutation rate is increased by the action of X-rays, beta-particle emission and gamma rays, and exposure to certain chemicals. An increased mutation rate results in greater variety.

Radiation is deliberately used by plant breeders to increase the variation between plants of the same species. Some of the variants will have undesirable characteristics and these plants will be destroyed. Plants which have desirable characteristics will be selected for breeding. Once a new variety has been established, it can be propagated by any of the normal methods which are used to propagate the particular species: pollination and the subsequent planting of seeds, planting of cuttings, grafting on to an existing root system and stem, budding, etc.

Large-scale mutations can occur during meiosis if the chromosomes separate incorrectly when they migrate towards opposite ends of the cell. Normal separation occurs when each group of four chromatids divides into two equal halves, each consisting of two chromatids. In mutated separation, this division is not equal and results in some gametes having matching pairs of chromosomes instead of the normal single chromosomes. When gametes with this type of mutation fuse to form zygotes, the characteristics determined by the genes on these 'giant' chromosomes will have a greater effect, because there are more of them.

Mutation and the natural selection of those which have an advantage over the normal are important aspects of evolution (see Chapter 14).

Test your understanding

1. Where would you expect to find DNA?
2. What differences would you expect to find between the cell of a bean and the cell of a cat?
3. How many chromosomes are there in the sperm cell of a horse?
4. What is the difference between mitosis and meiosis?
5. In plant and animal breeding, what is the significance of the ratio 3 : 1?
6. Why is it easier to produce guaranteed true-breeding dwarf plants than guaranteed true-breeding tall plants?
7. A roan cow is mated with a red bull. Draw a diagram to show the possible coat colours of the calf.
8. Draw a diagram to show why males are more likely to suffer from colour blindness than females.
9. Draw a diagram to show all the possible effects on the children of a married couple where the father suffers from haemophilia and the mother is a carrier.
10. John and Mary are brother and sister and both have blue eyes. Their parents both have brown eyes and their four grandparents all have brown eyes. Draw a diagram to show how John and Mary inherited their eye colour from their parents and grandparents.
11. 'Tuberculosis runs in families—therefore it is inherited.' Explain why this 'old wives' tale' is not true.
12. Assume the following:
    (a) Bloom size is controlled by a single pair of genes and the gene for large size is dominant over the gene for small size.
    (b) Bloom colour is controlled by another single pair of genes and a 'red' gene is dominant over a 'yellow' gene.
    A plant breeder has two plants: one produces large yellow blooms and the other produces small red blooms. Draw a diagram to show how he could attempt to obtain plants which will produce large red blooms.

Chapter 14

Evolution

14.1. Earth and its crust

While scientists are not certain how the Earth began, most are now agreed that it is approximately four and a half thousand million (4.5×10^9) years old and that during this time, it has undergone continuous change. Man is believed to have emerged about one million years ago.

Conclusions such as these can only be reached as a result of much scientific 'detective' work; by collecting as much evidence as possible and then piecing the evidence together to give a reasonable explanation. In this chapter, we shall consider some of the ways in which the Earth and its inhabitants have changed over the years. This is the study of evolution.

The centre of the Earth is believed to consist mainly of a mass of very dense molten material. Only the outer layer, or crust, is solid and relatively cool. This crust provides us with most of the materials which we need in order to live and to build our civilization. Those materials which cannot be found on or in the Earth's crust are provided by the envelope of air surrounding it.

Among the rocks forming the crust, we find the metallic ores and some metals in their pure state (see Chapter 6). We can use some kinds of rock for building and, from chalk and limestone, we are able to manufacture lime and cement (see Chapter 5). Using clay, we are able to make bricks for our houses. In the crust, we find deposits of coal, oil and gas, which we use to heat our homes, to cook our food and to provide fuel for our cars.

14.2. The three main types of rock

You will know from Chapter 1 that the Earth's crust is made up of igneous, sedimentary and metamorphic rocks. These rocks are not homogeneous, that is, they do not consist of one chemical compound alone. In them, we find many different substances, including some materials which have been formed from the remains of living matter, both plant and animal.

249

14.3. Dating the rocks

One of the substances found in rocks is the element uranium. This is a radioactive element and if a piece of it is left for a period of time, it is found to undergo radioactive decay, emitting radiation and ultimately leaving a form of lead. The time taken for one half of the atoms in a lump of uranium to decay in this way is known as the half life of the element. The half life of uranium is about 4 500 million years. If, when it was formed, a mass of rock contained 100 g of uranium 235, then 4 500 million years later it would be found to contain only 50 g of uranium 235 and about 43 g of lead. After another 4 500 million years, there would be only 25 g of uranium 235 and about 65 g of lead. By examining a piece of rock containing uranium 235, it is therefore possible to estimate the age of the rock by comparing the proportions of uranium 235 and lead. Examinations of this kind show that some of the oldest rock strata are more than 2 000 million years old.

14.4. Fossils

Any evidence found in the earth's crust that indicates that an animal or plant once existed is called a **fossil**. Types of fossils include:

a. Whole preservation in amber

Amber is a hard, transparent material which has been formed from the resin from coniferous trees, which covered vast areas many millions of years ago. Sometimes a piece of amber is found with a small creature, such as a spider, embedded in it. It is easy to imagine drops of resin falling to the ground and, a little later, some small animal becoming trapped in this sticky material. Over the course of many years, the resin would be converted into amber, with the perfectly preserved animal body still inside it.

b. Moulds and casts

Sometimes the body of a creature, covered with sediment, would gradually be dissolved away, leaving only a cavity where the creature had been. This is a mould fossil. Sometimes the cavity would become filled with another material, which would harden to form a cast of the original animal. Fossils formed in these ways are usually of shelled animals.

c. Carbon films

Many creatures have no internal skeleton but only a horny external covering (exoskeleton) with a soft body inside. Often, the only evidence left by such creatures is a thin film of carbon, formed from the exoskeleton.

d. Tracks and trails

Sometimes the impression made by an animal is found in a rock. Perhaps the creature would make a footprint in soft soil. This might remain undisturbed for many years and then, under the influence of heat or pressure, the soil would be converted into hard rock, leaving the footprint preserved.

Fossils may be dated, approximately, by dating the rock in which they are found. Fossils have been found showing that life has existed on the earth for more than 500 million years. More recent fossils,

Figure 14.1 Some fossils

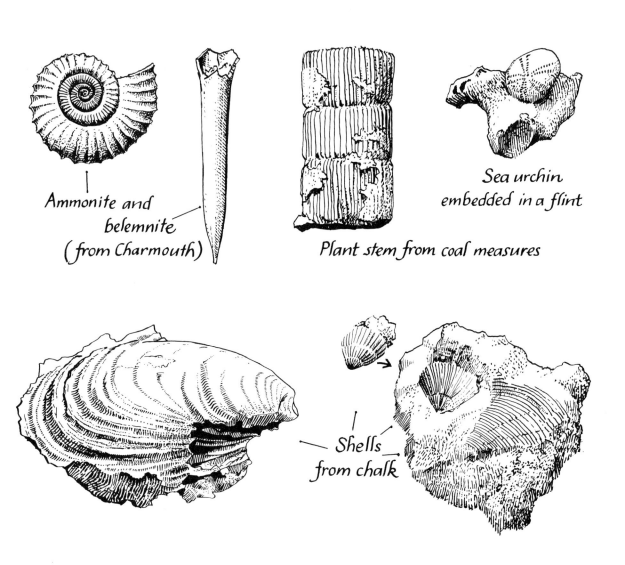

Ammonite and belemnite (from Charmouth)

Plant stem from coal measures

Sea urchin embedded in a flint

Shells from chalk

251

produced by animals during the last million years, show that the creatures which formed them were similar to creatures found living today. Older fossils are frequently quite unlike any living animal. Figure 14.1 shows some typical fossils.

14.5. Coal and oil

Both of these materials have been formed from living matter. Because they do not, by themselves, give any clear indication of the organisms from which they were formed, they are not classified as fossils. However, the leaf patterns which are often found in coal are fossils.

Coal was formed from the remains of vegetation. These remains have undergone varying degrees of decomposition and have been subjected to pressure, resulting in the formation of a hard, brittle substance, rich in carbon. Some coals were formed from a great variety of plants, while others were formed mainly from one type of plant. Nearly all types of coal retain traces of the plant tissue from which they were formed. The pressure required to form coal is very great indeed, and it has been estimated that a coal seam one metre thick required a layer of plant debris about twenty metres thick to form it.

Mineral oil is believed to have been formed by the action of heat

Figure 14.2 An oil-bearing rock formation

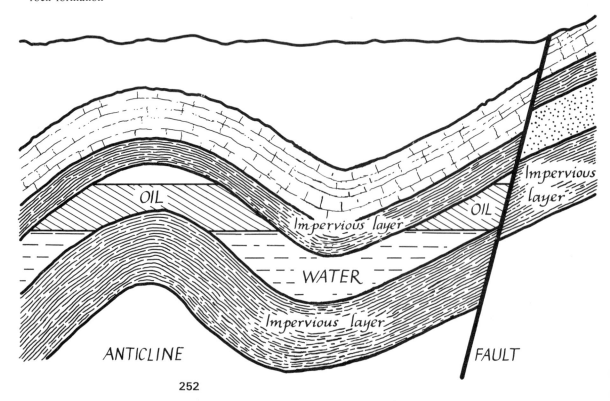

ANTICLINE

OIL

Impervious layer

WATER

Impervious layer

OIL

Impervious layer

FAULT

and pressure on animal remains. This oil is a black, sticky liquid which is found underground in many parts of the world, but principally in the Middle East, the Far East, the Americas, the U.S.S.R. and, more recently, under the North Sea.

Figure 14.2 shows a typical oil-bearing rock formation. Often, there is a layer of compressed gas trapped above the oil surface. If an oil well is drilled so that it passes through the gas layer, the gas will escape and the oil will then have to be pumped to the surface. If, however, the well is drilled so that it enters the oil directly, then the gas pressure is often sufficient to force the oil to the surface, making pumping unnecessary.

14.6. Geological time

For convenience, geologists have divided the age of the earth into six **eras**. The changeover from one era to the next is marked by some important geological change, such as mountain building or continental uplift. Each of these eras is divided into a number of **periods**, denoting the times when changes of lesser significance occurred on the face of the earth.

The earliest era is called the **azoic** era. During this era, which is estimated to have lasted for more than a thousand million years, there is no evidence that any form of life existed; the word azoic means 'no life'.

During the second era, there was intense volcanic activity and mountain building took place. This is known as the **archeozoic** (primitive life) era. Rocks of this era contain a small amount of materials containing carbon, but very little else to indicate that life existed. It is likely that the only form of life at this time consisted of primitive algae.

Great evolutionary changes must have occurred in the **proterozoic** (first life) era, for at the end of it there is evidence that a wide variety of life existed, though very little fossil evidence has been found to indicate the kind of creatures which must have lived during most of this era.

During the **paleozoic** (ancient life) era, the forms of life which developed included fishes, amphibians, the earliest reptiles and the first mammals. The first land plants also appeared at this time.

The **mesozoic** (middle life) era saw the appearance of the great reptiles, such as the dinosaurs, and the most primitive birds.

The **cainozoic** (recent life) era has seen the evolution of all modern forms of life, including man, but it is important to note that although this era began almost 70 million years ago, man only appeared in the last million years or so.

Table 14.1 shows the major geological time divisions, together with the principal forms of life which emerged.

TABLE 14.1. GEOLOGICAL TIME SCALE

Era	Date/millions of years ago	Periods	Principal Life Forms
Cainozoic	1	Pleistocene	Man
	25	Pliocene Miocene Oligocene	Mammals, birds, modern plants, molluscs
	70	Eocene	
Mesozoic	225	Cretaceous Jurassic Triassic	Dinosaurs, cycads, earliest birds, sea urchins, ammonites
Paleozoic	600	Permian	Earliest mammals
		Carboniferous	First reptiles
		Devonian Silurian Ordovician	Tree-ferns, first insects, fishes, first land plants
		Cambrian	Trilobites, graptolites
Proterozoic	1 200		Invertebrates evolved but little fossil evidence
Archeozoic	2 000		Simplest living organisms
Azoic	3 000		No evidence of any living organism

14.7. The meaning of evolution

Evolution implies change. Any change in the form or structure of a living organism will only persist if the variation from the normal is better than the normal. Any change which is not an improvement will die out and become extinct.

The geological evidence of fossils and their dating indicates that the earliest forms of life were very simple in structure, and that they evolved into more complex structures with the passing of geological time.

To illustrate the essential features of evolution, Figure 14.3 shows some of the major stages in the evolution of the bicycle from 1790 to the present day.

Notice the following facts in this chain of evolution:
a. Each vehicle is an improvement on its predecessors.
b. Each vehicle evolved from a common ancestor.
c. The penny-farthing did not develop into anything better, therefore it became extinct.
d. All of the vehicles have certain features in common, e.g. two wheels and a saddle.

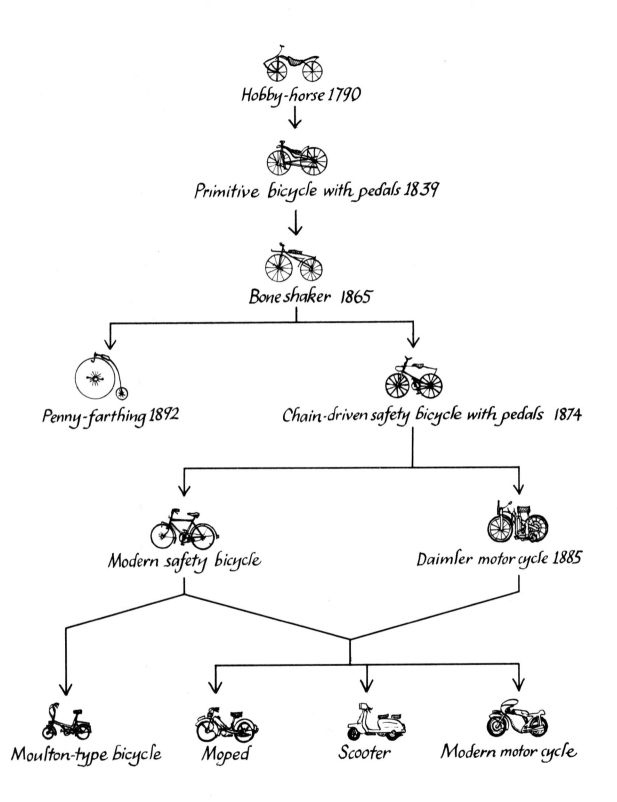

Hobby-horse 1790

Primitive bicycle with pedals 1839

Bone shaker 1865

Penny-farthing 1892

Chain-driven safety bicycle with pedals 1874

Modern safety bicycle

Daimler motor cycle 1885

Moulton-type bicycle

Moped

Scooter

Modern motor cycle

Figure 14.3 The evolution of the bicycle

In the plant and animal kingdom, many species have certain features in common. This indicates that these species have a common ancestor. Three such features in the animal kingdom which provide evidence that evolution has taken place are the stages in the development of the embryo, the presence of vestiges and the general pattern of the skeleton.

14.8. Comparative embryology

All organisms which reproduce sexually start life as a zygote, formed by the fusion of the nucleus of a male gamete with the nucleus of a female gamete. Once a zygote starts to divide by mitosis, it becomes an embryo. The early stages in the development of the embryos of many species are very similar indeed, so similar, in fact, that it is very difficult to determine what the final product will be. Figure 14.4 shows some of the features of a typical animal embryo in an early stage of development.

Figure 14.4 Features of an animal embryo

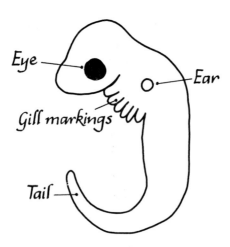

After these very early stages, development begins to vary from species to species. These differences become more obvious as development continues (see Figure 14.5), until the embryo reaches the stage at which it can be born (or hatched, in some cases) and is able to survive. At this stage, the embryo is called a **foetus**.

Notice that in the first two stages, (a) and (b) in Figure 14.5, all of the embryos have gill markings and a tail, which will only develop in organisms which have them when they reach maturity. In the organisms in which these features do not develop, they remain in their undeveloped state, and are known as **vestiges**.

Even after birth, or hatching, development is not complete; the organism grows and its proportions alter, until it reaches maturity. Figure 14.6 shows the differences in the body proportions of an infant and an adult human.

256

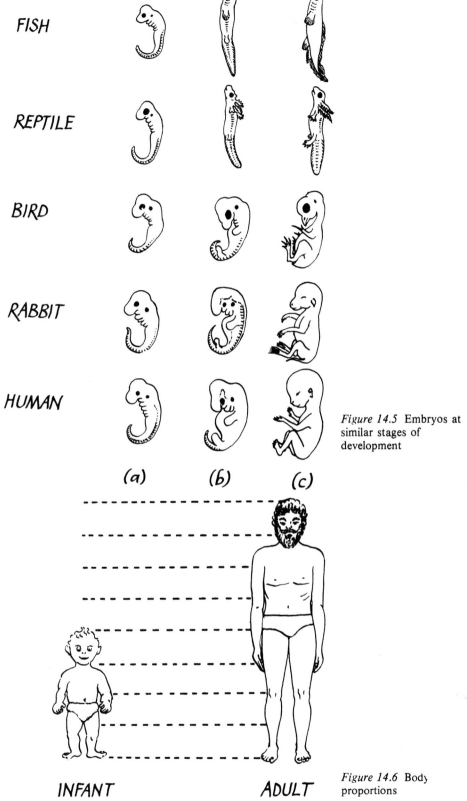

FISH

REPTILE

BIRD

RABBIT

HUMAN

Figure 14.5 Embryos at similar stages of development

(a)   *(b)*   *(c)*

INFANT   ADULT

Figure 14.6 Body proportions

14.9. The evidence of vestiges

All animals have vestiges, which were probably functional in their ancestors. Examples of such vestiges are:

a. The third eyelid in the inner corner of the eye of all vertebrates is used by birds, some reptiles and some amphibians to clean and protect the surface of the eye. This remains as a vestige in mammals.

b. One of the earliest ancestors of the modern horse was **Eohippus**, a small animal about 0·3 m high, which lived about 65 million years ago. Eohippus had four toes on each of its fore legs and three toes on each of its hind legs. **Hipparion**, a later ancestor which lived about 20 million years ago, had three toes on each leg. The embryo of a modern horse has three toes on each leg at one stage but, at birth, only one remains; the others are vestiges.

c. The muscles which move the ears are functional in many mammals, but are not used by man.

Figure 14.7 Darwin's point

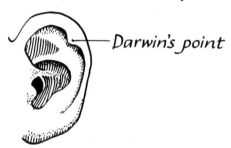

d. Some people have a small irregularity on the inner edge of the fold of the ear. This is known as **Darwin's point** (see Figure 14.7) and is a vestige of the pointed tip on the ears of many mammals. Darwin's point is more pronounced in the human embryo than in the human adult.

14.10. Comparative anatomy

The basic design of a modern car has four wheels, an engine compartment, a passenger compartment and a luggage compartment. The shapes and sizes (and even positions, in some models) of these

Figure 14.8 Modifications of a basic design

ENGINE

LUGGAGE

basic requirements vary from model to model, as shown in Figure 14.8.

To the basic design of a car, a number of systems are fitted: engine, cooling system, fuel system, lubrication system, braking system, ignition system, steering and suspension systems, etc. These systems perform the same functions in all models, but are modified to suit a particular model.

In a similar way, all vertebrates have a basic design, which is modified from one species to another. Compare the simplified skeletons of a reptile and man shown in Figure 14.9. The major features

Figure 14.9 Skeletons of a reptile and a man

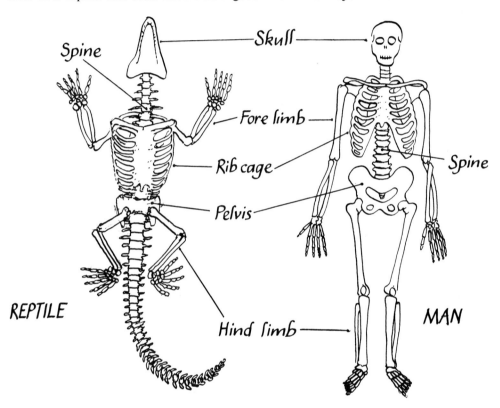

common to both skeletons have been indicated. How many other similarities can you find? It is these (and many other) similarities which indicate that these vertebrates originated from a common ancestor. In what respects do the two skeletons differ? The differences suggest that evolution may have taken place.

Figure 14.10 shows the bones in the front flipper of a whale, the hand of a man and the front leg of an amphibian. Notice the similarities in the arrangement of the bones. A limb which has this general arrangement is known as a **pentadactyl** (five-fingered) limb. All vertebrates have pentadactyl limbs. These have been modified in the course of evolution, some bones being longer, others being shorter, and others being mere vestiges.

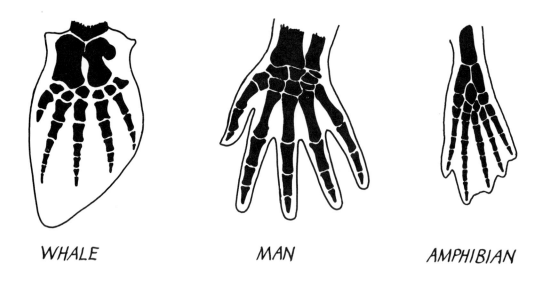

WHALE   MAN   AMPHIBIAN

Figure 14.10 Fore limbs

14.11. Lamarck's theory

There have been many theories put forward to try to explain how evolution has occurred. Lamarck's theory is only one of them and can be summarized as follows:

a. Simple organisms evolve into complicated organisms.

b. All characteristics are inherited.

The first of these two concepts can be justified by the evidence of fossils, comparative embryology, vestiges and comparative anatomy.

The second concept, however, is only partly true. The only characteristics which an organism can pass on to its offspring are those controlled by genes. Lamarck was wrong in his claim that skills and knowledge acquired during a lifetime could be passed on from one generation to the next.

Let us consider an example of the Lamarckian explanation of evolution. *Remember, this is theory only, not fact.*

a. Giraffes are descended from an animal the size and shape of an antelope.

b. Because the giraffe's ancestors were herbivorous, when the available grass and leaves became insufficient to keep them alive, they stretched upwards to reach leaves higher up. This stretching increased the length of their forelegs and necks.

c. These increases were passed on to the next generation which, in turn, stretched and further increased the length of their forelegs and necks until, eventually, the giraffe had forelegs and a neck long enough to reach all the food that it required (see Figure 14.11).

If we took Lamarck's theory to its extreme, children would be born with all the skills and knowledge of their parents and all of their ancestors. You know, from your own experience, that skills have to

260

be practised and knowledge has to be learned. Skills and knowledge which are acquired during a lifetime do not affect the genes and, consequently, cannot be transmitted by inheritance.

Figure 14.11 Lamarck's explanation of the giraffe's neck

Because it cannot survive the test of scientific investigation, Lamarck's theory is now not acceptable.

14.12. Darwin's theory of evolution

After much observation of plants and animals in their natural environments, **Charles Darwin** published the results of his observations in 1859, under the title *On the Origin of Species by means of Natural Selection*. In his book, Darwin put forward a possible explanation of evolution. This explanation is known as **Darwin's theory**, although the same explanation was put forward by another scientist, **Alfred Wallace**, who was working entirely independently.

These are the main points of Darwin's theory:

a. All organisms produce more potential offspring than can possibly survive. Consider the following examples:
(i) A poppy plant produces so many seeds that if they all germinated and grew, there would be little room for any other plant.
(ii) A female cod lays over one million eggs per year. If they were all fertile, hatched, survived to maturity and continued to breed, the seas would be so full of cod fish that there would be no room for any other fish.
(iii) A tapeworm lays over 1 000 million eggs per year.

b. Many of these offspring are unable to survive because there is a struggle for existence. Survival depends upon an organism being able to obtain sufficient food and to avoid being killed by its natural enemies. Consider the following examples:
(i) The roots of plants must obtain water and mineral salts from the soil; plant stems must grow upwards to ensure that the leaves can receive sufficient sunlight for photosynthesis.
(ii) Of the one million eggs laid by a female cod, many will not be fertilized and will be eaten by small fish. Those that are fertilized and are not eaten will hatch into fry. Many of the fry will be eaten by larger fish and seabirds. The few which survive must still avoid being eaten, in order to reach maturity.

c. In all species of living things, there is variation. The kittens in a litter are not identical; some are more vigorous than others. In many litters, one is often weaker than all of the others; this weak one is called the **runt** of the litter and is unlikely to survive.

Investigation 14a. Variation in runner beans

Take about 30 or more runner bean seeds and examine them. Can you find two that have identical patterns on the testas? Find the mass of each bean separately. Do they all have the same mass or do they vary? Measure the length and width of each seed. How many have the same measurements?

Plant all of your seeds under identical conditions of depth, type of soil, moisture and temperature, and wait until the seedlings begin to break through the surface. Do all of the seedlings break through the surface at the same time? When your plants have reached a height of *about* 5 cm, measure the height of them. Are they all the same height or do they vary?

Carefully, dig up all of your plants, wash the soil away from the roots and measure the length of the longest root of each plant. How many plants have the same length of root? Find the mass of each plant separately. How many plants have the same mass?

d. Individuals of a species which are better adapted to their environment are more likely to survive and breed. Those which are not able or less able to adapt will be less likely to survive and, consequently, less likely to breed. This 'weeding out' effect is known as the **principle of natural selection**, or, more commonly, **survival of the fittest**. Consider the following examples:
 (i) Poppy seedlings which grow vigorously in the early stages will be able to obtain more moisture from the ground and more sunlight than those which grow more slowly. The slow-growing seedlings will be overshadowed by the vigorous plants, become deprived of these essentials and die.
 (ii) In a population of rabbits, any that cannot detect the presence of a prowling fox or run fast enough to escape are likely to be eaten. Those with the most acute hearing and the ability to run fastest will live longest.
(iii) When D.D.T. was first introduced as an insecticide, many millions of houseflies (and other insects) were killed. Those that survived had a genetic immunity, which was transmitted to their offspring. Because of this, D.D.T. is a less effective insecticide now than when it was first used.

e. Variations which give an advantage are transmitted by inheritance. Variations which put the individual at a disadvantage will become extinct, because such individuals are unable to compete successfully in the struggle for survival.

262

The Darwinian explanation of the giraffe's neck is as follows:

a. Giraffes are descended from an animal about the same size and shape as an antelope.

b. The food that was available to them was from ground level to the lower branches of trees.

c. From time to time, mutations could have occurred to the genes controlling the growth rate of the neck and the forelegs, possibly at the same time or, more probably, at different times.

d. The longer-necked and longer-legged variety was at an advantage, because it could feed from higher levels which were not available to the normal variety.

e. Because of the abundance of food at these higher levels and the lack of competition for it, the long-necked and long-legged variety survived and bred.

f. The occurrence and increasing numbers of the long-necked and long-legged variety reduced the competition for food at the lower levels, so the normal variety could survive side by side with their taller relatives.

Figure 14.12 shows, in a very simplified form, Darwin's explanation of the evolution of the giraffe's neck.

Figure 14.12 Darwin's explanation of the giraffe's neck

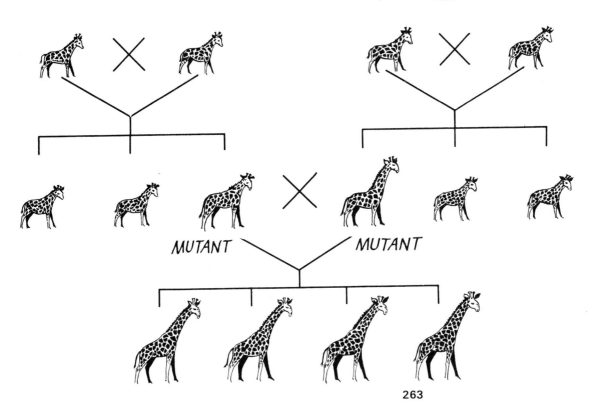

263

14.13. Extinction

In the course of evolution many species have become extinct. Extinction of a species usually results from changes in the environment which do not favour the species. The consequence of an unfavourable environment is that the number of offspring surviving gradually decreases until, eventually, extinction occurs.

If a mutation occurs at the same time as the change in the environment and the resulting mutant is capable of existing in the changed environment, the mutant will survive and breed, while the original variety will gradually become extinct. If, on the other hand, no advantageous mutation occurs at the same time as the change in the environment, there will be complete extinction of the species.

An example of extinction is the fate of the dinosaurs, which existed for over a hundred million years. The name dinosaur comes from two Greek words, 'deinos' meaning 'terrible' and 'sauros' meaning 'lizard'. Dinosaurs varied in size and diet: some were very small, while others were over 27 m long; some were herbivorous, while others were carnivorous. About 70 million years ago, the dinosaurs began to die out. Their extinction may have been caused by a number of factors, some of which were:

a. The climate became colder and the dinosaurs were unable to maintain their body temperature.
b. The colder climate reduced the growth of plant life. This led to the death of many of the herbivores and, consequently, to the death of many of the carnivores.
c. The natural environment of some of the dinosaurs was swamp. As the food supply dwindled, perhaps because the swamps gradually dried up, the dinosaurs had to roam farther from their natural homes. Away from the support of the water in the swamps, the movement of these dinosaurs was slow and cumbersome, thus making them easy prey for their natural enemies.
d. The large proportion of time spent by some of the larger dinosaurs in obtaining food to maintain life left very little time for rest.
e. Large animals take longer than small animals to reach maturity and the time when they are capable of producing offspring. Even when they reach maturity, they produce a relatively small number of offspring.
f. Compared with the size of their bodies, the brains of dinosaurs were very small indeed.

14.14. Artificial selection

Without the influence of man, evolution has occurred through natural selection. Man has been able to improve many species of plants and animals by two methods:

a. By restricting breeding to varieties which have desirable characteristics.
b. By providing an environment which is suitable for these varieties.

Wheat crops produce a better yield than they did in earlier times. This is partly because of selective breeding of heavy-yield, disease-resistant varieties, and partly because of improved cultivation methods. Selective breeding involves the saving of seed from plants in a crop which has these desirable characteristics, planting them, and thereby increasing the stock of seed. Cultivation involves the improvement of the environment to encourage the growth of the crop. This involves factors such as: better drainage of the soil; more effective tillage by ploughing, harrowing, rolling, etc., to improve aeration; the addition of suitable fertilizers; the elimination of undesirable plants (weeds) by the use of selective weed-killers; and the protection of plants by the use of suitable pesticides. By cross-breeding different varieties, combinations of characteristics suitable for a particular environment can be produced. For example, in a field exposed to strong prevailing winds, a heavy-yield, long-stemmed variety would be beaten down thus making harvesting difficult, so a short-stemmed variety would be more suitable.

Modern cultivated roses are very different from wild roses or briars. There are many thousands of varieties of the rose, some of which originated as 'sports' (plants with desirable characteristics resulting from natural pollination), and others as the result of selective cross-pollination. Once a new variety has been produced, it is propagated (increased in numbers) by the process of budding, in which buds of the new variety are inserted into slits in the bark of a stock. A **stock** is the root system and stem of another plant. In the case of roses, English briar (*Rosa canina*) and *Rosa rugosa* are often used. The stock determines the vigour of growth, while the bud determines the flower characteristics. Other methods of propagation include grafting and the striking of cuttings. You may have noticed long, spindly growths with seven leaflets per leaf (instead of the normal five), pale green in colour and with many sharp thorns growing from near the base of a cultivated rose. These are called suckers and are outgrowths from the stock. These suckers would produce blooms of the wild rose type and should be removed as soon as they appear.

Fruit trees are also propagated by grafting a small, trimmed branch of the required variety, known as a **scion**, on to a suitable stock. By using this method of propagation, it is possible to produce a tree bearing several different varieties of the same fruit on a single tree, one variety on each branch.

Cattle are reared for two purposes: to provide beef and to produce milk. Beef cattle are heavy breeds with well-rounded bodies, such as the Hereford, Shorthorn and Aberdeen Angus. Dairy cattle are lighter in build with lean angular bodies, such as the Jersey, Guernsey and Friesian. By cross-breeding, it is possible to produce dual-purpose cattle which have the advantages of both types. A dual-purpose cross-breed will not produce as high a milk yield as a pure-bred dairy cow or as much high quality beef as a pure-bred beef steer. Intensive veal production is achieved by rearing calves in an artificial environment, in which temperature, humidity, light intensity, quantity of food and quantity of water are regulated to promote rapid growth.

Poultry are also reared for two purposes: to lay eggs and as table birds. By selective breeding, it is possible to produce birds with a high egg output or with good table-bird qualities. Cross-breeding can produce a dual-purpose bird. By providing a suitable artificial environment, the output per bird can be increased to over 300 eggs per year, compared with about 120 eggs per year by birds in an outdoor flock. A part of this increase is caused by shortening the length of the birds' 'day' by reducing the time of the 'light and darkness' cycle to less than twenty-four hours. Most table birds are reared in broiler houses in which the environment is controlled to encourage a high growth rate.

Dogs are all members of the same species and are all descended from a common ancestor. Natural selection has produced many varieties but, by selective breeding, man has been able to produce many more varieties which will breed true (see Figure 14.13).

14.15. The evolution of man and the future

Man has not evolved from monkeys and apes but it is thought by many scientists that man, monkeys and apes all evolved parallel with each other from a common ancestor, sometimes popularly called the 'missing link'. The evolution of man to his present position of supremacy over all other forms of life is the result of many factors. These factors include:

    a. Compared with body size, man has a larger brain than other animals.

    b. Man is able to make and use tools, ranging from simple weapons, such as spears, knives, etc., to complicated machines, such as aircraft and computers.

    c. Man is able to survive in almost any natural environment.

266

COLLIE

COCKER SPANIEL

CAIRN TERRIER

ALSATIAN

AFGHAN HOUND

Figure 14.13 Some breeds of dog

d. Man is able to make and control fire, and harness natural sources of energy.

e. Man is able to control his environment.

What of the future? Evolution has taken place since the beginning of time and, no doubt, it will continue; but it would be impossible to forecast the course that future evolution will take. We cannot forecast events and changes that will take place in 100 years any better than men of 100 years ago could have forecast the events of today. One thing is certain, the future evolution of man will become more and more dependent on his ability to apply his technology to everyday problems and situations.

Figure 14.14 An impossible scene

1. Why would it be difficult (if not impossible) to bore a tunnel from the British Isles through the centre of the earth to Australia?
2. Why do we not find fossils in granite?
3. Why could man never have ridden on Eohippus?
4. Penicillin is used to treat certain bacterial infections but, in some cases, it is less effective than when it was first used. Why is this so?
5. Which features are out of place if Figure 14.14 represents a scene (a) 100 million years ago, (b) 800 000 years ago, (c) in the sixteenth century, (d) today?
6. Explain how the zebra got its stripes: (a) according to Lamarck's theory, (b) according to Darwin's theory.

Chapter 15

The Earth in Space

15.1. Stars and planets

From the beginning of history, men have studied the heavens and have noticed that although the positions of the stars in the sky are continually changing, certain groups always appear to maintain the same position relative to one another. Such groups of stars are called **constellations**. Figure 15.1 shows some well-known constellations.

It was also noticed that certain heavenly bodies appeared to behave in a different manner, by moving among the constellations. These were called **planets**.

We now know that the planets are very much nearer to the earth than any of the stars in the constellations and that the planets, of which the earth is one, together with the sun, which is itself a star, form the **solar system**.

15.2. The solar system

The solar system consists of nine planets, five of which have been observed for many centuries. These are Mercury, Venus, Mars, Jupiter and Saturn. The more distant planets were discovered only after the invention of the telescope. Uranus was discovered in the year 1781, Neptune in 1846 and Pluto in 1930. In addition to the nine major planets, there is a region, known as the asteroid belt, situated between the orbits of Mars and Jupiter. This consists of a very large number of small bodies, called **asteroids**, very few of which have a diameter much greater than 100 km.

All the planets rotate around the sun in orbits, which are elliptical in shape. Figure 15.2 shows the relative distances of the planets from the sun, as they orbit around it.

As well as moving in their orbits, the planets also revolve on their axes. One complete revolution of the earth is called one day, and it is this revolution which causes the sun to appear to rise and set, giving rise to day and night.

The time taken for the earth to complete one orbit of the sun is called a year, and takes a little more than 365 days to complete.

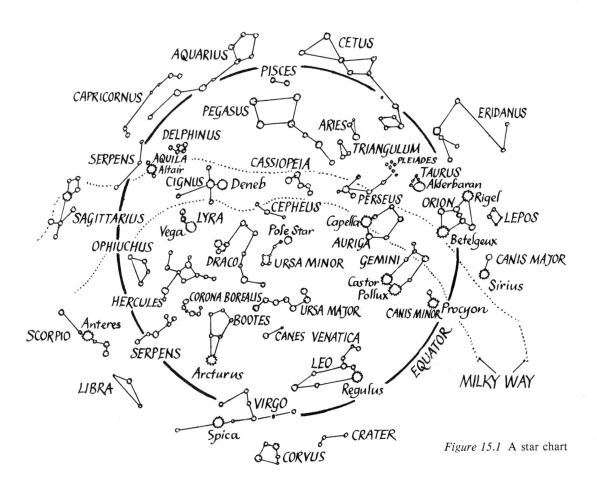

Figure 15.1 A star chart

Figure 15.2 The relative distances of the planets from the sun

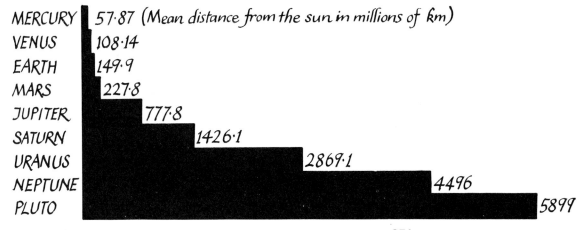

MERCURY	57·87 (Mean distance from the sun in millions of km)
VENUS	108·14
EARTH	149·9
MARS	227·8
JUPITER	777·8
SATURN	1426·1
URANUS	2869·1
NEPTUNE	4496
PLUTO	5899

Table 15.1 gives the length of the 'days' and 'years' of the other planets, in terms of earth days and years.

The planets vary considerably in size and composition (see Figure 15.3 and Table 15.1). Although most planets would appear to be solid, it is likely that Saturn, which has an average density less than that of water, is largely gaseous.

The average surface temperature of a planet depends very largely on its distance from the sun; so that Mercury has a temperature of around 400 °C, while the distant planets have very low temperatures.

The moon is a satellite of the earth. It orbits the earth once every twenty-eight days and spins on its axis, taking twenty-eight days to complete a single spin. For this reason, the same 'side' of the moon always faces the earth. Mars, Jupiter, Uranus, Saturn and Neptune each have more than one satellite, but the other planets have none which have been observed.

The sun is very much larger than the biggest of the planets. It consists of a vast mass of very hot material. Its mass has been calculated as being 332 000 times that of the earth, and the temperature at its centre has been estimated at 20 million degrees Celsius. This temperature is believed to be produced as a result of nuclear reactions occurring within the sun, causing matter to be converted into energy. The power radiated into space is of the order of 40 000 million million million kilowatts (40×10^{21} kW).

Much of this energy is in the form of heat and light. The sun is the only luminous body in the solar system; the planets and their satellites being visible *only* because they reflect light from the sun.

TABLE 15.1. THE SOLAR SYSTEM

Name	Distance from Sun*/ millions of km	Diameter*/ thousands of km	Density*/ kg m^{-3}	Length of† Day	Length of† Year
Sun	—	1391·0	1414	—	—
Mercury	57·9	4·9	5600	58 d	88 d
Venus	108·1	12·2	5150	247 d	225 d
Earth	149·5	12·8	5516	24 h	365·25 d
Mars	227·9	6·8	3940	24·5 h	687 d
Asteroid belt	Consists of more than 100 000 minor planets, very few of which are greater than 100 km in diameter.				
Jupiter	777·8	142·8	1337	10 h	12 y
Saturn	1426·1	120·8	690	10·3 h	30 y
Uranus	2869·1	49·8	1350	10·8 h	84 y
Neptune	4496	44·6	2240	15·8 h	16·5 y
Pluto	5899	6·0	?	6 d	248 y

* These are average values.
† Given in terms of hours (h), earth days (d) and earth years (y).
Note: The density of water is 1 000 kg m^{-3}.

272

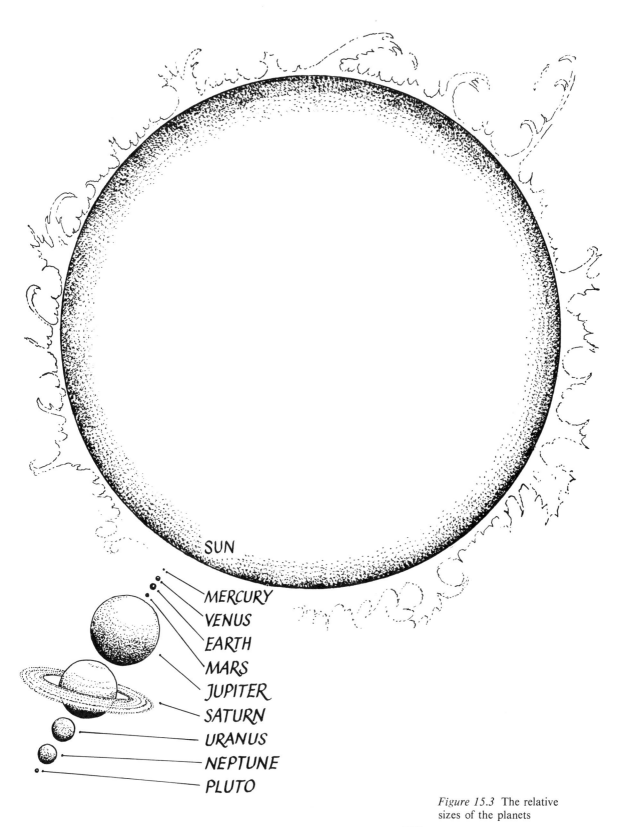

SUN

MERCURY
VENUS
EARTH
MARS
JUPITER
SATURN
URANUS
NEPTUNE
PLUTO

Figure 15.3 The relative
sizes of the planets

273

An **eclipse of the sun** occurs when the moon is in a position between the sun and the earth, so that the shadow of the moon is cast on the earth. If the earth and moon are in such a position that the shadow of the earth is cast on the moon, an **eclipse of the moon** is said to occur (see Chapter 7).

15.3. The galaxies

The sun is just one of a countless number of stars in the universe. On a clear night, a band of light can be seen in the sky. This band is in the shape of a circular arc and may be seen from both the Northern and the Southern Hemispheres. On examination with powerful telescopes, this band is found to consist of an enormous number of stars, separated by huge distances. A cluster of stars of this kind is called a **galaxy**, and this particular galaxy, of which the sun is a member, is called the Milky Way.

The Milky Way appears to be in the shape of an enormous wheel, and is rotating about its centre at such a speed that one rotation would take about 250 million years. This apparently slow rotation means that the stars near the edge of the galaxy must be moving at a speed of almost 300 kilometres per second!

One of the nearer stars in our galaxy, Sirius, is at such a distance from us that its light takes about 8·6 years to reach the earth. The velocity of light is almost 300 000 km s^{-1}. Even at this velocity, light would take about a quarter of a million years to cross from one side of the galaxy to the other!

Even this is not the end of the story, for the Milky Way is just one of many galaxies, each separated from the other by vast expanses of nearly empty space. Light from the Andromeda nebula, a relatively near galaxy, takes about a million years to reach us.

Another most important feature is the relative motion of the galaxies. These all appear to be moving away from us at a very high speed, so it appears that the universe is expanding in all directions.

15.4. The age of the earth

By studying the materials found in the crust of the earth and calculating the rate at which radioactive elements decay to become inert elements, it is possible to estimate the age of the crust. This appears to be at least 4 500 million years ($4·5 \times 10^9$ years).

15.5. How old is the universe?

The age and the origin of the universe are problems which have fascinated philosophers and astronomers throughout the ages. The two main theories of the origin of the universe are the 'Big Bang' theory and the 'Steady State' theory.

The 'Big Bang' theory states that the universe began by the explosion of a relatively small, but extremely dense, piece of matter. All the galaxies are supposed to have originated as a result of this explosion. This would explain why the galaxies are receding from one another. If one accepts this theory, it is possible to trace the motion back and reach the conclusion that the 'Big Bang' occurred about 10 000 million years ago.

The 'Steady State' theory states that the overall pattern of the universe remains constant. Stars, and even galaxies, may explode and die, but new ones are constantly building up to replace them, so that the overall picture remains the same. This theory implies that the universe had no beginning and will have no end!

15.6. Is there life anywhere else?

It seems most unlikely that intelligent life, as we understand it, can exist anywhere in the solar system except on the earth. The only other planets in the system where any form of life seems remotely possible are Mars and Venus, our nearest neighbours. Two conditions necessary for life, as we know it, are a suitable atmosphere and a suitable temperature. Of the other planets, Mercury is much too hot and the others are far too cold. The atmosphere of Mars is probably too rarefied to support anything other than the simplest forms of plant life.

The question of whether there is intelligent life on the planets of other stars is a very different problem. When one considers the vastness of the universe, it seems probable that life has occurred not once but many times in different places. It is most unlikely that we are the only intelligent beings in the universe, but it may be that our nearest neighbours are so far away that the solar system may cease to exist before man can become aware of their existence.

Test your understanding

1. What is the difference between a star and a planet?
2. List the planets which make up the solar system.
3. What is a galaxy? Name one.
4. If light travels across space at a velocity of 300 000 km s^{-1}, and the light from the moon takes 1·25 s to reach the earth, how far from the earth is the moon?
5. Using the information given in Table 15.1, calculate how long it takes sunlight to reach the earth (answer correct to the nearest second).
6. The moon always presents the same face to the earth. Why is this?

Appendix 1

Units of Measurement

Quantity	Unit	Symbol	
Mass	kilogram gram	kg g	1 kg = 1 000 g (1 tonne = 1 000 kg)
Length	metre millimetre kilometre	m mm km	1 m = 1 000 mm 1 km = 1 000 m (*Note:* The centimetre (cm) is sometimes used.) 1 m = 100 cm
Time	second hour	s h	1 h = 3 600 s
Area	square millimetre square centimetre square metre square kilometre	mm^2 cm^2 m^2 km^2	
Volume	cubic millimetre cubic centimetre cubic decimetre cubic metre	mm^3 cm^3 dm^3 m^3	
Density	kilogram per cubic metre gram per cubic centimetre	$kg\ m^{-3}$ $g\ cm^{-3}$	
Velocity	metre per second kilometre per second kilometre per hour	$m\ s^{-1}$ $km\ s^{-1}$ $km\ h^{-1}$	
Acceleration	metre per second squared	$m\ s^{-2}$	
Force	newton	N	A force of 1 N will produce an acceleration of $1\ m\ s^{-2}$ in a mass of 1 kg 1 MN = 1 000 000 N
Work and Energy	joule kilojoule	J kJ	Energy is the capacity for doing work 1 MJ = 1 000 000 J
Power	watt kilowatt	W kW	Power is the rate of doing work 1 W = 1 joule per second 1 kW = 1 000 W 1 MW = 1 000 000 W
Temperature	degree Celsius kelvin	°C K	Temperature in K = temperature in °C + 273
Electromotive force	volt kilovolt	V kV	1 kV = 1 000 V
Electric current	ampere	A	1 milliampere = $\frac{1}{1000}$ ampere
Electric charge	coulomb	C	
Electrical resistance	ohm	Ω	1 kΩ = 1 000 Ω 1 MΩ = 1 000 000 Ω

Appendix 2

The Elements

Element	Symbol	Mass No.	Atomic No.	Element	Symbol	Mass No.	Atomic No.
Actinium	Ac	277	89	Neodymium	Nd	144	60
Aluminium	Al	27	13	Neon	Ne	20	10
Antimony	Sb	122	51	Nickel	Ni	59	28
Argon	A	40	18	Niobium	Nb	93	41
Arsenic	As	75	33	Nitrogen	N	14	7
Astatine	At	210	85	Osmium	Os	190	76
Barium	Ba	137	56	Oxygen	O	16	8
Beryllium	Be	9	4	Palladium	Pd	107	46
Bismuth	Bi	209	83	Phosphorus	P	31	15
Boron	B	11	5	Platinum	Pt	195	78
Bromine	Br	80	35	Plutonium	Pu	239	94
Cadmium	Cd	112	48	Polonium	Po	209	84
Caesium	Cs	133	55	Potassium	K	39	19
Calcium	Ca	40	20	Praseodymium	Pr	141	59
Carbon	C	12	6	Promethium	Pm	145	61
Cerium	Ce	140	58	Protoactinium	Pa	231	91
Chlorine	Cl	35	17	Radium	Ra	226	88
Chromium	Cr	52	24	Radon	Rn	222	86
Cobalt	Co	59	27	Rhenium	Re	186	75
Copper	Cu	64	29	Rhodium	Rh	103	45
Dysprosium	Dy	162	66	Rubidium	Rb	85	37
Erbium	Er	167	68	Ruthenium	Ru	101	44
Europium	Eu	152	63	Samarium	Sm	150	62
Fluorine	F	19	9	Scandium	Sc	45	21
Francium	Fr	223	87	Selenium	Se	79	34
Gadolinium	Gd	157	64	Silicon	Si	28	14
Gallium	Ga	70	31	Silver	Ag	108	47
Germanium	Ge	73	32	Sodium	Na	23	11
Gold	Au	197	79	Strontium	Sr	88	38
Hafnium	Hf	179	72	Sulphur	S	32	16
Helium	He	4	2	Tantalum	Ta	181	73
Holmium	Ho	165	67	Technetium	Tc	99	43
Hydrogen	H	1	1	Tellurium	Te	128	52
Indium	In	115	49	Terbium	Tb	159	65
Iodine	I	127	53	Thallium	Tl	204	81
Iridium	Ir	192	77	Thorium	Th	232	90
Iron	Fe	56	26	Thulium	Tm	169	69
Krypton	Kr	84	36	Tin	Sn	119	50
Lanthanum	La	139	57	Titanium	Ti	48	22
Lead	Pb	207	82	Tungsten	W	184	74
Lithium	Li	7	3	Uranium	U	238	92
Lutetium	Lu	175	71	Vanadium	V	51	23
Magnesium	Mg	24	12	Xenon	Xe	131	54
Manganese	Mn	55	25	Ytterbium	Yb	173	70
Mercury	Hg	201	80	Yttrium	Y	89	39
Molybdenum	Mo	96	42	Zinc	Zn	65	30
				Zirconium	Zr	91	40

The mass numbers quoted are those of the most common isotope.

Appendix 3

Solutions

The Table below gives the quantities of solutes required to make 1 dm³ of solution.

Solution	Strength (molarity)	Quantity of Solute
Sodium hydroxide	1·0 M	40 g solid sodium hydroxide
Potassium hydroxide	1·0 M	56 g solid potassium hydroxide
Ammonia solution	1·0 M	52 cm³ ammonia fortis (0·88)
Sulphuric(VI) acid	1·0 M	55 cm³ conc. acid (Add acid to water. *Care!*)
Nitric(V) acid	1·0 M	64 cm³ conc. acid
Hydrochloric acid	1·0 M	95 cm³ conc. acid
Silver nitrate(V)		15 g (Store in dark glass bottle.)
Barium chloride		100 g
Methyl orange		1 g
Phenolphthalein		2 g (Dissolve in 500 cm³ industrial spirit, then add water.)
Lime-water		Saturated solution (Mix calcium hydroxide with water, then filter.)

Note: Where the strength of a solution is given as 1·0 M (molar), the gram formula mass of solute is dissolved in water to make 1 dm³ of solution.

If a solution of different strength is required, a proportionately different mass of solute is used. Thus, 4 g of solid sodium hydroxide would make 1 dm³ of solution of strength 0·1 M, and 80 g of solid sodium hydroxide would make 1 dm³ of solution of strength 2·0 M.

Appendix 4

Common Chemical Substances

Common Name	Chemical Name	Formula
Baking soda	Sodium hydrogencarbonate	$NaHCO_3$
Borax	Sodium tetraborate	$Na_2B_4O_7 . 10H_2O$
Caustic potash	Potassium hydroxide	KOH
Caustic soda	Sodium hydroxide	$NaOH$
Chalk (limestone and marble)	Calcium carbonate	$CaCO_3$
Chrome alum	Chromium(III) potassium sulphate(VI)	$K_2SO_4Cr_2(SO_4)_3.24H_2O$
Common salt (table salt)	Sodium chloride	$NaCl$
Condy's crystals	Potassium manganate(VII)	$KMnO_4$
Epsom salts	Magnesium sulphatc(VI)	$MgSO_4$
Glauber's salts	Sodium sulphate(VI)	Na_2SO_4
Hypo	Sodium thiosulphate(VI)	$Na_2S_2O_3$
Nitre	Potassium nitrate(V)	KNO_3
Oil of vitriol	Sulphuric(VI) acid	H_2SO_4
Plaster of Paris	Calcium sulphate(VI)	$CaSO_4$
Potash alum	Aluminium potassium sulphate(VI)	$K_2SO_4Al_2(SO_4)_3 . 24H_2O$
Quicklime	Calcium oxide	CaO
Sal ammoniac	Ammonium chloride	NH_4Cl
Sal volatile	Ammonium carbonate (soln.)	$(NH_4)_2CO_3$
Slaked lime	Calcium hydroxide	$Ca(OH)_2$
Water glass	Sodium silicate(IV)	Na_2SiO_3

Appendix 5

Some Famous Scientists

This is a list of some famous scientists. It is important to realize that it is not a complete list—many other men and women have contributed to the advance of scientific knowledge and understanding.

Archimedes (287–212 B.C.) was a Greek mathematician and physicist who first stated the principle of levers and discovered the laws of flotation (Archimedes' principle).

Aristotle (384–322 B.C.) was a Greek philosopher, who taught that all happenings should be investigated before any conclusions were reached. He also suspected that man had developed from very simple forms of life, although he could not prove it.

Baird (1888–1946) developed the first television system and gave his first demonstration in 1926.

Becquerel (1852–1908) discovered the existence of radioactivity.

Bell (1847–1922) invented the telephone.

Bohr (1885–1962) made valuable contributions to the development of the atomic theory.

Boyle (1627–91) stated the relationship between the pressure and the volume of a given mass of gas.

Brown (1773–1858) was a Scottish botanist who first discovered the movement of particles, which we now call 'Brownian movement'.

Bunsen (1811–99) invented a number of devices, the best known being the bunsen burner.

Celsius (1701–44) divided the thermometer scale between the fixed points into a hundred equal degrees.

Chadwick (born 1891), together with Bohr, Rutherford and others, made contributions to the theory of atomic structure.

Clerk-Maxwell (1831–79) first put forward the possibility of the existence of electromagnetic waves.

Cockcroft (1897–1967) succeeded in splitting the atom, thus enabling further advances to be made in the theory of atomic structure.

Copernicus (1473–1543) was a Polish astronomer who first developed the theory that the planets, including the earth, revolved around the sun.

Curie, Marie (1867–1934), together with her husband, discovered the existence of polonium and radium.

Dalton (1766–1844) put forward an atomic theory in the early nineteenth century.

Darwin (1809–82) is famous for his theory of natural selection.

Davy (1778–1829) was a president of the Royal Society, and is best known for the Davy miners' safety lamp.

Edison (1847–1931) was an inventor, most famous for his invention of the phonograph, the carbon microphone and the electric filament lamp.

Einstein (1879–1955) predicted the relationship between matter and energy.

Faraday (1791–1867) discovered the principles of the transformer and the dynamo, and stated the laws of electrolysis.

Fermi (1901–54) was largely responsible for the first successful nuclear chain reaction.

Fleming, Alexander (1881–1955), observed the mould, penicillin, and realized that it had medical value. Together with Florey and Chain, he developed this mould to produce the first antibiotic.

Fleming, John (1849–1945), invented the thermionic diode.

Franklin (1706–90) was an electrical experimenter who showed that lightning was an electrical spark.

Galileo (1564–1642) was the inventor of a telescope. He also investigated pendulums and the laws of acceleration.

Gilbert (1540–1603) is famous for his work on magnetism.

Harvey (1578–1657) first discovered that blood circulated round the body.

Hertz (1857–94) carried out work which confirmed Clerk-Maxwell's suspicions of the existence of electromagnetic radiation.

Hooke (1635–1703) was a mathematician who developed a compound microscope. He also stated the relationship between the extension of a spring and the load applied to it.

Huygens (1629–95) invented the pendulum clock and formulated a wave theory of light.

Jenner (1749–1823) discovered the method of vaccination against smallpox.

Joule (1818–89) did work on the relationship between heat energy and mechanical energy, which led to the hypothesis of the conservation of energy.

Lavoisier (1743–94) first gave the correct explanation of combustion.

Linnaeus (1707–78) is famous for his work on the method of classifying animals, diseases, minerals and plants.

Lister (1827–1912) made surgery safer by his use of antiseptics.

Marconi (1874–1937) was the first man to send radio signals across the Atlantic.

Mendel (1822–84) discovered the laws of heredity.

Newton (1642–1727) was one of the greatest scientists. Among his many achievements are his statement of the laws of motion, the law of cooling, the laws of optics and the development of a reflecting telescope.

Ohm (1787–1854) was famous for his work on electricity, which established the relationship between the current flowing through a conductor and the potential difference across its ends.

Pasteur (1822–95) showed that diseases could be transmitted by micro-organisms. He developed inoculation treatments for hydrophobia and anthrax, and discovered that heat killed bacteria.

Priestley (1733–1804) discovered the gas oxygen.

Röntgen (1845–1923) discovered the existence of X-rays.

Rutherford (1871–1937), together with others, was responsible for a theory of atomic structure.

Salk (born 1914) developed a vaccine against poliomyelitis.

Scheele (1742–86) discovered oxygen, independently of Priestley. He also discovered the element chlorine.

Soddy (1877–1956) originated the theory of atomic disintegration and is famous for his work on isotopes.

Thomson (1856–1940) developed the electron theory.

Volta (1745–1827) invented the voltaic cell.

Watt (1736–1819) experimented with a Newcomen engine and, as a result, was able to develop a more efficient steam engine.

Analytical Contents List

12 Reproduction

12.1 Asexual reproduction 12.2 Sexual reproduction
12.3 Flowers 12.4 Pollination
12.5 Fertilization in flowers
12.6 Fruits 12.7 Fruit and seed dispersal
12.8 Seeds 12.9 Germination of seeds
12.10 Sexual reproduction in animals
12.11 Reproduction in human beings
12.12 Early growth of the baby
12.13 Growing up 12.14 Menstruation

13 Genetics

13.1 What is genetics? 13.2 The work of Mendel
13.3 Some terms used in genetics 13.4 The cell
13.5 Mitosis 13.6 Meiosis 13.7 Incomplete dominance
13.8 The sex chromosomes 13.9 Sex-linkage
13.10 The functions of the genes
13.11 Heredity and environment
13.12 Eye colour and heredity
13.13 Height and heredity
13.14 Disease and heredity 13.15 Mutation

14 Evolution

14.1 Earth and its crust
14.2 The three main types of rock
14.3 Dating the rocks 14.4 Fossils
14.5 Coal and oil 14.6 Geological time
14.7 The meaning of evolution
14.8 Comparative embryology
14.9 The evidence of vestiges
14.10 Comparative anatomy 14.11 Lamarck's theory
14.12 Darwin's theory of evolution
14.13 Extinction 14.14 Artificial selection
14.15 The evolution of man and the future

15 The Earth in Space

15.1 Stars and planets 15.2 The solar system
15.3 The galaxies 15.4 The age of the earth
15.5 How old is the universe?
15.6 Is there life anywhere else?

Appendices

1 Units of Measurement
2 The Elements
3 Solutions
4 Common Chemical Substances
5 Some Famous Scientists

Analytical Contents List for Book 1

For the convenience of the users of this book, we are setting out below the contents of the companion volume, *Matter and Energy*, SSS General Science Book 1.

Index

Where the subject is illustrated, the page number is shown in bold type